D1270713

Implementing and Integrating Product Data Management and Software Configuration Management

For a complete listing of the *Artech House Computing Library,*
turn to the back of this book.

Implementing and Integrating Product Data Management and Software Configuration Management

Ivica Crnkovic
Ulf Asklund
Annita Persson Dahlqvist

Artech House
Boston • London
www.artechhouse.com

Library of Congress Cataloging-in-Publication Data
Crnkovic, Ivica.
  Implementing and integrating product data management and software configuration management / Ivica Crnkovic, Ulf Asklund, Annita Persson Dahlqvist.
      p.   cm.—(Artech House computing library)
    Includes bibliographical references and index.
      ISBN 1-58053-498-8 (alk. paper)
      1. Computer integrated manufacturing systems.   2. Production contro—Data processing.   3. Concurrent engineering.   4. Management information systems.   I. Asklund, Ulf.   II. Dahlqvist, Annita Persson.
III. Title.   IV. Series.
    TS155.63.C76 2003
    670.285'—dc21   2003049579

British Library Cataloguing in Publication Data
Crnkovic, Ivica.
  Implementing and integrating product data management and software configuration management. — (Artech House computing library)
    1. Industrial management—Data processing   2. Software configuration management   3. Product management—Data processing   I. Title   II. Asklund, Ulf   III. Dahlqvist, Annita Persson
    658.5'00285
    ISBN 1-58053-498-8

Cover design by Igor Valdman

International Standard Book Number: 1-58053-498-8
Library of Congress Catalog Card Number: 2003049579

10 9 8 7 6 5 4 3 2 1

Contents

Part II   Similarities and Differences Between PDM and SCM

4   Comparison of technical principles and key functionality

5   Analysis and general findings   109

Part III   Integration and Deployment   131

6   PDM and SCM integration   133

Foreword

I had been working for years in the SCM field when, in the mid 1990s, one of my customers, Dassault Systems, a major CAD vendor, asked me to make a study of PDM tools and concepts and specifically of AP203 (STEP Application Protocol). I had no previous knowledge of PDM and was due for a series of surprises.

The first surprise was seeing how difficult it was for newcomers to enter the field. It was necessary to read large piles of obscure documents and standards (STEP), and, through discussions with a PDM colleague, to slowly understand what were the underlying concepts and the intentions behind these concepts. It took me a few years of effort (not full time!).

The second surprise was to see that PDM, fundamentally, addresses the same issue as SCM, (i.e., the control of the evolution of complex systems). This logically resulted in PDM consisting of concepts and tools similar to those found in SCM, such as data modeling, versioning, and concurrent engineering.

The third surprise was the realization that despite the many similarities between PDM and SCM, my unawareness of PDM was not an exception. Most, if not all of my colleagues working in SCM were equally ignorant of PDM. I subsequently learned that the reverse was also true; PDM specialists were just as unaware of SCM. I could find no one who was a specialist in both fields. Both areas were ignoring each other (and still do) and were essentially (re)discovering, (re)developing, and (re)inventing the same things. A huge amount of expertise was being wasted.

The next surprise was to learn that, behind the apparent similarities, at least some of the differences between PDM and SCM were deep and fundamental. I learned that though these two fields have similar global objectives, each addresses specific concerns, thus resulting in differences between concepts and incompatibilities between solutions.

At this point it was clear to me that, for many reasons, both fields would benefit from closer cooperation. For example, considerable expertise had been accumulated in both fields and some of the original solutions found and validated in one camp were clearly relevant to the other camp, and vice versa. For scientific and technical reasons, such closer cooperation would be very beneficial. The major reason, however, for cooperation is that today, all major projects include hardware and software. All analysts forecast an ever deeper interdependency between hardware and software, and potentially a complete merger between both, as exemplified by the system-on-a-chip (SOC) domain, in which the designer is free to decide if a function is to be provided by hardware or software or both, and in which such decisions can be changed at any time during design and even during the commercial life of the chip. This trend clearly illustrates the need for a tool (or tools) that can handle the design and maintenance of systems containing both hardware and software in the same way.

A further surprise was to note that at that time, there was no interest in addressing the development of a tool capable of supporting the design and maintenance of systems combining hardware and software. I therefore made a first assessment of the difficulties of realizing such a tool. Indeed, the difficulties were many and there was no obvious way to achieve the goal. A successful solution would require serious research and technical investment, and would potentially require years of rework, calibration, and debugging. Nevertheless, I was very disappointed to see that this work was not passionately undertaken.

Without a common understanding of both fields, at all levels (goals, concepts, and techniques), it is not likely that the SCM and PDM communities will meet on common ground, and therefore, there is little hope that the tool(s) we desperately need will be produced. Considering the amount of time that would be required for such an undertaking, its initiation should be delayed no longer.

This is what this book intends to do (and it succeeds). It first presents both fields clearly, precisely, and concisely. In itself, this is valuable because no clear survey of both fields is available; but the major contribution of this book is its point-by-point analysis of their similarities and differences. The authors present an honest assessment of the current state in both fields; they make no attempt to show that one domain subsumes the other, nor attempt to "sell" one solution or one technology. Indeed, they clearly show the contrary—that PDM and SCM tools are successful in their respective domain, but are unable to satisfy the needs of the other.

The real goals of this book, and its strength, are a thorough analysis of what an integration of PDM and SCM could mean and a presentation of what it might look like. The authors describe different possible approaches and comment on their strengths and weaknesses. This analysis is state of the art and is based on real experience.

The authors are the right people to write this book, as the case studies clearly show. They worked for years in industry at Ericsson and ABB or in close cooperation with them; they were mostly in the SCM camp, while their respective companies were primarily involved in PDM. They had become experts in SCM but were asked to solve the issue of PDM and SCM integration. It is then that they realized, as I did myself, how difficult the integration is, and a few years later they decided to write this book.

I am sure that this book will satisfy those wanting to learn about PDM, SCM, and their differences, as well as those involved in trying to work in both fields. I personally hope that it conveys to researchers and practitioners that this is a very challenging and fundamental topic and that it will foster serious work in finding a satisfactory solution towards integration.

Jacky Estublier,
Research Director
Laboratoire Logiciels, Systemes et Reseaux LSR
LSR, Grenoble University
Grenoble, France
June 2003

Preface

Product data management (PDM) is the discipline governing the control of the product data and processes used during the entire life cycle of a product. Companies developing and manufacturing hardware products have traditionally used PDM. Software configuration management (SCM) is the discipline encompassing the control of the evolution of software products. Over the years, PDM and SCM have evolved in parallel with little or no communication between the separate developers of software and hardware. Today, products are often complex systems consisting of hardware, software, and related documentation, placing new demands on the system integration. Such complex products are often developed by several groups, each developing its part of the product, making use of either PDM in the case of hardware or SCM in the case of software components. At the point in time at which the components must be integrated to constitute the final product, information controlled by PDM and SCM must also be integrated. This is not easy, as considerable information of different formats is involved. Without direct support such as that provided by PDM and SCM tools, it is almost impossible.

Indeed, at this point many companies experience serious problems—information integration is found to be difficult to achieve, especially when managed by different tools from different domains. Why is this so? There are many reasons, technical and nontechnical. Technically, it is difficult to transfer information between different systems in an efficient way and to keep information in many systems consistent. The interoperability of PDM and SCM could thus be a key factor in the efficient management of total product information. However, PDM and SCM tools are not designed to communicate. Nontechnical factors can have even more serious results. System and hardware engineers frequently do not understand software engineers and their demands on a configuration management (CM) system, and vice versa. PDM users and SCM users may use the same or similar terms, but these terms often have different meanings to each category and are understood differently. Companies have serious problems in using PDM and SCM together. The degree to which their engineers, developers, and project mangers have knowledge of both disciplines is typically low, the overall development process is usually complex and not properly defined, and the integration possibilities provided by PDM or SCM vendors are limited.

The purpose of this book is to build a bridge between PDM and SCM and between the users of these tools. The first step towards this is to create a common understanding of the two disciplines. The book aims at this by providing an overview of PDM and SCM separately and in relation to each other. In this way, both PDM and SCM users can learn and understand the needs and requirements of the other discipline from their own perspective. Comparing and analyzing key functions of tools from both disciplines gives a deeper insight into both the use of the tools and how they can be integrated. Further, the book discusses the possibilities of their integration. As integration is not only a matter of the integration of the tools but also of the processes in which these tools are used, the book describes and discusses product life cycle processes and their relation to PDM and SCM. The principles of integration and the information that can be integrated are discussed in particular. To provide a more concrete understanding, several cases of integrated tools and processes are presented in the book. Case studies from several large international companies demonstrate the state-of-practice use of PDM and SCM and provide a basis for discussion.

Organization of this book

The book is divided into five parts, each of which explores a theme through several chapters. The parts are organized in such a way that a concept of PDM and SCM, and their integration, is developed from the ground up.

The first half of the book consists of three parts and describes the theoretical principles and concepts of PDM and SCM and their integration. The book begins with an introductory text explaining why PDM and SCM support is essential in any development process. The following chapters introduce PDM and SCM principles and discuss their similarities and the principal differences between them. The last chapters of the first half of the book describe possible alternative integrations of PDM and SCM and provide useful procedures for the deployment of PDM and SCM tools.

The second half of the book consists of two parts and is of a more practical nature: The first part includes several case studies from prominent U.S. and European companies. These case studies illustrate the use of PDM and SCM in the companies' development and manufacturing processes. The second half functions as a reference book. It includes many references to PDM, SCM and document management tools and their vendors, Web resources, and finally overviews of the most important standards used in PDM and SCM.

The five parts are organized as follows:

- Part I, *Basic Principles of PDM and SCM*, consists of three chapters. The first chapter is an overview of the complexity of product development and explains the need for the support provided by PDM and SCM. It is aimed at readers unfamiliar with PDM or SCM, (e.g., students or engineers not experienced in developing large systems). The second and third chapters describe in detail the basic principles of PDM and SCM.

- Part II, *Similarities and Differences Between PDM and SCM*, compares PDM and SCM, and describes their ability to support particular processes in software or product development.

- Part III, *Integration and Deployment*, contains two chapters. The first chapter discusses the possibilities of integrating PDM and SCM, describes the concepts of integration, and presents certain examples of integration. The second chapter contains a detailed description of PDM and SCM evaluation and deployment processes.

- Part IV, *Case Studies*, gives examples from the industry of development processes and the practical use of PDM, SCM, and document management tools. Overviews of particular projects and organizational units in large multinational companies are presented. The studies illustrate the complexity of development processes and the ongoing efforts of the companies to improve these processes by using PDM and SCM.

- Part V, *Tools and Standards Survey*, consists of comprehensive lists of references to PDM, SCM and document management tools, and vendors and their Web resources. Short surveys of selected PDM and SCM tools are used to exemplify the different types of such tools. Finally, standards closely related to PDM, SCM, and document management are described briefly.

Who should read this book?

The book is oriented toward several reader categories. The main purpose of this book is to build a better understanding between PDM and SCM users. Software developers and engineers in particular would be interested in descriptions of PDM, while system and hardware engineers would learn about basic SCM principles. Both user categories will find useful principles and concepts for PDM and SCM. Project and company managers are likely to be interested in the process and organizational aspects of the deployment and use of these tools. The case studies will provide useful information about challenges, pitfalls, and successes in the practical use of PDM and SCM and will be of interest to engineers, project managers, and system administrators. The book is also appropriate as a course book, primarily for graduate students or for undergraduate students in the later years of their studies. Researchers, within the fields of both PDM and SCM, would be interested in topics related to integrated environments and to integrated support of PDM and SCM.

How to use this book

The most straightforward way is to read the book from beginning to end! This is, however, not the only way.

Those mostly interested in the practical use of PDM and SCM could begin with Part IV, *Case Studies*, which describes relevant practical experiences of leading companies in the United States and Europe in the fields of software, telecommunication, and hardware development, as well as manufacturing. At the end of each case study, cross references to relevant chapters in the book help the reader to guide further reading. In Part V, extensive information about Web resources and references to tool providers are available for readers requiring up-to-date information about PDM, SCM, or document management tools and vendors. Similarly, the references to many standards related to PDM, SCM, and product life cycles may be of interest to engineers, project managers, and quality assurance departments.

If a new SCM or PDM tool, or a tool of a similar nature, is to be introduced, very useful and practical information about tool evaluation and deployment is available in Chapter 7.

Those interested in the basic principles and theory of PDM and SCM and their integration may prefer to focus on the first half of the book, from Chapter 1 to Chapter 6. These chapters provide useful and thorough information for engineers and others new to the use of PDM or SCM or for those already using one of these tools but who have no overall picture of development processes, product life cycles, and the support of these processes. Those with experience with SCM only may be interested in gaining insight into PDM, and vice versa. System and hardware engineers often have working experience of PDM and may wish to learn about SCM.

As course literature, reading could begin with the first parts and continue with a study of some of the case studies or standards.

For researchers, apart from Chapters 1 to 5, the most interesting would be Chapter 6, which discusses many open questions about the integration of PDM and SCM.

Web site

A Web site, www.cs.lth.se/pdm-scm/book, includes a set of presentation slides and additional material for personal study and to support the use of this book in teaching. Instructors may freely use and modify the presentation material.

Acknowledgments

We developed this book while working in three different places. We wrote in parallel, read and commented, or directly changed the text that another just wrote. Sometimes each of us worked on separate chapters, sometimes we worked together on the same chapter. It was literary a distributed development project. To make it possible to work in this way, we used the concurrent versions system (CVS) SCM tool. Over time, we realized more and more that CVS was an enormous help—and that we could not have finished our work without such support. We wish to thank all enthusiastic developers of this simple and yet so powerful tool.

Many people have contributed to the development of this book. First, we wish to thank Daniel Svensson and Allan Hedin, who actively contributed in several chapters. The inspiration for the book came from our work on the project PDM and SCM: Similarities and Differences, organized by the Association of Swedish Engineering Industries. The final report of that project was the basis for many parts of this book. We wish to thank the project participants for many fruitful discussions and for important input to the book. Many thanks to Göran Östlund, Johan Ranby, Jan-Ola Krüger, Magnus Larsson, Thomas Nilsson, Olle Eriksson, Daniel Svensson, and Allan Hedin. Special thanks to Göran Östlund, the representative of the Association of Swedish Engineering Industries, who kindly offered all the project material for the work on the book. Jacky Estublier and Geoffrey Clemm read the project report and an early version of the text for the book and greatly encouraged us to continue to work on the book. Many people from the ABB, Ericsson, Mentor Graphics, SAAB, and SUN companies have helped us greatly to make the case studies up to date, accurate, and interesting. We are obliged to them very much. Special gratitude goes to Peter Lister, an active member of International Council on Systems Engineering (INCOSE), who reviewed the entire book in detail and whose comments led invariably to its improvement. We wish to thank Victor Miller, who did a great job of reviewing all chapters and enhancing the writing style. We are particularly indebted to Tim Pitts and Tiina Ruonamaa from Artech House for their enormous and sustained support during the writing. Finally, we wish to express to our families our gratitude and love, to the children Tea and Luka, Johan and Emma, and Fredrik, Emma, and Kaspar, and to our spouses, Gordana, Maria, and Roger, without whose indefinite, unfailing, and generous support this book could not have been written.

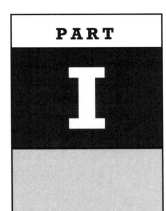

PART

I

Basic Principles of PDM and SCM

CHAPTER

1

Contents

Requirements of complex product development

There are two ways of constructing a [software] design; one way is to make it so simple that there are obviously no deficiencies, and the other way is to make it so complicated that there are no obvious deficiencies. The first method is far more difficult.

—C.A.R. Hoare

1.1 Products are all around us

In our everyday life, we are surrounded by an enormous number of products. Their number and their diversity are much greater than we can imagine. Take as an example a short moment in your daily life: the time occupied when walking from the parking lot to the entrance of a shopping center. You leave your car, close the door, and lock the door with a remote-control key. You pay your parking fee by entering your credit card in the parking meter. You approach the building, noticing briefly the lighting spots and the advertisements on a giant screen mounted on the wall of the building. You enter the shopping center through a glass door that is automatically opened as you move towards it. How many products have you been in contact with? Think for a while. It is even more fascinating to think of the number of parts from which these products are built. For example, the glass door: 5, 10, 20, perhaps up to 100 different parts? It depends on which way you count, how far you go with dividing the products into their constituent parts, and those parts into their parts, and so on. For a car,

3

you can begin to count from a 100, or maybe a 1,000. And all of these parts are products themselves, produced in thousands, millions, perhaps billions.

What is a product, then? In principle, all things manufactured or built are products. A product can be a bridge, a car, a watch, a telephone, a sweat-shirt—anything that has been built or manufactured. Different types of services can also be considered products. In their own way, software applications such as word processors, operating systems, and computer games are also products. Software is interesting in this context because an increasing number of products previously considered to be hardware now incorporate software. Examples of such are mobile phones, cars, washing machines, and television sets. Even more, for such products, the cost of developing the software component is a considerable proportion of the total development cost and is increasing. For example, the development cost of software in the industrial robot industry was one third of the total development cost 10 years ago; today it is about two thirds, and this trend is expected to continue (see Figure 1.1). We observe similar trends in the mobile phone industry and in the automobile industry.

It is also fascinating that most of these products actually work the way we expect. How is it possible for a product consisting of thousands of parts to function as one monolithic entity? And what supporting procedures are indispensable for their functioning?

 Two things are crucial for the proper functioning of a product: <u>manage-ment of its complexity</u> and the <u>provision of support</u> during its entire life. The more complex the product is, the more complex are the procedures for its development and support during its life.

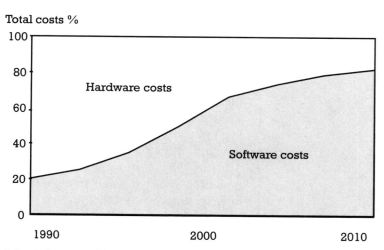

Figure 1.1 Software and hardware development costs in the industrial robots.

1.2 Product life cycle

Many products have a long life, of which the "normal" user (so-called end user) only sees a small fraction. To be aware of an *entire life* of a product, we must understand all of the processes involved in the product's development and operation, and all activities of the people involved in the processes. The mechanism used to structure these processes and to identify the major activities is called a *product life cycle* (PLC) *model.* Usually, we divide a life cycle into several life cycle phases. Each phase is characterized not only by its inputs and final results, but also by its activities, support provided, the roles of the different people involved in the activities, and the different technologies and techniques used in them. Independent of the product type, we can identify six generic phases [1]: the business idea of the product, requirements management, development, production, operation and maintenance, and finally disposal (see Figure 1.2).

The *business idea* phase begins with a perception for a new product. It continues with an assessment of the market and technology and with the identification of the key requirements of the product. At this stage a feasibility study is performed (e.g., all available information is collected and, with this as a basis, it is decided if it is feasible to develop the product). An example of feasibility study is when a company receives an inquiry from a customer for a new radar for the next generation of aircraft. The space available for the new radar is specified in the inquiry as approximately one third of that occupied by today's smallest possible radar. After months of work the feasibility study concludes that it can be done, assuming current trends in computer-aided design (CAD) and application-specific integrated circuit (ASIC) technology are extended some five to six years, and provided that the company buys a patent for 14 layer cards. The estimated risk factor is 30%.

The *requirements management* phase focuses on a further identification of requirements, their analysis, and their specification. The result of this phase is a product requirements specification.

The next phase, *development,* includes design and implementation activities. The result from this phase is the implementation of all of the artifacts needed for production. The types of artifacts can vary considerably,

Figure 1.2 Generic PLC.

depending on the type of product concerned. A typical hardware product includes prototypes and all the material needed for the product production (for example tooling and test equipment). In principle, the development phase for software will complete with the product itself.

The *production* phase (also called manufacturing phase) is significantly different for software and hardware products. In the case of pure software products, this phase is automated to a high degree and has very low costs in comparison with the other phases; at an absolute minimum, it becomes a matter of only downloading the software product. On the other hand, for a product with hardware elements, this is probably the most demanding and the most costly of all the phases. Therefore, for hardware products, much effort is invested in coping with the production requirements and in keeping production costs low.

Operation and maintenance is the phase in which the product is used by consumers and often the only phase they will see. To ensure correct operation, the product may require continuous support and maintenance. Many products have a short lifetime and require no maintenance. Some products such as jewelry have a long lifetime but require almost no maintenance. Other products require maintenance for years or even decades (e.g., houses and bridges).

The final phase of the life cycle of a product is its *disposal*. Again, the significance of this phase depends very much on the product. Different aspects related not to the product itself but to its surroundings must be taken into consideration (e.g., its impact on the environment and the question of its replacement). Examples of disposal of products are the delivery of a car to the junkyard. This is actually only the beginning of its disposal—there is disassembly, recovery of recyclable materials, and disposal of nonrecyclables. Another disposal process example is the management of nuclear waste, which lasts over thousands of years. In some countries, the producer of a product is responsible for its final disposal. Many modern products are being designed to be recycled as a result of such legislation.

1.2.1   The development phase

Generic PLC models can be implemented in different ways. There will be particular differences in the cases of software and hardware products. Let us further analyze the development phase for two different types of products: pure software products and pure hardware products.

To describe the main steps of pure hardware development, we can adopt a generic development process from Ulrich and Eppinger [1]. The process contains six steps, as depicted in Figure 1.3 (the lower part). The

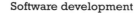

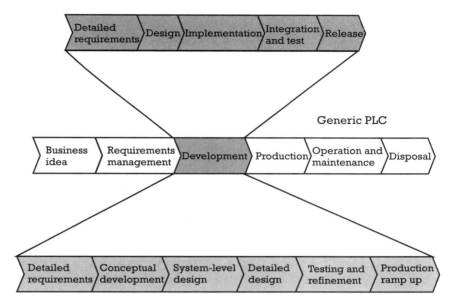

Figure 1.3   Software and hardware development processes.

development phase is preceded by the *detailed requirements management*. Although the requirements management phase can be treated separately and independently of how the product is realized (e.g., in hardware or software), a detailed requirement solicitation and specification is closely connected to the development, in particular to the *conceptual development* in which the product concepts are generated. At the *system-level design*, the architecture of the product is decided, including the identification of subsystems and components. The components are further designed during the *detailed design*. *Testing and refinement* includes the building of product prototypes to test both the product and the production system. During the *production ramp up*, the production system is used for serial production of the product, beginning at a low rate but then increasing to full production.

The software development process consists of similar phases, expressed in a most illustrative way in the waterfall model [2], shown in Figure 1.3 (the upper part). The model includes the following phases: requirements analysis, design (overall and detailed), implementation, integration and test, and finally release. The *detailed requirements* analysis phase is completed with a requirements specification. This specification is an input to the system *design* that consists of two steps: the overall design where the system architecture is designed and the components and their interfaces are identified, and the detailed design in which the component implementations are specified. In the *implementation* phase, the developers follow the design documentation and implement the system in the form of algorithms and data structures specified and written in different programming languages. If it is possible, components are tested independently. In the *integration and system test* phase, the integrators build the system from the components. The system is then ready for the system test. The final development phase in this model is the *release* management, in which the product is packaged in an appropriate form for delivery and installation at the customer's premises.

1.2.2 Different variants of PLCs

The hardware and software PLC models described here exhibit many similarities. The phases are similar; in many cases, there are no visible differences and the inputs and the goals of the corresponding phases are the same or very similar. Are there any differences then? If so, what are they? To answer these questions, we must analyze these processes in more detail. We must also understand that these models are abstractions and idealizations of the real world. For example, there are many different models that define different software development processes. The waterfall model is known to be a rigid, inflexible, and in many cases inappropriate model, but suitable for explaining and understanding software development process. It has often been used to manage large development processes. Other models (e.g., the unified process [3]) take another approach; the process is divided into a number of incremental stages in which the product is built progressively.

Finally, we should mention that there are many other PLC models that relate particularly to different aspects of product life, such as marketing issues, supply chain, and life cycles for particular products. However, all of these models have needs in common: the possibility of access to correct information, support for information generation, and the possibility of information integration.

1.3 Complexity increases

We are aware that many products meet our expectations, but also that some are afflicted with problems, such as malfunction or inadequate performance. One reason for such negative experiences is that products are becoming increasingly sophisticated and complex (e.g., the incorporation of software in different types of products improves the functionality of the products significantly, but at the cost of increased complexity and decrease in robustness). This is because software does not follow physical laws, and consequently its behavior is less predictable. Complexity makes it harder, and more expensive, to maintain high quality and is consequently most important to master. The first step toward mastering complexity, however, is to understand what actually makes a product complex.

A product can be complex for many reasons, some of them more obvious than others. A hardware product may be mechanically complex (e.g., a mechanical watch). No one doubts there must be extreme precision during the production and that maintenance (repair) is expensive. But what makes building a bridge or developing a software application complex?

Some examples of the parameters that influence complexity are:

▸ *Complex functionality.* Many products being developed today have complex functionality. Cars, airplanes, industrial control systems, mobile phones, television sets, and computers are some of examples of products with complex functionality. In addition to complex main functions, very often the products must fulfill a number of requirements to make the product more usable, adaptable, configurable, or more attractive. There are products in which properties such as reliability, robustness, availability, and performance are of crucial importance. These types of requirements specify not particular functions, but a behavior of the product. For this reason, these types of requirements are designated as nonfunctional or extra-functional requirements, sometimes quality of services. There is also another type of nonfunctional requirements, which refer to the development process. Examples of these requirements are modifiability, testability, reusability, and traceability. A large number of requirements and a large number of different types of requirements, often incompatible, lead to many difficulties in the development process. One of the problems is traceability of requirements: Which requirements are fulfilled and to which extent in a product? Transition of information from one phase to another is one of the largest problems in a development process.

▸ *Complex structure.* To avoid the difficulties in solving complex problems, a well-known principle, *divide and conquer,* is usually applied. By this, a large problem is divided into many small problems that are easier to solve. Different principles and methods can be used in such a process. Examples of these methods are top-down structural refinement, object-oriented approach, data flow analysis, unified modeling, and component-based approach. There are many references in the literature, old and new, addressing this problem [4–7]. However, transforming a large problem to many small problems usually implies that relationships between the parts become complex. The relationships between components can be so complex that it is almost impossible to grasp them. Changes in one component or its replacement can have a significant impact on other components.

▸ *Complex operational behavior.* In some cases the interaction between a product and its consumers can be complex, which makes it difficult to predict the behavior of the product in its operation. It is known that systems can excel at things that they were never designed for. The customers may want to use the products in a particular way or for a particular purpose that may require redesign of the product. This will further require extensive service, maintenance, or new development of the product.

▸ *Product and component versions and variants.* A product may consist of many components, and each component may exist in many versions. If, for example, a product consists of three components and each component exists in two versions, by combining all versions of the components, we have eight different versions of the product (as illustrated in Figure 1.4). If the product consists of four components and every component is produced in three versions, then we can build 81 versions of the product. Mathematically, the number of combinations grows n-powered with the number of components and versions. For n components in k versions, we get k^n possible versions of the product. Many of these versions are valid, but it may also happen that particular combinations of component versions are impermissible (because the versions are not compatible). Some may be managed as variants (i.e., they exist in parallel both during development and during maintenance). Keeping track of the versions and configurations of their products is a big challenge for many companies today.

▸ *Complex development process.* When the products are complex, then the development process tends to be complex as well. When many people with different roles are involved in the development process, it is important for them to have access to accurate information. In smaller groups, information can be spread in an informal and direct way. However, when the group grows, direct exchange of information is impossible to achieve. As Brooks observed [8], communication between people

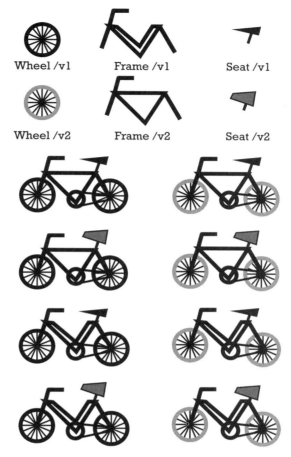

Figure 1.4 Component versions and product versions.

in a group becomes rapidly more complex when the group grows. When two people communicate directly with each other, there is one communication *link* between them; when they are three, there are three links, and for four people, the number of links grows to six. For a group of n people, there are $n(n-1)/2$ direct communications links. It is obvious that for larger groups, and for processes active under longer periods, there must exist well-defined and efficient ways to access information (see Figure 1.5).

▸ *Distributed development and production.* Both development and production may be geographically distributed. For software, the developers are often dispersed to several sites, often in different countries, while developing the same system. The production of hardware is often out-sourced (i.e., produced by another company). In some cases, many different producers are involved, producing different parts of the final product.

▶ *Need for maintenance.* Demand for maintenance and further development of a product means we must keep track of the status of all products released—sometimes even when the customer makes modifications.

▶ *Products containing both hardware and software components.* When a product consists of both hardware and software, it is important to understand the problems of both hardware and software development, production, and maintenance processes. Although these processes might be quite different, they must work together in the end. We will give some further, more concrete examples to explain some types of complexity.

▶ *Maintenance.* After 6 months of extensive selling of a new car model, a major mechanical failure in the brake system is proven after several accidents. Investigations have found that brake pads are not strong enough. The company must now replace this part in all cars already produced and delivered and on the production line. They are lucky—three independent suppliers produce this part for them. They now "only" need find out who the responsible supplier is and exchange

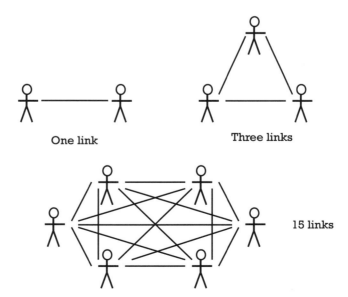

One link   Three links

15 links

Figure 1.5   Direct relationships between group members.

all parts from this supplier with a part from any of the other two suppliers. Fortunately, they treat each produced car as an individual and can trace and determine which cars have the part that must be replaced from their serial numbers. Within a few days, they send a letter to the known owners of the cars sold during the current time period and even prepare a Web page in which the owners can enter their car serial numbers and learn for themselves if they should visit the garage. Unfortunately, it may be that the responsible supplier also produced this part for previous models. The company must now investigate if this part must be replaced in these cars as well. If they are fortunate, it is only the new environment (the new car model) that stresses the part to failure.

▸ *Development—Scenario 1.* During the development phase, it was noticed that some of the requirements required modification. The requirements documents therefore had to be updated and approved by authorized people. In addition, the test cases affected by these requirements had to be modified accordingly. The result was the generation of many updated documents, followed by a document flow through the organization in order to assure that all steps in the predefined process were followed. It is a complex task to assure that all documents are updated and that all people concerned are aware of the changes concerned.

▸ *Development—Scenario 2.* Kevin in Austin, Texas, and Martin in Lund, Sweden, live in different places but work in the same company and develop the same software product. Kevin reorganizes some code in order to improve the product performance. Martin suddenly experiences a problem with his part of the code; the program crashes unaccountably. After several days of testing and frustration, he learns that another person has changed the code he is using, thus causing the crash. After further investigation, it becomes known that Kevin's optimization of his code caused the problem on Martin's part. Why could Martin not see, at once, that he was using code that had been changed and that this change might cause unpredictable behavior of his code? He should be able to see and easily find out what kind of change had been made and by whom.

1.4 PDM and SCM

Different people with different roles are engaged in the development or use of a product. These people are often interested in certain data about the product that are important for a specific phase or particular process in which they are involved. Examples of such data are requirement documents created during the early phases of the product development but also used during test phases to verify the product's function and to validate the product. Common to all data, irrespective of the phase in which it is created, is that it belongs to the product. More precisely specified, it should be related to the product, or, even better, to the correct part of the product. And vice versa—for a given product, it should be possible to find all data relevant to it.

The domain managing such product data during the product's entire life cycle is called PDM. PDM is an engineering discipline that includes different methods, standards, and tools. First, it manages data related to products: structures of the products, including lists of their components, and product configurations that identify all artifacts (components and documents versions) belonging to a particular product version. Second, it supports procedures during the PLC (e.g., peoples' roles in the processes, including their authorities and assigned activities, change management, workflow management, and even project management). PDM also deals with the development and production infrastructure, which means that it provides information for all activities. This means, for example, that PDM does not include design methods, but makes possible the availability of all information needed for a successful design process. Traditionally, PDM deals with hardware products, while it usually has not been used in development of software products.

As previously mentioned, the software development phase is frequently characterized by collaboration and coordination of many developers. To cope with this type of complexity a domain called SCM was established. The scope of SCM is to keep track of all of the files and modules constituting the product and—especially—all of the changes made to these items during their entire lives. It also takes care of all documentation related to the product.

As the alert reader now understands, PDM and SCM must have many requirements and much functionality in common. Also, even though these areas have a different history, they are both growing and increasingly incorporate more and more of the total need for managing product data, resulting in a significant overlap. This overlap is now so extensive that some people advocate that they need only one of them, their choice being determined by whether software or hardware is being developed. Our experience, however, is that there are still differences originating from the nature of the artifacts and differences in the processes. Hardware products are visible as their components. The product structure defined at design time corresponds to its physical structure. Software products are not visible in the same way as hardware products. They are embedded in specific (special purpose computers) or in standard hardware (common desktop computers). The structure of software systems during design is often very different from the structure of the system during its execution. Because the production phase of hardware products is extremely important and demanding, the focus of PDM on the production phase is very high. For software products, the production is much simpler than the development phase. The implementation process for software systems is extremely dynamic; that is why SCM focuses mostly on the implementation phase.

As long as the hardware and software development processes are isolated from each other, we can accept that PDM and SCM, although similar in principle, are different in implementation. We use one or the other tool depending on the development and production process we have. The real problem begins when we produce products that consist of both hardware and software. The first thing we would consider is the question of whether we can reduce costs by using one tool instead of two. The second question would be how we can achieve an integrated support during the entire PLC independently of whether we develop software or hardware parts. This is what this book is about! In the rest of this book, we will give a more detailed description of PDM and SCM and their respective goals and functionality. We will compare them function by function, and we will compare the use of their respective tools. After this analysis, we will arrive at a conclusion, whether we need support from both domains or we can manage with one of them, and certainly explain why. Studies of several cases will illustrate use of PDM and SCM in practice. Where both PDM and SCM are used, we will discuss the possible solutions to their integration.

References

[1]   Ulrich, K. T., and S. D. Eppinger, *Product Design and Development*, New York: McGraw-Hill Education (ISE Editions), 1999.

[2]   Sommerville, I., *Software Engineering*, Sixth Edition, Harlow, UK: Addison-Wesley, 2001.

[3]   Jacobson I., G. Booch, and J. Rumbaugh, *The Unified Software Development Process*, Reading, MA: Addison-Wesley-Longman, 1999.

[4]   Wirth, N. E., "Program Development by Stepwise Refinement," Communications of the ACM, Vol. 14, No. 4, April 1971, pp. 221–227.

[5]   Parnas, D. L., "On the Criteria to Be Used in Decomposing Systems into Modules," Communications of the ACM, Vol. 15, No. 12, December 1972, pp. 1053–1058.

[6]   Henderson-Sellers, B., and L. L. Constantine, "Object-Oriented Development and Functional Decomposition," *Journal of Object-Oriented Programming*, Vol. 3, No. 5, January 1991, pp. 11–17.

[7]   Dori, D., *Object-Process Methodology*, Berlin Heidleberg, Germany: Springer-Verlag, 2002.

[8]   Brooks Jr., F. P., *The Mythical Man-Month*, Reading, MA: Addison Wesley Longman, Inc., 1995.

Contents

General description of PDM

It is a capital mistake to theorize before one has data.
                                     —Sir Arthur Conan Doyle

2.1 Introduction

Hardware design is not only about hardware. Modern design environments are highly computerized, containing a wide variety of tools producing vast amounts of information. This information produced in different formats, in widely dispersed locations, on heterogeneous computer networks, needs to be stored and related to other data. Furthermore, geographical dispersal of design teams has made the management of design data much more complex—a pile of plans in a single location is no longer an option. Gone are the days when the design of a product and related information could be found in a central location in drawing filing cabinets, using a manual process for storing, managing, and controlling documents.

PDM systems have been developed to manage the large volumes of information created in modern design environments more effectively and to meet demands for faster development of more complex products. These systems provide access to and control of information and support different kinds of processes (e.g., approval of documents and storage of documents in archives). Typically, PDM is used for work with files and database records. These include information such as product configurations, specifications, CAD drawings, images (in the form of scanned drawings), general documentation, and numerical control part programs. In short, all product information required throughout the life cycle of a product can be managed by PDM systems.

PDM functions can be classified in different levels, as shown in Figure 2.1. All basic functionality within PDM is divided into user functions and utility functions. A PDM application is a combination of one or more PDM basic functions. Examples of applications include CM and project management. It may be necessary to establish principles and practices for PDM applications to be able to use PDM efficiently. These principles, business rules, and best practices constitute the business solution for the company.

The description of PDM in this chapter is an overview for those working within the SCM area and for beginners. A survey of PDM is provided in [1], and more information can be obtained from the PDM Information Center [2]. For a more comprehensive description from a research perspective, we recommend [3, 4]. We give a list of most commonly used PDM tools in Chapter 10.

We begin this chapter with a survey of the history of PDM (Section 2.1.1). We provide a definition of PDM (Section 2.1.2) and describe all of its functions (Section 2.2). We then present the more technical details of PDM—the information architecture (Section 2.3) and the system architecture (Section 2.4). Some applications are discussed in Section 2.5, and we finally consider certain trends in the use of PDM (Section 2.6).

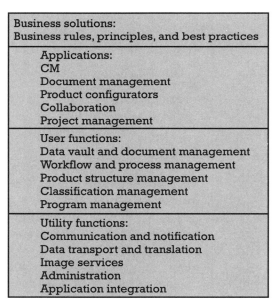

Figure 2.1 A PDM business solution model.

2.1.1 History overview

The management of product data is not a new activity. Traditionally, text documents and drawings have been archived on paper. These had to be identified and classified. Provided that the amounts of information produced were reasonable, the storage of documents in filing cabinets was manageable—even if the manual work associated with physical archives could be inconvenient. As computer technology evolved, more and more product data was created in digital form. This could be stored on file servers, thus creating a demand for systems for managing such files.

When PDM systems were introduced, the management of design documents was the most common task. For example, many companies began using PDM for more effective control of their CAD documents. PDM functions were developed both as separate systems and as data management modules in CAD systems.

Manufacturing is another area that has influenced PDM. Product structures were previously defined in text documents. When the use of databases developed in the 1970s, before the use of digital documents became wide spread, many companies began to store their product structures in databases. Companies developed their own database applications, and the design departments were responsible for feeding the databases with information. As design departments and production facilities were frequently located separately, and designers and manufacturing engineers had different demands on the content and breakdown of information, the design and manufacturing departments used separate databases. In the late 1980s, commercial PDM systems became available. The PDM systems used a product structure similar to the manufacturing structure to organize the documents. Product structure management became an issue for PDM. Initially, systems developed in-house were used to manage product structures, with the PDM systems being mainly used as advanced file systems to manage design documents. This is still the situation within some companies; legacy systems are hard to replace because they handle critical data and have many users and multiple connections to other systems.

2.1.2 PDM definition

One definition of PDM is:

> PDM is the discipline of controlling the evolution of a product and providing other procedures and tools with the accurate product information at the right time in the right format during the entire PLC.

As depicted in Figure 2.2, this involves supporting processes, such as development, manufacturing, marketing, sales, purchasing, and extended enterprises (e.g., suppliers, subcontractors, customers, and partners). Even though much of the information in the PDM system is created in the design phase, other people with different roles (e.g., partners, suppliers, and customers) use and create information during other phases. Figure 2.2 shows how the different support activities are gathered around the product and its life cycle.

Other designations on this area are collaborative product definition management (cPDM), product information management (PIM), PLC management (PLM), and electronic product data management (ePDM). Even if there are differences in the definitions, the terms and the meaning are still the same.

Note the difference between the concepts *PDM* and *PDM system*. PDM is a generic name for a set of rules, principles, and methodologies that comprise functions from different systems. A PDM system is an implementation (i.e., a set of particular tools) for managing product information and the

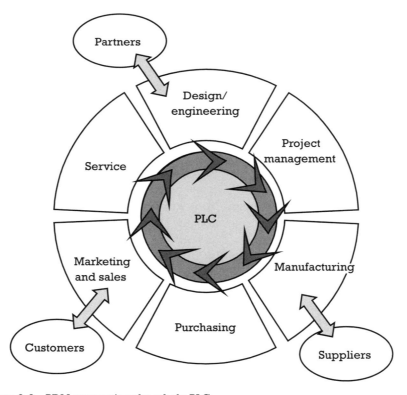

Figure 2.2   PDM supporting the whole PLC.

implemented processes. In this book, we use the term PDM to refer to a PDM system unless otherwise stated.

In the context of today's PDM vision, a PDM system is more accurately described as an information infrastructure—an infrastructure that provides users with support in performing their tasks by means of the different functional models that it incorporates and by means of other integrated software systems. PDM is therefore both a base for different systems and an information management system into which other applications can be integrated. Some applications present in PDM will be discussed in Section 2.5 as separate applications.

2.2 Basic functionality

The functionality of PDM systems is often divided into two categories: user functions and utility functions. *User functions* provide functionality for the user to access the PDM system. Different types of users may work with different subsets of these functions. A user may be a consumer (viewing information) or a producer (creating information). User functions can be divided into five categories:

1. Data vault and document management;
2. Workflow and process management;
3. Product structure management;
4. Classification management;
5. Program management.

Utility functions provide an interface between different operating environments and encapsulate their complexities to the users. Utility functions can be divided into five categories:

1. Communications and notification;
2. Data transport and translation;
3. Image services;
4. Administration;
5. Application integration.

Both user functions and utility functions will be further described in the following sections.

2.2.1 Data vault and document management

PDM systems consist of central locations, referred to as data vaults, used in the control of all types of product information. Data vaults are either physical locations in the file system (any kind of folder or directory) or databases. They provide data access control, data security, and integrity. Two types of data are stored in data vaults:

1. Product data generated by various applications, such as specifications, CAD models, computer-aided engineering (CAE) data, software executables, maintenance records, services, user and operating manuals, or any kind of information that permits users to access the data. This information is stored in the file system or in a database.

2. Metadata, which describes different properties of the product data (e.g., who created a specific piece of information and when) and index and definition information about products so that changes (new versions), approval authorizations, and other data can be tracked and audited. The PDM system also offers the functionality to query for a document, either by searching for key metadata (e.g., document title or document number) or free text search.

Users have access authorization to one or several data vaults, where they can check in documents to the data vault and control the alteration of documents after they have been checked in to these locations. To modify a data item, a user checks it out to a local work structure. Check-in and check-out functions provide secure storage and access control to data stored in the data vaults.

When a PDM system is deployed in an organization or in a project, the system administrator must define how the data vaults are to be used. One example of the use of data vaults is shown in Figure 2.3. When the user checks out a document, it will be under PDM control in a work location—a personal physical file location. Only one specific user is permitted to read and write in this work location. Any change made in the document here will not be visible to other users. The document may be changed several times before it will be checked in again into another data vault, the work in process (WIP) vault. All of the members of the project team are provided with access to the WIP vault for viewing or altering the information it contains. When the document has passed the approval process, it will be submitted and stored in the release vault, a file location where users have only read access. The approval process automatically stores information in the

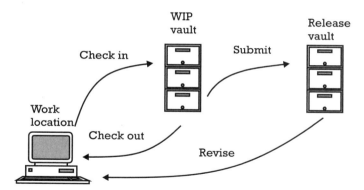

Figure 2.3 Example of data vault usage.

release vault to which only the PDM system (a very specific user with system authorities) has write access.

PDM offers many more functions than storage, check in, and check out for managing documents. A more detailed description of document management is given in Section 2.5.2.

2.2.2 Workflow management

All companies must manage their changes effectively, whether using a tool for managing changes and workflows for strict change control or using manual procedures for managing all changes on paper. Thus, workflow management is a critical part in the product definition life cycle to ensure that the right information is available to the correct users at the proper time. It includes defining the steps in the process, the rules and activities associated with the steps, the rules for approval of each step, and the assignment of users to provide approval support. PDM workflow management provides the mechanisms for modeling and managing defined processes automatically. Data can be submitted to the appropriate workflow for processing. The workflow can transfer the data to nominated users, groups, or project roles to carry out a specific business process. Appropriate information is routed automatically. At any location, the data can be assessed as it progresses through its life cycle.

PDM systems record information at each step in a process, and users can review the change history at any time. Audit and historical records are maintained. Workflow management can help define and control changes in any kind of product data.

2.2.2.1 Change approval—An example of workflow and process management

Figure 2.4 [5] shows an example of an approval process. All documents in which work is in progress are stored in the WIP vault. A work order is sent to the designer when review is necessary. The designer sends the document to designated users for reviewing. The change review board will take care of the comments. When the document is approved, it will be stored in the release vault. Upon approval, the new and modified documents and all data are sent from the WIP to a release vault, and the item now revised becomes generally available. After the work is completed, the newly revised items continue to refer to the work instructions and work orders by which they were generated. This provides a valuable history of the evolution of the design, which allows users to learn from design approaches that have been implemented in the past.

2.2.3 Product structure management

When designing a complex product, the management of its component parts is as important as the management of the documents that describe the product. A product structure comprises components (elements), the

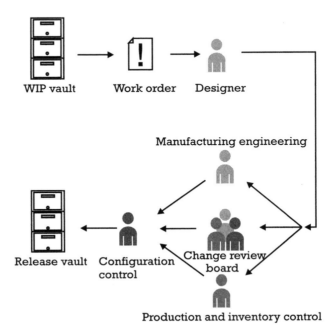

Figure 2.4 Example of a workflow for change approval.

externally visible properties of those components, and the relationships between them.

Product structure management includes the following activities:

▸ Identification and control of product configurations;

▸ Management of the development and selection of product variants, including platforms, options, alternates, and substitutes;

▸ Linking of product definition data to the structure;

▸ Allowance of various domain-specific views of a product structure, such as design and manufacturing views;

▸ Transfer of product structure and other data in both directions between PDM and manufacturing resource planning (MRP) or enterprise resource planning (ERP) systems.

A product structure most often forms a hierarchical structure. A traditional mechanical design-oriented definition of a product structure is:

> A product structure is a division of parts into a hierarchy of assemblies and components. An assembly consists of other assemblies (subassemblies) and/or components. A component is the lowest level of the structure.

This definition also describes a bill of material (BOM), which is used in manufacturing to collect all the objects and information for building the final product. Figure 2.5 depicts an example of a BOM of a bicycle, which consists of pedals, handlebars, a saddle, a frame, and wheels. In the figure, each of the parts is quantified (e.g., there are two wheels and one saddle).

The business items in a PDM system (defined in Section 2.3.1) can be used to represent any kind of object (or data) describing a product (e.g., requirement objects describing the requirements of a product and functional objects describing the functions of a product). Various kinds of relationships can be used to connect the business items (e.g., described by, requirement for, designed as, built as, and planned as).

In an enterprise, product structures are used in different procedures, which can have different requirements for the breakdown and information content of a product structure. A designer and a manufacturing engineer need to see a product from different perspectives, which results in multiple product structures, as shown in Figure 2.6. Examples of other groups that could need their own structures are business planners, or maintenance, purchasing, and sales departments. These variants of a product structure are

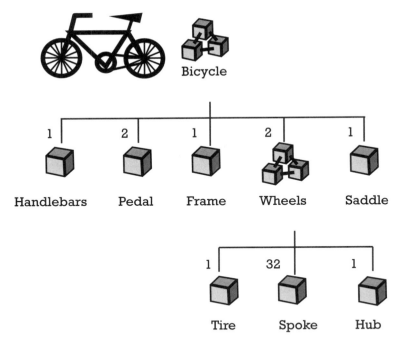

Figure 2.5   Quantified BOM of a bicycle.

often referred to as *views*, even if this is not a correct usage of the term, as they are often separate structures stored in separate information systems.

Figure 2.7 shows a more detailed example of a product structure. Each business item is of a certain type (e.g., part, assembly, or subassembly), has a name (e.g., can, lid, or container), a unique part number (e.g., 1111, 2222, or 3333), a revision (e.g., 1, 2, or 3), and perhaps also variants (e.g., small, medium, or large). For the variant "cylinder large," all three revisions are shown to illustrate that an object can exist in several revisions. Revisions are described in Section 2.3.3, and variants are described in Section 2.4.1.

PDM systems also identify variants of parts. The can in the example is manufactured in three sizes. The cylinder part has three variants: small, medium, and large. The relationships between the parts may contain rules used for the selection of alternative parts. The three different container variants (large, medium, and small) can be selected with rules. A rule can be, for example, "if volume larger than 2 dm^3, then use cylinder large." This kind of rule defines what to include in a product. There are also other (exclusive) rules defining invalid combinations of parts and assemblies.

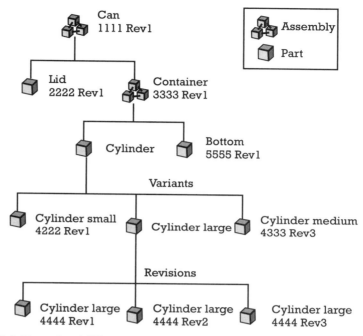

Figure 2.6 Example of different product structures.

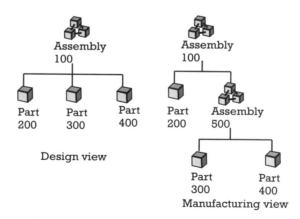

Figure 2.7 Example of a product structure describing a can with variants and revisions.

Effectivity is used to define when a part is valid in a product configuration and to select the correct revision of the part. Configuration *effectivity* is defined in Section 2.5.1.

2.2.4 Classification management

Classification management is the classification of standard components in a uniform way. To support reuse of standard components, the components are classified and information about them is stored in the PDM system as common attributes (attributes defined in Section 2.3.1). Examples of information relating to components are supplier, supplier part number, release date, revision, and material. These attributes are used for querying and retrieval of standard components, items, or objects.

To ensure that a new product reaches the market in the shortest possible time, the reuse of parts of products is essential. Reuse is supported by the possibility of classifying components and attaching attributes to them. These attributes can later be used for querying and retrieval of components to be used. Reuse also leads to greater product standardization, reduced redesign, shorter time to market, savings in purchasing and fabrication, and reduced inventories. Reuse can be at any level of a product in the product structure (e.g., engines, wheels, antennas, software modules, screws, and bolts).

When a PDM system is installed, libraries with standard components (with searchable attributes) are often included. User-defined attributes created for specific objects can also be added to these standard components. To make good use of the reuse of components, an organization should define the structure of the available reuseable components.

2.2.5 Program management

The support for project management provided by a PDM system involves standard functions such as definition of work breakdown structures (WBS), resource allocation, and project tracking. The purpose of this kind of functionality in a PDM system is that it enables the relation of the project data to the product data. This makes it possible to see with which parts of a product a specific project is working and the extent to which resources have been expended on this particular part of the product. The usage of PDM systems for project management is further explained in Section 2.5.5.

Today, most PDM systems are integrated with specialized project-management tools. Effective support for project management is then provided with the possibility of relating product and project data with each other.

2.2.6 Communication and notification

As part of the implementation of workflow support, notifications can be automatically sent to the users. A notification can be sent to make a user aware of a specific operation (e.g., check in) or when a specific state has been reached (e.g., when a change has been approved). Each user, or role, can decide to which types of notification he or she wishes to subscribe. Typically, a user is interested in everything happening within a specific project or part of the product, or a user may be interested in all parts that reach a specific state. A sufficient level of awareness may be achieved by subscribing to the appropriate notifications. Electronic mail is often used as the medium for notifications.

2.2.7 Data transport and translation

PDM stores and manages data produced by many different applications. This information is often retrieved for reading or changing in the same application, but there may be a need to (at least) read the data in another application.

In a PDM system, predefined translators can be used for converting data from one application for use in another and for displaying information. The system administrator sets up the translators and the users therefore do not need to know which data translators to apply. Events can trigger automatic data translation from one application format to another.

2.2.8 Image services

Visualization tools support collaborative work by making it possible for all users to view images. Images can be stored and accessed as any other data in the PDM systems or in, for example, CAD systems. Scanned documents, two-dimensional drawings, and three-dimensional CAD models can then be viewed and marked up using standard visualization capabilities. The PDM system has add-on functionality for interoperability between CAD systems and the PDM system. For example, information represented by raster and vector images, together with portable definition file (PDF) viewing, allows users to view drawings and other design data in the PDM system, even though the data is stored in a CAD system. PDM solutions may also provide visualization capabilities within the products. View, markup, and annotation functions are commonly used during change reviews. This function can significantly improve communication between reviewers and others.

2.2.9 System administration

PDM systems, like any other computer system, need system administration. For PDM systems, this administration is more complicated and contains more tasks. The system administration functions include installation and maintenance, role management, workflow definition, operational parameters, system performance monitoring, database and network configuration, access and change permissions, user authorizations, setting up new projects and authorization of project team members, approval procedures, data backup and security, database migrations to later versions, customization, and data archival. These systems can be customized in many ways: matching business needs, tailoring the user interface to satisfy particular needs, integrating third-party applications (tools), adding new functionality, changing terminology, tailoring system information messages, and extending the standard data model to include company-specific data types. The customization, and the consequent requirements for education and maintenance, will need resources and efforts to be successful.

2.2.9.1 Role management

Role management is a part of system administration. Many roles, mechanical designers, software designers, project managers, and service support people are involved in the life cycle of a product, performing only particular tasks and therefore needing different access rights to product data. Role management includes such functions as setting up user accounts, groups, access rights, and security levels and the maintenance of all users and corresponding roles and groups.

2.2.10 Application integration

Integration with authoring, visualization, and other collaborative tools is important to establish a single source of product data. Information is created once for use throughout the product development process, and one source electronically colocates geographically dispersed authors and users.

Integrations range from the less complex, such as that with text editors, to tight integrations as with CAD/computer-aided manufacturing (CAM) and ERP systems. Integration with text editors (e.g., Microsoft Word and Adobe FrameMaker) includes the addition of such functions as check in and check out of documents to and from the text editor. This supports the user with automatic transferring of documents without manual work and detailed knowledge of the PDM system. Integration with CAD/CAM systems is more difficult because CAD/CAM systems manage various relationships between the parts, both parts structures and system-specific relationships, resulting in a network of interrelated files. Integration with ERP systems includes the transfer of parts structures with attributes. This kind of inter-domain integration is often the most difficult to achieve.

2.3 Information architecture

Information architecture has been defined as follows [6]:

> An information architecture describes salient phenomena and their static relationships to each other in a defined context.

2.3.1 Data representation

The information in a PDM system is structured to follow an object-oriented product information model. Objects are of two different kinds: *business items* and *data items*.

Objects used to represent parts, assemblies, and documents are designated business items or *business objects*. (To avoid confusion, we will use the terms business item and data item.) A business item contains attributes and metadata, described in Section 2.2.1, which define the properties of the item (e.g., its name or revision). An *attribute* has a name and one or several values. A PDM system also manages files. A file is represented in the database as a data item. The metadata is separated from the content or actual data (file). This is to enable replication of metadata without necessarily replicating the file. A data item can be reused from several business items. A business item can have a relationship with several data items. This is not possible in a standard file system.

In many cases, PDM extends a function, which is performed on a business item to apply automatically to the data item or data items. For example, when a business item is copied in PDM, the data item is also copied, given a new name, and attached to the new business item.

Relationships are used between objects (both business and data items) to relate them to each other. A product structure consists of objects and relationships together with attributes. Product structures use a special class of business items (*structured business items*) with special relationships to support BOM requirements for usage, described in Section 2.5.1, and physical identification. An attribute can be defined either on an object or on a relationship.

Figure 2.8 shows how a document is managed by its metadata through the business item and the file itself in the data item.

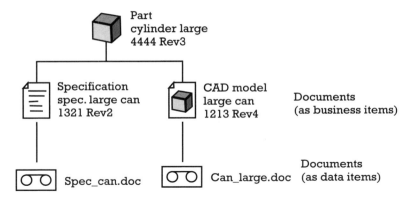

Figure 2.8 Illustration of representation of documents by both business items and data items.

2.3.2 Information model

An information model is a logical organization of real-world objects, constraints on them, and the relationships between objects (i.e., a network of objects related to each other). An object-oriented information model consists of the following basic object-oriented concepts [7, 8]:

> ▸ *Object and object identifier.* Any real-world entity is uniformly modeled as an object. An object is associated with a unique identity with which it can be pinpointed.
>
> ▸ *Attributes and methods.* Every object can have a state (the set of values for the attributes of the object) and a behavior (the set of methods—program code—that operate on the state of the object). The state and behavior encapsulated in an object are only accessed or invoked from outside the object through explicit message passing.
>
> ▸ *Class.* This is a means of grouping all of the objects that share the same set of attributes and methods. An object may belong to only one class as an instance of that class.
>
> ▸ *Class hierarchy and inheritance.* This is the derivation of a new class (subclass) from an existing class (super class). The subclass inherits all of the attributes and methods of the existing class and may have additional attributes and methods.

The PDM information model utilizes this object-oriented approach. The PDM information model describes the types of objects, relationships, and attributes used to represent business items, data items, and relationships between them. The information model can be changed to better suit the needs of a particular business solution in a company.

A database system implements an information model, or, in other words, a database language is a concrete syntax for an information model. In most database systems, the object-oriented information model is implemented in tables, concealed from the users by both a graphic interface and several functions on a higher abstraction level. Alternatively, an object-relational database, an object-oriented database extended with relationships, can be used. Transactions provide support for concurrent usage of the objects.

Figure 2.9 depicts an information model described by a generic product structure. This example is selected from Metaphase [5]. Several PDM systems (e.g., [5, 9, 10]) have an information model partly based on the Standard for the Exchange of Product Model Data (STEP) standard [11]. Most of them, however, only follow this standard to a certain degree.

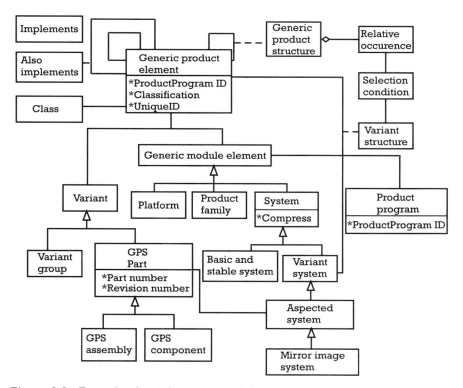

Figure 2.9 Example of an information model.

2.3.3 Version management

Version management is mostly about revisions and versions—how to create them, store them, and retrieve them. Within the PDM system, all items are under version control management.

Versions are at the lowest level. The main characteristic of a version is that when frozen, it can no longer be changed (i.e., it is immutable). It must be checked out instead, which means that the system creates a new, succeeding version (with identical contents), from it which can be edited. When editing is completed, the user checks in the item, making the new version also immutable. Versions are identified with a sequence number starting from one (see Figure 2.10).

Revisions are superimposed on versions. Revisions of business items are often identified with a letter (e.g., A, B, or C). To work with an item, the user checks it out, edits it, and then checks it in again (freezing it), creating a new version with the same revision name. A revision can be revised, which means a new succeeding revision is created and assigned an increased revision letter.

The versions and revisions of an item together constitute its evolution history and can later be viewed by any user. However, only the latest revision and version can be changed (i.e., checked out—B;2 in the Figure 2.10 example).

PDM does not support concurrent development. When a user checks out an item, this version is locked to prevent other users from checking out the same version. Thus, there is no possibility of creating several versions of an item to exist in parallel with each other. When the item is checked in again, the new version is stored, and the lock is released. That support of concurrent editing of items is not provided is of no great significance for hardware

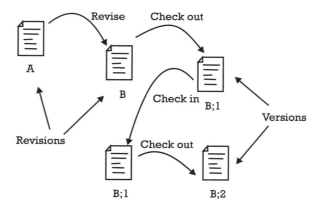

Figure 2.10 Example of the connections between revisions and versions.

development, but is a clear disadvantage for software development, where concurrent development is more common.

2.4   System architecture

Figure 2.11 depicts a PDM system containing both a metadata database and data items managed by the system but stored in an ordinary file system. The figure also depicts an example of metadata stored in a business item. Note the reference to the data item file location.

Figure 2.12 [5] shows an example of PDM architecture. The example shows how a corporate server (one master server within the company)

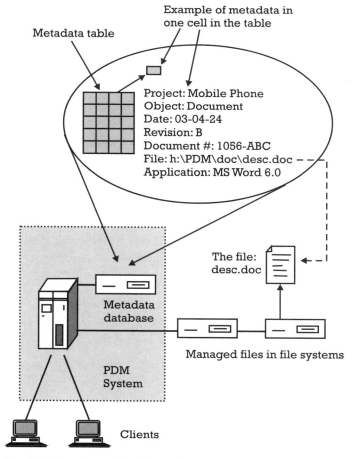

Figure 2.11   A PDM system with data vaults.

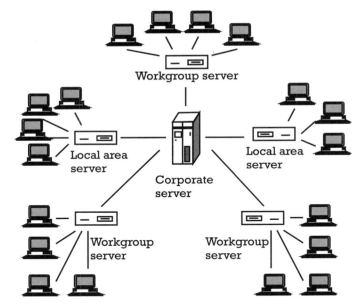

Figure 2.12   Example of a system architecture in a PDM system.

stores common information used by other servers. This information in the corporate server defines what the other servers must be able to access and what kind of data they may modify. The corporate server information also includes the location of all other servers in the network. The local area server provides services to networks geographically separated from the corporate server. Locally, a workgroup server runs one or more database servers. The purpose of the workgroup server is to provide better performance when the data is stored locally. The workstation runs the client software. In another solution, the server runs the client application, and in this case the client is only a Web browser.

2.4.1 PDM database

A PDM system uses a database to store data in a structured way. A database offers a query language, which is used to make queries to the database to extract information. A database can also manage multiple users, security, and backup of data. PDM manages metadata and file data, where the metadata is stored in the database, and file data is stored in PDM-controlled file locations, as can be seen in Figure 2.11. Metadata is used to support PDM functions, such as search for information. Relevant attributes must be stored with the data item for a user to be able to make relevant search criteria.

2.4.2 Data vault

A data vault is used as a repository to control product information represented as business items and data items in the database. The vault is logical data storage used to store and manage access to documents and files stored electronically and produced by various applications. Depending on the chosen installation strategy, the administrator may choose either to incorporate all files (data items) in the PDM database or just to store the references to the actual file in the file system in the database.

2.4.3 Data replication in a distributed environment

To be able to perform distributed development, where project team members are located at various geographically dispersed sites, data has to be available at all of the sites. This must be done in a controlled way to avoid inconsistency of data. PDM systems have distributed replicated databases, in which it is possible to replicate metadata or both metadata and files throughout the network, as shown in Figure 2.13. In a distributed environment, administration and user data is always replicated. Other metadata is replicated as needed. Files (data items) are also replicated as needed. Performance problems are distributed by event-driven replication. For example, if a change is performed and a check in is done, the changed document will not be distributed to all other servers until a query is done to avoid unnecessary network load.

The metadata must always be distributed upward in the hierarchy, toward the corporate server. Figure 2.12 depicts the server hierarchy. Metadata stored on a workgroup server is first distributed to the local server and then to the corporate server. When a user searches for metadata, the workgroup server is searched first. If this metadata is not found on the workgroup server, the local area server is searched, and finally the corporate server is searched. If the metadata contains a link to a data item, this link can be used to fetch the data item from its location.

The data items are always stored locally on the workgroup servers. These gives the teams located at the sites good performance, as each file can be quite large, resulting in disturbing download times. In some PDM configurations, data items are distributed to other sites (or servers) as well, which may cause performance overhead. This is used when the local site needs all data with good performance, fast downloading of data, and guaranteed availability of data even when the central server is not up and running.

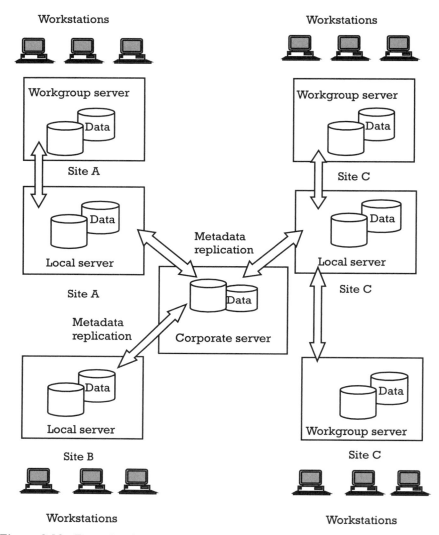

Figure 2.13 Example of a distributed environment in a PDM system.

2.5 Applications

Over the years, many different solutions for supporting PLCs have evolved. Many different applications (e.g., CM, document management, change control, and product configurators) have been developed. PDM vendors provide these applications to different degrees. They have taken user functionality and utility functionality and extended the capabilities by developing applications focused on specific problems.

PDM solutions are built upon different applications, together with business methods and processes, business-tailored PDM information structures, and the specific PDM system architecture.

In this section, we present an overview of the most common and important applications used in PDM systems.

2.5.1 CM

CM is a domain that originated in military and space applications in the late 1950s, where complex products were built from detailed specifications. Traditional CM is a coarse-grained document management [12], where configuration identification and control is directly on product level.

CM is a huge domain, related to PDM, with its own definition and standards [12–15]. Parts of CM are implemented in many PDM systems.

CM is both a management discipline and a process. Its purpose is simply to ensure that organizations have the information they need to ensure that their products perform as intended. The CM processes span the PLC, including the supply chain, and must play a comprehensive role in enterprise management. A more thorough description of CM from a Swedish point of view [13] is given in Chapter 3.

CM support, from a PDM point of view [1, 2, 5, 16] provides the tools needed to more effectively communicate with the disparate workgroups and business partners that comprise the supply chain to:

- Instantly communicate and control engineering changes, and determine which changes have been implemented; minimize the number of changes after production begins, reducing delays, and rework; trace problems back to their origins and forward to locate faulty or out-of-date components or documents that may have been or will be placed in use; and manage different product variants and versions—changes drive CM;

- Plan and control product configurations (supported by the product structure), especially in supporting mass configure-to-order manufacturing and high levels of customization, using several supply sources; provide different views of the product structures to support multiple disciplines (e.g., design engineer and manufacturing engineer); control the product baselines; manage available options and combinations for ordering; and manage alternatives and substitutes for parts in the structure;

▶ Synchronize parallel/concurrent or collaborative product development at geographically dispersed sites, reducing lead-time without propagating errors, and provide awareness of product progress;

▶ Synchronize multisource procurement and multisite manufacturing through centrally controlled and distributed BOM and related specifications to yield a product consistent with a single set of specifications;

▶ Reconfigure a complex supply chain to respond to rapidly shifting customer requirements;

▶ Optimize the maintenance of highly varied technical assets and products by ensuring that repair or upgrade crews are provided with the correct parts, tools, and drawings to perform their work;

▶ Configuration effectivity to meet the needs from different users—designers use revisions; manufacturers use changes to date, lot, serial numbers, or as-maintained details; vendors use a com-bination of effectivities to determine designs used and as-built/as-maintained details. The configuration effectivity of a part is either a time frame $[t_1, t_2]$, a version interval [$revision_1$, $revision_2$], or a number interval [$number1$, $number2$]. Effectivity is particularly used for manufacturing purposes. The configuration effectivity is an attribute on the relationship, not an attribute on the part objects themselves, as a part may exist in several configurations with different effectivity.

2.5.2   Document management

As document management is important in product development, and therefore in PDM, document management is important in any type of business—software development, information services, publishing businesses, all type of administration, and any kind of production. For this reason, the existence of different types of document management tools outside PDM is expected. The main objectives of document management tools are similar to the goals of PDM (i.e., to provide a structure for the storage, selection, and retrieval of information). According to [17]: "Document management is functionality for managing documents that allows users to store, retrieve, and share them with security and version control."

Like PDM systems, document management systems use a relational database to store data about documents. This data (i.e., metadata) defines the information structure and different views for presentation and accessing documents. Further, it includes information about authorization, ownership, history, and other data related to documents. Document management systems provide version management similar to PDM. In addition, a workflow management, also designated issue management, is usually provided in document management tools. The histories of documents are available (i.e., it is possible to access previous versions of documents, but only the latest version of a document can be modified). Similar to PDM systems, document management systems support distributed development by managing distributed databases where different replication mechanisms are used for the updating of local databases.

Is the focus on documents specific to document management? Not really. Most of the functions implemented in document management are also present in PDM. Most of the functions implemented in document management are present in PDM. However, there are several functions that are developed to a greater extent in document management:

- *Extensive search functions.* Document management tools make possible not only the specification of an extensive range of search keys, but also searches through different types of documents.

- *Virtual document.* A set of documents must often be assembled for a particular purpose. Such a set is not necessarily defined as a part of the document structure; it can be an ad hoc collection of different documents. Document management tools provide support for the assembly of documents, or specific versions of documents, in a so-called virtual document. A virtual document may later be handled in the same way as any other document.

- *Automatic translation into different formats.* The same information must very often be presented in different forms. In some cases, certain information in one document is to be used in another. Document management tools provide sets of conversions tools for the most popular document formats.

- *Web-oriented approach.* Because Web publishing has become of enormous importance in any type of business, document management tools show a strong trend to the support of Web publishing. Functions such as automatic document translation to Web pages, organization of Web servers, Web page organizers, and Web page editors are standard parts of modern document management tools.

- *Standard formats.* The differences between the formats of documents are hindrances to the seamless integration and exchange of information. Integration tool providers call for a common format for metadata and other types of data. A solution to these problems is separating documents formats from their contents. Several standards are based on this principle. Standard generalized markup language (SGML) or the more popular extensible markup language (XML) differentiate between content and format and in this way enable the presentation of the same contents in different formats. XML is less general than SGML (actually it is a specific implementation of SGML), but much simpler. XML has become a de-facto standard for describing different formats and for describing protocols for exchanging information. Document management tools use XML today as a basic standard for specification of structures and document formats.

In the same way as PDM, the scope of document management tools is being extended. In addition to documents, they manage all types of information items, referring to them as digital assets. Multimedia assets are typical examples of digital assets that require specific treatment. To indicate that the tools manage any type of digital asset, there is a trend to replace the term *document management* with *content and document management*.

2.5.3 Product configurators

Product configurators are used to assemble a product, offering choices between alternative components. The configurator contains a set of rules for selecting the correct component.

Configurators are used to guide users with insufficient in-depth knowledge to otherwise configure a product. For examples, salesmen can use a configurator to automatically configure a product based on a customer's requirements, and a configurator can be used in manufacturing to select the correct components to build a specific product.

Throughout the various stages of a product's life cycle, use is made of rules based on experience, best practices, company standards, and knowledge of how the product can be sold, manufactured, packaged, maintained, and disposed. Historically, these rules have been available in different kinds of paper documents, and even as generally accepted unwritten rules. The product configurator manages the various constraints and dependencies using the product structures and relationships.

2.5.4 Collaboration

PDM has traditionally been associated with design and release in preparation for production, while the PDM of today aims to manage product data throughout the complete PLC, from the early phases until manufacturing and maintenance. Many users with different roles need the information managed by the system. Within many of today's companies, organizations, or functions are outsourced. Companies focus on their supply chains, extended enterprises, strategic partnerships, and virtual teams [18]. All of these functions need access to certain defined product information. For example, a supplier will provide the company with new information about an old component. A company partner must know the most recent requirement of a product; a manufacturer needs the latest documents for manufacturing the product; developers must exchange information, often on a daily base during the development phase; and a customer may be interested in how far the product has come in the development phase. This calls for collaborative tools to bridge geographical distances and enable users to work in virtual teams, and it has made collaboration support an essential component of a PDM system. Commercial PDM systems of today support what they call collaborative product management (CPM) or collaborative product commerce (CPC).

PDM systems contain functions that can be used in a distributed environment to provide necessary information to the different roles concerned at the right time. Examples of different roles are suppliers, partners, manufacturers, developers, and customers. Examples of processes supported by collaborative tools are, according to [18]:

▸ *Change management and design review.* Information has to be sent several times between the sites, when the design of a product that was developed at several sites is reviewed. If the information is stored at a single location and the process is controlled by a workflow, less information is sent between the sites and control is gained over the process. The next step is to add synchronous collaboration and enable virtual team members to work together simultaneously. A group of designers, working at separate locations, can view the same model, annotate it, and communicate with each other using text messages, audio, and even video communication.

▸ *Sales and bidding.* To make it easier for customers, the customers can be given access to product information. The request for quotation (RFQ) process can be automated. The customer sends in a request, its validity is checked, and an answer is generated. If the request results in an order, this can be followed on its way through design and manufacturing.

▸ *Maintenance and support.* Engineers, operators, and maintenance staff need access to up-to-date maintenance information. Animated illustrations can be used to assist in understanding documentation. Feedback is also important; personnel in the field can send in fault reports and recommendations.

> ・ *Manufacturing planning.* Manufacturing personnel can use collaboration for many purposes, such as reviewing design and change orders in consultation with the design team. They can interface early with tool designers to verify tooling assemblies and operations, reviewing manufacturing process plans and factory layouts, discussing manufacturing problems with suppliers, and coordinating tooling at different sites.

2.5.5 Project management

Modern project management began in the late 1950s and early 1960s, when the magnitude of new projects, their scope, duration, and the resources required began to demand more than a flow chart and a conference table. At the same time, literature on the subject of *management by projects* began to emerge [19]. The phrase *project management* crept into the vernacular, although it was mostly limited to the engineering and designing industries.

According to [19], project management is the application of knowledge, skills, tools, and techniques to a broad range of activities in order to meet the requirements of the particular project.

The project team manages the work of the project, and the work typically involves:

> ・ Planning, or deciding what is to be done;
> ・ Organizing the resources through the activities;
> ・ Directing the activities towards the project goals;
> ・ Controlling the activities concerning project constraints where the most critical constraints are time, cost, and performance;
> ・ Motivating the project members to accomplish the project objectives.

In product development processes, the work is often divided into phases, where each phase is related to some kind of decision making. When starting up a new project, the project manager breaks down the project into subprojects. Each subproject manager then breaks down the subproject into smaller tasks and activities. Tasks are ordered within work breakdown structures (WBSs), which can be grouped into hierarchical structures of dependencies. This provides a convenient way to allocate resources and to track the project's progress. For example, requirement specifications, verification plans, drawings, and software executables can be linked to a WBS to make tracking possible when work has been completed against project plan activities.

Most PDM systems manage product data and processes, which by integration with third-party project management systems can be tied to project activities and milestones. The advantage of incorporating project management capabilities within a PDM system stems from the knowledge that the PDM system has of the processes and data needed to complete specific activities within the project plan.

2.6 Trends in PDM

This chapter contains a short survey of trends in PDM research and development and of the use of PDM in industry.

2.6.1 Trends in research and development of PDM

PDM as a research field is not yet fully consistent. There are no unifying theories and the definitions are sometimes vague. This may be because the scope of PDM is wider than that of many other research areas. PDM aims at managing product development information throughout the entire PLC and intersects with several other disciplines, such as requirements management. It is difficult to develop theories and knowledge in a comprehensive domain, and few PDM researchers and developers use PDM systems on a daily basis for their ultimate purpose (i.e., to assist in the design of products).

Research in the field of PDM has a wide scope and has to cover more areas than information systems and data management methods only. How data is represented and structured is an important issue. To be able to discuss these matters, theories for the structuring of the things represented—the products—are needed. This has become a separate area of research, known as product models, dealing with how products should be represented by information models and represented in databases. This area and other important areas of research on PDM will be presented in the following section.

2.6.1.1 Deployment of PDM systems

The deployment of PDM systems is more than a question of technology. Sufficient knowledge of company-specific processes and what they require of PDM systems is crucial, as several processes in the PLC are affected by a PDM implementation. Research in this field mainly deals with the technical aspects of product data management, such as computer systems and data representation. More research is needed into the deployment of PDM systems, system strategies, and applications of PDM, such as CM and document management. This section lists some of the research into system deployment and strategies.

Pikosz et al. [20] discuss different strategies for the deployment of PDM systems. PDM can be introduced by beginning with limited functionality, implemented companywide across several projects, or as a complete PDM system introduced in a single project. Risks were observed with the introduction of a complete system. Many introductions are therefore now performed in a phased manner, with the functionalities implemented in steps, beginning with a few basic functions.

Companies using PDM have differing objectives. Some are operational, such as improved support for information management, but PDM solutions may also address business drivers, such as time to market, product quality, and product development cost. The operational effects of PDM are more evident than the effects on a company's business performance. Harris [21] states that there has been little research performed on the connection between PDM system strategies and a company's overall business strategy, either directly or through a higher level information system strategy.

PDM systems can play an important role in a high-level information system strategy through their integration capabilities. It has earlier been observed that PDM systems are mostly used by the design discipline [22]. This situation is likely to change, especially on the tool side. This is because the aim of PDM system suppliers is to support a larger part of the PLC, but the integrational capabilities of the PDM systems are not yet fully exploited. The main challenge in future research in this area will be to merge all local solutions used in the PLC phases using an integrated approach in supporting the entire life cycle. PDM technology will have a key role in such a system.

2.6.1.2 Collaboration

Ways that PDM can be applied to support collaboration was mentioned earlier in this chapter. Collaboration is supported not by adding new data management functionality to the system, but by packaging already existing functionalities together with methods for data access via Web interfaces (from inside and outside firewalls). The trend here is about applying standard functionalities and improving access possibilities, and then marketing these under the keyword *collaboration*. Commercial PDM systems of today support what is designated CPM or CPC.

2.6.1.3 Product structure management

Product structure management (PSM) plays a key role in product data management in the manufacturing industry, which uses product structures in both design and manufacturing activities. The aim of PDM with respect to PSM is similar to the overall aim of PDM: support for the complete PLC. The trend in product structure management is therefore to provide improved support for the various types of product structures used throughout the PLC, such as design structures, manufacturing structures, and delivery structures.

PSM research is focused on the support of manufacturing activities. The use of BOMs has been quite extensively covered [23–26]. One challenging problem is the handling of variants of products (see Section 2.5.3).

Another issue is the handling of domain-specific structures and views of structures. Various types of product structures are used by different disciplines in a company, each having different requirements with respect to the decomposition of the product structure. Designers are likely to prefer decomposition into systems and subsystems, while manufacturing uses an assembly decomposition of a structure [23]. Svensson and Malmqvist [26] discuss strategies for cooperation between systems containing different views of a product structure, concluding that the conflicting demands have led to a multisystem environment. All changes in a product structure must (automatically) propagate to all information systems containing this product structure, which calls for information system strategies that involve more than the PDM systems used.

2.6.1.4 CM

PDM systems offer possibilities that are not fully exploited by existing CM methods. Traditional CM is a coarse-grained document management, while PDM enables product-centric, fine-grained CM [12], in which configuration identification and control is directly on the product level.

An important part of CM is configuration control, also referred to as engineering change management (ECM). Even if a company does not perform CM in accordance with the standards, companies need to control the changes in their products. PDM technology offers fine-grained ECM and allows changes to be effected at the finest grained object/attribute level. The impact of changes can be identified through relationships, minimizing the overall disruption of a change. This is one example of the possibilities of PDM systems that can be exploited more effectively.

ECM is a part of CM that has been subject to research (e.g., Wright [27] has performed a thorough review of research into ECM). One of the questions asked was how engineering changes drive incremental and step-wise design in different types of companies. While engineering changes can be seen as a source of expense from a manufacturing perspective, they can actually have a positive impact on the product design process. Pikosz and Malmqvist [28] have made a comparative study of ECM to find company-specific factors in the performance of ECM.

2.6.1.5   Product configurators

A product configurator is used to solve complex problems. It should be able to configure and optimize a product despite restrictions that may be contra-dictory. In the 1980s, artificial intelligence was a popular approach to the solution of the configuration problem. The problem to be solved has since broadened and now includes knowledge management. To configure a prod-uct, the ability to handle both the process of configuring the product and the data and knowledge associated with it is essential [25]. Product configura-tors are often in-house-developed software and are difficult to update with new products and rules. Mesihovic and Malmqvist [29] suggest that the information needed for configuration could be handled by the PDM system during the development phase. Configuration data would then be available to all needing, it and it would be easier to change data.

In manufacturing, the problem is associated with production control issues and forecasting. The BOM must be able to manage variants. A generic BOM [25, 24] is a BOM capable of managing variants of a product in a sin-gle structure, which simplifies the work of keeping structures up to date when a change occurs. Forecasting is another issue that is complicated by variety in products. It is difficult to plan the component if it is difficult to predict which variants of product customers will order. The manufacturing planning system must therefore be able to work on the basis of aggregate information [24].

2.6.1.6   Product models[1]

Until relatively recently, an engineer's view of product modeling has been of a purely technical nature, concerned with the problems of creating a robust geometric model in a CAD or CAE system. However, as CAD and CAE environments have developed further and data management systems facilitated the distribution of data, new problems have emerged.

1. Sections 2.6.1.6 and 2.6.1.7 are partially taken from a report [30] written by a group of researchers within the Swedish national graduate school Engineering Design Research and Education Agenda (ENDREA).

In order to generate a sound product model, it is important to have a clear idea of how to decompose a product. The science of engineering design has created elegant theories, such as the Theory of Technical Systems (TTS) [31], describing the correct structuring of product models, but these are hardly, if ever, used in industry. A more widely implemented technique used to organize and structure information is systems engineering [32, 33]. It was initially created to support the development of complex systems, while the TTS is the result of European research into engineering design. Sharing some features with TTS, system engineering is more concerned with analysis and life cycle management and has been formalized in at least two standards, IEEE 1220 and EIA 632. The European design research has a more product-oriented view, decomposing a specification into a component structure using a so-called chromosome model of a product [34].

These techniques are concerned with high-level structuring of product data. At a more detailed level, interest is increasing in techniques for formalizing engineering know-how, often referred to as knowledge-based engineering (KBE). KBE has been in use a number of years; one of the best-known systems is iCAD, which dates from the mid 1980s.

The need for a systematic way to describe products is clearly increasing in importance as product models now include complex constructs such as rules, variants, requirements, and product configuration possibilities.

2.6.1.7   Product data representation and modeling

Product modeling theory deals only with the structuring of the product, not its representation, for which we need some kind of language. The capabilities of representation have evolved with the development of object-oriented techniques. The capabilities have progressed from lists of values defined by text documents to product models that also take care of the semantics and internal relations within the model. The modeling language that describes the product model must therefore also be able to define these semantics. It is important that both humans and computers can interpret the modeling language to avoid misunderstandings and misuse.

A number of languages are capable of handling product information with semantics. The two languages most frequently used today are the lexical (the language is expressed in text, but can be visualized with the appropriate tools) language EXPRESS [35] and the visual (the language is expressed in graphics and has no lexical representation) language Unified Modeling Language (UML) [36]. Both of these languages are defined by international standards and are not based on any specific implementation technique or specific programming language.

The advantages of EXPRESS, as compared with UML, are its capacity to handle rules and the fact that it was specifically designed to describe product information. UML was originally designed to describe software development projects, but the general structure of the language also makes it suitable for describing product information. It also has the capability to describe processes and display different views of the product information.

2.6.1.8 Databases

Database technology has existed since the early 1960s [37] and is a mature area from both a practical point of view and a scientific point of view. However, handling product data in a database is different from other applications:

- Many different types of objects and attributes are needed to describe a product.
- Large hierarchical structures must be stored.
- The frequency of creation and change of data is high.
- The data models differ between companies.

Most databases used today are relational or object-relational databases, in which data is best stored when structured in lists. Hierarchical structures are best represented by object-oriented concepts. Object-oriented databases are a relatively mature technology but have not been successful to date, mainly because of performance problems.

2.6.2 Trends in industry

Many companies today consider the implementation of a PDM system to be of strategic importance. PDM investments (software and services) in industry increase continuously, from $1.1 billion in 1997 to $1.7 billion in 1999 [38]. Implementations have often been associated with problems and high costs, with services accounting for the greater part of the implementation cost. Even if there is strategic importance in PDM systems, PDM projects are today subject to more strict requirements for well-defined business cases and faster return on investment than they were previously. During recent years, more successful implementations have been achieved, partly as a result of better control of implementation projects, better applications and hardware, and the growing interest in PDM in industry, which results in a stronger commitment to the PDM projects.

In this section, the situation in two larger companies is described: Ford Motor Company and Boeing. The description is based on a report from a study visit to those companies by a group of researchers within the Swedish national graduate school ENDREA [39].

2.6.2.1 Ford Motor Company

Ford is a global company in the automotive industry, producing a wide range of cars: Lincoln, Ford, Mercury, Volvo, Mazda, Jaguar, Aston Martin, and Land Rover. About 60 car programs are developed in parallel. The PDM activities at Ford are mainly coordinated by a project called C3P (CAD, CAE, CAM, and PIM). Ford used an in-house-developed system to manage product data for many years, but finally decided to develop a new computer-supported environment for product development, which also involves partners and suppliers. One year later, EDS was chosen as the provider of the CAD system I-DEAS, and the PDM system Metaphase. About four years after the decision, all new car programs were developed in C3P, and the first cars developed in the C3P environment were introduced on the market.

2.6.2.2 The goals of C3P

The vision of C3P is to obtain integration of Ford Enterprise Product Development through Global PIM and Advanced CAD, CAM and CAE functionality. The main forces behind this investment are the demands of concurrent SE and supply chain integration. The measurable targets of C3P were ambitious:

• Lead-time reduction from 50 to 36 months;
• Prototype cost reduced by 50%;
• Reuse of components increased by 30%;
• Late product changes reduced by 50%.

The time-to-market (TTM) goals of C3P have been achieved at both Ford and Mazda.

2.6.2.3 The C3P concept

C3P involves more than information technology. Both the tools and the way things are processed had to be changed. Changing existing working procedures was the big challenge and a large part of the introduction involved training people at Ford and its partners and suppliers. The concept is divided into four CAE views. *Digital mock up* (referred to at Ford as digital buck) represents the product definition, *digital factory* represents the production process, *digital clay* is the styling surfaces, and *analytical prototypes* are the simulation models. Digital mock up is the most mature area of the four. A digital mock up is a simplified representation of CAD geometry and is used to represent large assemblies, which cannot be displayed in their native format due to performance problems. Ford uses digital mock up to study the fitting together of parts, specifically project manager use it to follow up projects and to support decision making at meetings.

PIM manages the information by means of Metaphase. The PIM installation is based on a tight integration with the CAD tool IDEAS and operates in a distributed environment. A team of designers (about 50) works with their CAD tools, which are connected to a team data manager (TDM). TDM is a miniature PDM system included in IDEAS. The CAD models in the TDM are grouped in master packages. These are copied to a central vault, to which other teams have access. The central vault is connected with the digital mock-up application. By means of this central vault, it is possible to visualize and analyze a complete vehicle, although developed by geographically dispersed teams. The product structure is not stored in Metaphase, only a list of the master packages representing the product. So far, release of parts is not supported in this Metaphase implementation and must be performed in another system.

2.6.2.4   Problem areas of C3P

PIM needs further development. The information infrastructure is causing problems. The connections with Eastern Europe (based on telephone lines) were too slow. Other performance problems were found in the TDMs, when large teams of designers worked with large assemblies. The release of product structures and integrations with legacy systems also need improvement.

2.6.2.5   Boeing

Boeing is in the aerospace industry with a variety of products, including commercial and military aircraft.

Boeing Military Aircraft has chosen to work toward the standardization of information instead of systems. STEP was chosen as the corporate standard for product data exchange and therefore Boeing Military Aircraft will only consider using products that comply with the STEP standard. The partners Boeing works with must be able to use STEP to exchange data.

Boeing Military Aircraft has to deal with a situation in which several CAD systems are used. Take an engine supplier as an example. It supplies engines to other customers, in addition to Boeing. It is not cost efficient for the engine supplier to remake the design for each customer with other preferences regarding the CAD tools used because it is a complex design. Boeing must therefore accept that suppliers use various CAD tools. To verify the complete product with fuselage, wings, and engine, a digital mock up is used, based on a neutral geometry format included in the STEP standard AP 203.

Boeing Military Aircraft uses several PDM systems: Metaphase, iMAN, Sherpa, and Windchill, among others. This does not conflict with the idea of having a single PDM system, but only if it fulfills Boeing's demands. No system available on the market is considered to do this. The use of STEP makes it easier to change or vary PDM systems.

Boeing Military Aircraft has tested the exchange of geometry, parts lists, and change data with STEP. The information is exchanged between engineering and manufacturing databases both within the company and between Boeing and its partners.

Boeing Commercial Airplanes improves the way it builds airplanes by implementing two critical initiatives, lean enterprise and define and control airplane configuration/manufacturing resource management (DCAC/MRM) [40]. Both activities will help Boeing meet its internal goals to reduce costs, cycle time, and defects, and consequently deliver more value to its customers. DCAC/MRM focuses on streamlining the way commercial airplanes are designed and built. The system support includes a PDM system (Metaphase), an ERP system, a product configurator, and a process-planning tool. Some facts about the implementation:

- A total of 39,250 users (July 2001), located in eight states, Canada, and Australia;
- Almost 1,000,000 part numbers in its databases;
- Twenty production databases ranging from 10 to 130 gigabytes in size;
- Estimated Boeing savings: $100M per month.

2.6.2.6 Problem areas and future work at Boeing

A common objection to the use of neutral formats is that they do not keep up with the progress of the tools. It can take up to 6 years before a new functionality in a CAD tool is introduced into the standard. There is a trade off between neutral formats and a high degree of functionality of the tools.

A time plan has been formulated, which outlines the introduction of STEP in various areas. Boeing Military Aircraft's vision is that all product data should be stored in open formats. At Boeing Commercial Airplanes, the DCAC/MRM initiative is planned to increase its number of users further to 50,000 users.

2.7   Summary

Product design is a fast-paced process that requires rapid access to large quantities of valid, coherent, and accurate product information. Nowadays, distributed developments with developer teams geographically dispersed worldwide are common. During the development, for manufacturing and maintenance, all product information has to be stored, managed, and controlled to provide all of the different functions within the company with access to the information when needed.

PDM is the discipline of controlling the evolution of product designs with the aim to control and manage projects and products and to provide different relevant disciplines with accurate product information at the right time in the right format. It also supports the entire life cycle of a product, from conception to obsolescence.

This discipline is realized in PDM tools. The PDM tool is a tool providing people with assistance in managing both product data and the product development process. All of the PDM tools mentioned constitute a complex set of functionality. The functionality can be grouped into two sets of functionality for the users: *user functions* and *utility functions*.

User functions provide access to PDM systems for different types of users, including data storage and management. Functionality for document management includes data vaulting, support for check in and check out, and versioning and revisioning of documents. PDM systems provide workflow support for different critical parts in the product definition process (e.g., the change process and the approval process). To manage complex products, it is essential to assemble the total product in a product structure, which contains all of the relevant information—including all components. In the structure, the documents are related to the product to which they belong. The PDM systems provide integration with different project management tools. The integration provides the project manager functionality for work breakdown structures, as well as follow-up activities.

Utility functions provide the user with functions for, among other things, notification. All of the data is stored and accessed under the control of the PDM system (i.e., the user does not need to know where all of the data is stored). Any kind of image is managed in the same way as any other data. The user may view these files. To simplify for the end user, and to provide the right access to the right user, different kinds of roles may be defined in the system. The system administrator will set up these accounts, groups, and access rights. Integration with authoring, visualization, and other collaborative tools is important and supported by PDM systems.

Research in connection with material from Ford and Boeing targets certain trends and common characteristics of PDM today. Commercial PDM systems have proven their capabilities in large-scale implementations. Behind these implementations, time and cost reduction are important drivers. PDM is evolving toward PLC management and collaborative product commerce, with greater emphasis on information evolution and life cycle management, global access, control, and collaboration. Therefore, PDM can now be used successfully to support distributed development. Standardization is a technical prerequisite for collaboration. Two main strategies for the exchange of data between systems have been observed: It is now possible to require partners to use the systems that your company uses, as exemplified by Ford, or to use a neutral formats in the same way that Boeing uses STEP.

The usage of PDM slowly introduces a more fine-grained control of information and a higher frequency of updates of information. To build a physical prototype (a physical model of the product as it will be manufactured) is time consuming. It is now possible to verify that the product components fit together directly in the computer, providing managers and project managers with immediate knowledge of the status of all geometry models in a project. This is somewhat similar to the daily build in software development and requires more frequent check in of new versions for the mock up to reflect the actual status of a project.

Information models and technical issues associated with PDM are subjects of intensive research. Product models are needed to represent products appropriately in information systems and are becoming increasingly important, as the use of information systems is a determining factor in product development today. Product models are also important to ensure compatibility between information models when exchanging data. Studies of implementation methodology issues, such as deployment and change management for organizations, are research topics awaiting attention.

References

[1] CIMdata, www.cimdata.com, 2003.

[2] The PDM Information Center, www.pdmic.com, 2003.

[3] Estublier J., J-M Favre, and P. Morat, "Toward SCM/PDM Integration?" *Proceedings of 8th International Symposium on System Configuration Management (SCM-8)*, Lecture Notes in Computer Science, No. 1439, Springer Verlag, 1998, pp. 75–94.

[4] Estublier, J., "Distributed Objects for Concurrent Engineering," *Proceedings of 9th International Symposium on System Configuration Management (SCM-9)*, Lecture Notes in Computer Science, No. 1675, Springer Verlag, 1999, pp. 172–185.

[5] EDS PLM Solution, vendor of the PDM system Metaphase, www.sdrc.com, 2003.

[6] Axelsson, K., *Metodisk Systemstrukturering—Att Skapa Samstämmighet Mellan Informationssystemarkitektur Och Verksamhet (A Method for Structuring of Information Systems—Information Systems Architecture and Organization in Concert)*, (in Swedish), Ph.D. Thesis, Department of Computer and Information Science, Linköping University, Sweden, 1998.

[7] Silberschatz, H., F. Korth, and S. Sudarshan, *Database System Concepts*, 3rd ed., New York: McGraw-Hill, 1997.

[8] Kroenke, D., *Database Processing: Fundamentals, Design and Implementation*, Upper Saddle River, NJ: Prentice Hall, 1996.

[9] MatrixOne, Inc., www.matrixone.com, 2003.

[10] ENOVIA Solutions, www.enovia.com, 2003.

[11] ISO TCI194/ SC4/WG5, "Overview and Fundamental Principles," *STEP Part 1*, November 1991.

[12] ANSI/EIA-649-1998, *National Consensus Standard for Configuration Management*, American National Standards Institute, New York, 1998.

[13] Swedish Standards Institute, *Quality Management—Guidelines for Configuration Management*, ISO 10 007, 1995.

[14] MIL-STD-2549, *Configuration Management Data Interface*, Department of Defense Interface Standard, Washington, D.C., June 1997.

[15] MIL-STD-973, *Configuration Management*, U.S. Department of Defense, Washington, D.C., April 1992.

[16] Configuration Management Information Center, www.pdmic.com/cmic/index.shtml, 2003.

[17] Open Document Management API, Version 2.0, Association for Information and Image Management, September 19, 1997.

[18] Miller, E., *Manufacturing Industries Move Toward Engineering Collaboration*, CIMdata, Ann Arbor, MI, 2001.

[19] Project Management Institute, www.pmi.org, 2003.

[20] Pikosz, P., J. Malmström, and J. Malmqvist, "Strategies for Introducing PDM Systems in Engineering Companies," *Proceedings of Advances in Concurrent Engineering—CE'97*, Rochester, MI, 1996, pp. 425–434.

[21] Harris, S. B., "Business Strategy and the Role of Engineering Product Data Management: A Literature Review and Summary of the Emerging Research Questions," *Journal of Engineering Manufacturing*, Institution of Mechanical Engineers, Vol. 210, Part B, 1996, pp. 207–220.

[22] Abramovici M., D. Gerhard, and L. Langenberg, "Application of PDM Technology for Product Life Cycle Management," *Preprints from 4th International Seminar on Life Cycle Engineering*, Berlin, Germany, 1997.

[23] Jansson, L., "Business Oriented Product Structures," Ph.D. thesis, Department of Production Control, Chalmers University of Technology, Gothenburg, Sweden, 1993.

[24] Hegge, H. M., "Intelligent Product Family Descriptions for Business Applications," Ph.D. thesis, Eindhoven University of Technology, The Netherlands, 1995.

[25] Schwarze, S., "The Procedure of Product Configuration and Handling the Configuration Knowledge," BWI Research Paper, No.3, Zentrum für Unternehmenswissenschaft, ETH, Zürich, Switzerland, November 1993.

[26] Svensson, D., and J. Malmqvist, "Strategies for Product Structure Management in Manufacturing Firms," *Proceedings of DETC'00*, Paper No. DET2000/CIE-14607, Baltimore, MD, 2000.

[27] Wright, I. C., "A Review of Research into Engineering Change Management: Implications for Product Design," *Design Studies*, Vol. 18, No. 1, 1997, pp. 33–42.

[28] Pikosz, P., and J. Malmqvist, "A Comparative Study of Engineering Change Management in Three Swedish Engineering Companies," *Proceedings of DETC'98*, Paper No. DET98/EIM-5684, Atlanta, GA, 1998.

[29] Mesihovic, S., and J. Malmqvist, "Product Data Management (PDM) System Support for the Engineering Configuration Process," *14th European Conference on Artificial Intelligence*, Configuration Workshop, Berlin, Germany, August 20–25, 2000.

[30] Isaksson, O., et al., "Trends in Product Modeling—An ENDREA Perspective," *Proceedings Product Models 2000*, Linköping, Sweden, November 7–8, 2001.

[31] Hubka, V., and W. E. Eder, *Theory of Technical Systems*, Berlin, Germany: Springer-Verlag, 1988.

[32] Blanchard, B. S., and W. J. Fabrycky, *System Engineering and Analysis*, 3rd ed., London: Prentice-Hall International, 1998.

[33] International Council on System Engineering (INCOSE), www.incose.org, 2003.

[34] Andreasen, M. M., "Designing on a 'Designer's Workbench' DWB," *Proceedings of the 9th Workshop on Qualitative Reasoning*, Rigi, Switzerland, 1992.

[35] Schenck, D., and P. R. Wilson, *Information Modeling the EXPRESS Way*, New York: Oxford University Press, 1994.

[36] Eriksson, H. E., and M. Penker, *UML Toolkit*, New York: Wiley & Sons, 1998.

[37] Elmasri, R., and S. B. Navathe, *Fundamentals of Database Systems*, Redwood City, CA: The Benjamin/Cummings Publishing Company, 1989.

[38] *CIMdata Europe'99—Conference Proceedings*, Nice, France, 1999.

[39] Fuxin, F., et al., "Product Modeling in the American Manufacturing Industry," Division of Computer-Aided Design, Department of Mechanical Engineering, Luleå University of Technology, Luleå, Sweden, 2000.

[40] "Lean Enterprise: Implementing Lean Practices," www.boeing.com/commercial/initiatives, 2003.

Contents

General description of SCM

... let's call him Ramses, too ...
—Ramses the 1st, inventor of versioning, at the birth of his son, 1784 BC

3.1 Introduction

SCM is a software engineering discipline for the control and management of projects and the synchronization of the work of different developers engaged in a project. SCM provides support during the entire development life cycle of a product. SCM is obtained by defining methods and processes, preparing plans, and using tools that help developers and project managers in their daily work in a development project. SCM is focused on supporting the software development phase. Although SCM is of use in all phases of a PLC, most SCM activities are concentrated during the development phase, when the program code is actually produced. The release of software products and their maintenance is supported by many other activities but these provide less support during the early phases. SCM is designed for use in software development, and it mainly supports functions required specifically by the software. The nature of the software determines both these requirements and the development process itself. The development of software products is separated into three parts:

59

1. Software design and development by the creation of documentation and source code;

2. Software building by compiling the source code and generating executables;

3. The manufacture of software distribution media such as CDs.

Specific properties of software include ease of modification, high cost of development but low or no production costs, the absence of concrete architecture in its final form, and a high degree of complexity during its development phase.

In this chapter, we shall give an overview of the most important characteristics of SCM. After a short historical introduction, we present its basic functions, such as version management, configuration selection, and workspace management. Modern SCM tools include the support of distributed development, change management, collaboration, and integration with other development tools. Like PDM, SCM contains many functions incorporated in other applications or tools. Its relationships with these applications are shortly described. The last part of the chapter contains an overview of trends in development and research in the SCM and related areas.

3.1.1   Historical overview

The history of SCM development follows that of software development. In the 1960s, when software consisted of monolithic programs mostly implemented as one source module, there was no need for SCM. The software engineering community was focused on the art of programming—the production of effective algorithms occupying as little memory as possible.

In the 1970s and the 1980s, software became more complex. Programs were built in two stages, compilation (producing binary modules from the source code) and linking (combining binary modules in a program or a binary library). The first generations of SCM tools appeared during this period: source code control system (SCCS) and Make [1], covering the basic SCM disciplines: CM, build management, and version management. Later, an improved version of SCCS designated revision control system (RCS) [2] replaced SCCS. At this time, SCM was focused on "programming in the large" (versioning, rebuilding, and composition) [3]. It is interesting to note that these tools have dominated the SCM market for many years and that the principles they introduced are still widely used in the majority of modern tools. Make exists today in many forms (e.g., imake, gnumake, and different project files), and RCS is used as a basis for many other, more advanced SCM tools.

During the 1990s, the focus of SCM moved to the "programming in the many," with emphasis on teamwork (process support, concurrent development, and concurrent engineering in general). Change management, workspace management, and process support became the new purposes of SCM tools. The complexity of SCM tools increased as software became more complex. Several new advanced SCM tools, very complex and very expensive, appeared at this time. In addition to their complexity, they were not easy to introduce into the development process. For this reason, many companies developed their own systems or used simple SCM tools, executing other SCM procedures manually.

The use of SCM increased significantly during this period for several reasons. The development of software became more complex, and a need for tools capable of managing this complexity became obvious. At the same time, software development became more important in business, and many new software companies appeared on the market. Finally, software development focused on development processes influenced by the well-known Capability Maturity Model® (CMM®) from the Software Engineering Institute (SEI) [4], which pointed out SCM as an important (*key process*) area. CMM® defines an SCM process as including a number of activities and their planning (with emphasis on the planning) during the entire PLC.

As the software industry continues to grow rapidly, producing larger and more complex software, the need for software management also grows. One example of the increasing complication of the situation is the demand for shorter time to market, which requires incremental and concurrent development process models, which in turn increase the burden on SCM. Another example is the increasing tendency for persons involved in the development of a system to be geographically dispersed. The new focus of software development is therefore on "programming in the wide" (Web-remote engineering, distributed development).

3.1.2 Definition

SCM can be defined as the controlled way to manage the development and modification of software systems and products during their entire life cycle.

The definition of SCM by Babich stresses that a system is often developed and supported by a group of developers: "Configuration management is the art of identifying, organizing, and controlling modifications to the software being built by a programming team" [5].

These are, however, only two of many definitions. Appleton has collected many for presentation on his home page [6]. One reason for there being many definitions is that SCM has two target groups with rather different needs: management and developers. Managers need control and measurement of the development and in particular of the releases of products. This need was previously met with manual routines often managed by an SCM librarian. Today, all developers of a project are involved in SCM, which is highly automated with sophisticated tools that meet the manager's needs and give developers a broader view of development within a project, increasing their efficiency.

It is important to stress that SCM also is about process management—control of the software development activities. This includes both defining these processes and setting up the necessary organization in order to control them. An example of the goal for such a process is to be able to ensure that a change request existed and had been approved for fixing and that the associated design, documentation, and review activities have been completed before allowed in the code to be checked in again. Later, in Chapter 6, a more thorough description of SCM processes is given.

3.2   Basic functions

SCM is very much about supporting developers in their daily routines. For developers, SCM maintains the current product components, keeps old versions and stores information of their history, provides a stable development environment, and coordinates simultaneous changes in the product. From the developer's point of view, much of this work may be considerably facilitated by the use of suitable tools. Of course, defined processes and detailed routines will help to guide developers. However, to do this efficiently, tool support is necessary. The most common functions supported by SCM tools are:

- *Version management*—making possible the storage of different versions and variants of a document and their subsequent retrieval and comparison;
- *Configuration selection*—providing functions for the creation or selection of associated versions (or branches) of different documents;
- *Concurrent development*—controlling simultaneous access by several users (either by prevention or by providing support);

- *Distributed development*—supporting geographically dispersed developers working on the same system;

- *Build management*—providing mechanisms for building software (for instance, compiling and linking) and keeping generated software up to date, preferably without unnecessary rebuilding;

- *Release management*—packaging software in a form suitable for distribution and generating documentation to inform users and developers of changes included in the product release;

- *Workspace management*—providing each user with a private sandbox in which the user can work in isolation but still under the control of the SCM tool;

- *Change management*—keeping track of changes introduced in the product and providing support for the process of entering and implementing changes in the product;

- *Integration with other tools*—the integration of SCM tools with the development environment and with other tools.

These functions are expanded on in further detail later. However, we will briefly discuss other SCM-related functionality first, that which is relevant to tool support. Specific terminology is frequently used in connection with some of the functions and is therefore introduced here:

- *Reporting status.* This is the reporting of current status with lists of the files that have been changed during a certain time period, by whom made the changes were made, and differences between products. These are important functions, particularly in the support of the overall view as seen by the project management.

- *Process support.* This is support made available to developers in following the development model and performing actions specified during the planning phase to ensure that the components are progressed through the chosen life cycle phases before being released.

- *Accessibility control (security).* This prevents inappropriate access to information without complicating everyday work.

3.2.1 Version management

Version management is central, the core functionality in all SCM tools. Many developers believe, incorrectly, that version control is the equivalent of SCM. Even though it is important, SCM is more than versioning, as explained in the other sections.

An element of software or a document placed under version control is designated a configuration item (CI). The most common example of a CI is a source code file, but executables, products, and documents are also CIs. A group of CIs can be defined as a CI (i.e., the group is version controlled itself). The ability to store, recreate, and register the historical development of CIs is a fundamental characteristic of an SCM system. The most important property of a version is its immutability (i.e., when a version has been frozen, its content can never be modified). Instead, new versions must be created.

As an important aid to developers, all SCM systems offer support for the synchronization of simultaneous, concurrent changes of the CIs from different users. Depending on the tool, this support is given in different ways according to different synchronization models (presented as CM models by Feiler in [7]). The most basic model is the *checkout/checkin model*, in which individual files are stored in a compact form on a version-control basis in a small database, a repository (also called a vault). The repositories contain only one complete version. The differences between the versions are saved using delta algorithms (i.e., the algorithms by which it is possible to recreate a complete file version by parsing saved differences). Many tools use line based delta algorithms, calculating the differences, in terms of lines, between two versions. There are also binary-based delta algorithms, calculating binary differences, byte per byte [8]. The main purpose of using a delta technique is to save disk space in the repository.

Files are not read or changed directly in the repository without being checked out first. To check out means that a particular version of a file is copied into the developer's working directory, and if write access is required, the file is *locked* in the repository. Locking prevents other developers from checking out that particular file (or, more specifically, that branch) in the write mode. When the file is checked in, a new version of the file is created in the repository and the lock is released. In this way, each file in the repository will be given its own version history with a new version for each check out and check in.

Versions of a file may be organized in a number of different ways. When organized in a sequence, they are often called revisions. They may also be organized as parallel development lines called branches. Branches can be merged into a new version, which then has two or more predecessors, as shown in Figure 3.1.

Revisions are usually deliberately created by a developer (e.g., when a developer completes a particular change in the file). In addition, many text

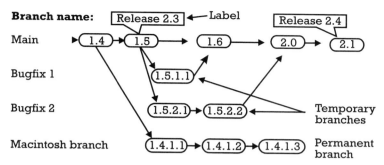

Figure 3.1 Basic version control.

editors maintain one or several microrevisions of a file to facilitate its recovery following unsuccessful editing. These revisions are not managed by the SCM tool.

Branches are created for several reasons. The primary branches are permanent, adjusting the file according to diverging demands, such as different operating or window systems. A second important purpose of branches is to enable parallel (concurrent) work. In the latter case, temporary branches are created and then merged when concurrent work is no longer required. Usually, a branch consists of a series of revisions and additional branches that can be created from the original branches. The development of strategies for creating and merging branches is often an important task for an SCM manager.

A tool for version control can identify revisions internally, usually utilizing a numbering technique in several stages. This may be user friendly to a greater or lesser degree. In addition, the users themselves can usually give the revisions one or several optional names in the form of text, often called a *tag* or a *label*. The tool can return a version identified by such a text. This facility (tagging) can be used to realize a simple selection mechanism (see Section 3.2.3).

3.2.1.1 Variants

The management of variants is a difficult problem, not yet completely solved. A common misunderstanding is to draw a parallel between a variant and a branch. Let us see what variants are and why are they used. The adjustment of entire products or configurations according to diverging demands is managed with variants. For example, different variants of a product may be developed for different operating systems or with different customer adaptations. These variants can be created and maintained in at least four ways:

1. *With permanent branches of the included files.* For a variant, file versions are primarily selected from the permanent branch created for the purpose. A file version from a variant independent branch is selected next. If this independent branch does not exist, a file version from a main branch can be selected. In this case, the main branch covers all variants.

2. *With conditional compilation (compiling directives).* This means that all variants are managed in the same version of the file and are therefore easier to keep together. However, the variant management will not be visible to SCM.

3. *With installation descriptions clarifying which functionality should be included in a certain variant.* Variant-dependent functionalities are implemented in different files, one for each variant.

4. *Run-time check.*

Thus, the creation of branches is only one way to implement variants. The most important thing is not the choice of implementation technique to be used, but the management of the many variants resulting from the combinatory explosion of several optional parameters. Read more about variants in [9].

3.2.2   Workspace management

Workspace management makes it possible for developers to work transparently with respect to SCM. When developers are focused on solving particular problems and have less interest in administrative tasks, a workspace functions as a sandbox in which they can work in isolation, remaining under the control of the SCM tool. Versions of files are checked out and temporarily stored in the workspace, with a mapping remaining between the versioned objects in the repository and the user files and directories in the workspace.

Files to be modified are not the only items are checked out to the workspace. Often all files needed in the build or test procedures, or those that are part of the product, are checked out (possibly, some of them read-only). Thus, the workspace also makes it possible for the files checked in to the common repository to maintain a certain degree of quality (e.g., that all files changed due to the same change request actually work together).

When several developers are working concurrently in their private workspaces, control is needed between the different copies of the same object, as described in Section 3.2.3.

Some tools also support cooperative versioning, as described in [10]. In short, this means that local versioning within the workspace is provided. When a file is checked in to the repository again, only the latest local version is checked in. The intermediate versions are deleted.

An example of integrated features is when the developer "logs in" to a project environment in which project structures and repositories are already prepared for the developer (e.g., by the SCM group). The developer then enters a transparent environment in which the development is done with SCM handled behind the scene. Examples of tools supporting this are Clear Case [11] through "Views" and CM Synergy (former Continuus) [12].

3.2.3 Configuration selection

As shown in Figure 3.1, a file can include a number of versions, and the one that should be used in a given situation is not always obvious. The situation is further complicated by the fact that a system consists of a large number of files such that the possible number of combinations is enormous. In everyday work during development, a developer usually wishes to have the latest revisions of the files being changed from a particular branch. For other unchanged files, the developer typically wants an older, stable version, such as that included in the latest product release or the most recently published stable version developed by another group. The development in the developer's own group should be particularly flexible to make it possible to change between different levels of collaboration. For example, a change may require the modification of more than one file. In all situations, a consistent selection, in terms of the inclusion of versions with related modifications should be ensured. A set of particular file versions, or, more generally, particular versions of CIs, is designated a *configuration*.

A useful technique for the specification of a configuration supported by several systems is to offer a rule-based selection mechanism. Typical examples of rules that can be advantageous to specify include:

- The latest revision in my own branch (for files that I myself/the group work with);

- The latest revision in a named temporary branch (for files that other groups work with);

- The latest revision in a named permanent branch (for files that differ depending on the product);

• The fixed, named, version (e.g., the latest release for other subsystems).

A system that is built using a rule specifying the latest version is called a partially bound (or generic) configuration, as the exact versions included will vary in time when new versions are checked in. A system built without such a rule is called a bound configuration and is particularly suitable for deliveries, as the versions of all files included are fixed and it can therefore be guaranteed that the system can be recreated.

A certain bound configuration can form a baseline that functions as a basis for further development with formal change management. It can also form a release that is delivered to an internal or external customer.

In the same way that individual files have a version history that describes their evolution, configurations create their own version history as they evolve. Users and customers see the development of a system in large steps, namely the configurations, releases, that are distributed. Developers and project managers see many more stages in the development of the system as well as the division into subsystems and configurations, each with their own version histories. Therefore, the perspectives in which a system and subsystem are regarded as the development of configurations in bound configurations may be useful at several levels.

The naming of versions (tagging) can be used to manage the selection of bound configurations in that all of the files in the configurations are tagged with the same name (e.g., release 2.3). This is illustrated in Figure 3.2.

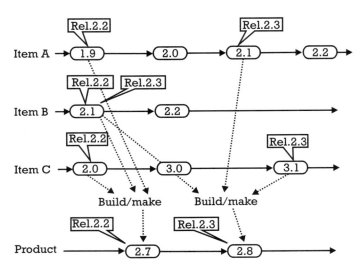

Figure 3.2 A bound configuration can be defined by tagging all files with the same label.

Relations between such configurations (e.g., that release 2.3 is a successor to release 2.2) are rarely supported by the SCM tools but must be managed in a different manner (e.g., in a release document).

Consistent naming may also be used to represent logical changes (i.e., changes arising from a change request and resulting in the modification of several files).

3.2.4 Build management

Build management supports the user in building the product or part of the product (e.g., a component or a library). Build tools such as Make [1] are used to create the product automatically. The correct versions of appropriate files are first collected for a particular build, as described in Section 3.2.3, and are then compiled and linked in the correct order. Make describes the dependencies between source code files at build time and ensures that the dependent source code is built in the correct order.

As building large systems may take days and an inefficient build process can waste hours of developer time, it is important to reuse components that have not changed since the most recent build as much as possible. This is particularly important during test and integration, when the entire system must be built to test a small change. An effective build process can reduce build time dramatically by reusing partially built items from previous builds.

Many SCM tools have further developed ideas from Make. The build procedure is automatically created by the tool and often stored in a project file managed by the development environment.

3.2.5 Release management

The identification and organization of all deliverables (e.g., documents, executables, and libraries) incorporated in a product release is designated release management. Release management is closely related to configuration selection, build management, and change management. A particular configuration of items selected is used in the build process, and the items created in the build process are inputs to the release process.

Release management has a double role. First, it must prepare deliverables and all documentation for the users. Information, which a deliverable contains, includes a list of (new) functions, changes implemented from the previous release, and demands on the run-time environment. Second, it provides information used internally—for test purposes, maintenance, or further development. For example, release support makes it possible to determine which users have developed which versions of which components, and therefore which of these will be affected by a particular change.

It is possible with appropriate release management to create installation kits automatically to ease the task of the build manager. The build manager is responsible for providing the packed product with the correct configuration and features. Products such as Windows installer [13] and Install shield can be used to create installation kits. Hoek et al. [14] describe a prototype, designated Software Release Manager (SRM), which supports both developers and users in the software release management process. SRM incorporates the notion of components and helps in assembling them into systems. Dependencies are explicitly recorded so that users can understand and investigate them.

3.2.6 Concurrent development

One major advantage of using a SCM system is that it enables teams to work concurrently on a single project. This is advantageous for many reasons. Different developers may be working concurrently on the same files, correcting different errors, or one developer may be working on the latest release while another is correcting an error in a previous release. A test team can test the latest stable version as the development team is working on the latest (unstable) versions (see Figure 3.3).

The SCM system makes this possible by providing:

  ▸ Selection of versions building specific configurations for different needs;

  ▸ A model for synchronization of concurrent changes (e.g., by locking the files edited or by permitting changes to be made at all times but detecting conflicts at check in and then at merge, often called optimistic check out).

For a more detailed description of synchronization models such as check out and check in, long transactions, and change sets and their use in different distributed development situations, we refer to [15].

3.2.7 Distributed development

The developers of a software system are often geographically dispersed. This situation is designated distributed development or remote development. Many SCM tools provide replicated repositories to support this process. There is no global master repository in most of the tools

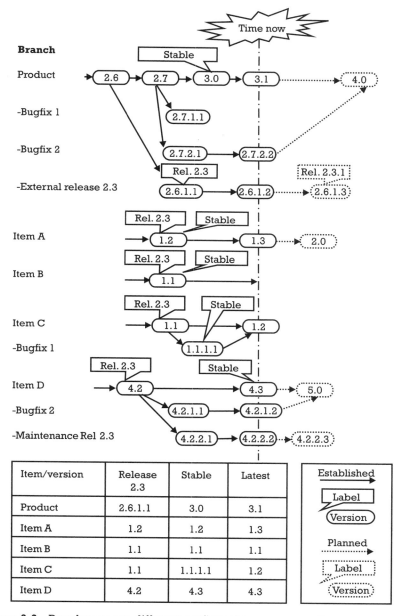

Figure 3.3 Developers use different configurations concurrently.

supporting replication, but all replicas are copies of the same repository, automatically kept synchronized. When a replica is modified by clients at one site, the updates are sent to the other replicas (in batches at a predefined frequency). When data is replicated between different servers for the first time, all the data in the repository must be sent/copied. Data sizes could be as large as several gigabytes. The next time synchronization/replication is performed, only update packages with a typical size of 4 to 5 MB need to be sent.

The implementation must avoid conflicts, and the synchronization can always be made totally automatic. In ClearCase [11], for example, the synchronization problem is left to the users by managing different branches at different sites. Only the site holding the ownership can create versions on that branch. In this way, it is always possible to send new versions created on a branch and "install" them at other sites without conflict. Versions on branches from other sites can still be viewed and used to merge from, creating a merged version on a branch owned by the site (see Figure 3.4).

3.2.8 Change management

Change management keeps track of all changes in a product under development. The reason for a change can be the correction of an error, the improvement of a component, or the addition of functionality. Change management is often supported by separate tools integrated with the main SCM tool. Examples of such tools are PVCS tracker [16], Visual Intercept [17], and Rational ClearQuest [11].

Change management has two main objectives. The first is to provide support for the processing of changes. Such processing includes change identification, analysis, prioritizing, planning for their implementation, decisions for their rejection or postponement, and decisions for their integration

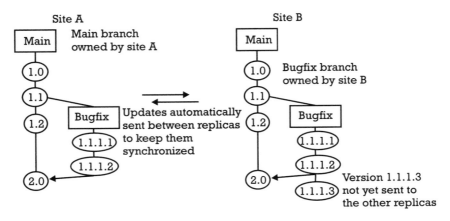

Figure 3.4 Replication of repositories.

in new product releases. The second objective is traceability (i.e., to make it possible to list all active and implemented changes). It should also be possible to track the modifications of different items due to a specific change.

3.2.8.1   Change management process

In a change management process, a change is usually identified by a *change request* (CR). When a change is initiated, a CR is created to track the change until it is resolved and closed. Figure 3.5 shows how a change proposal creates a CR as defined in [18]. The change control board (CCB), a group responsible for operational aspects of the project, analyzes the CR and determines the action to be taken. If the change is approved, the CR is filed to the developer responsible for implementing the change. When the developer has performed the change, its status becomes *implemented* and testing can be performed. The CCB also decides which changes are to be included in the new product release or if the change will be included in existing product versions in the form of a service pack. The latter is also part of release management.

3.2.8.2   Traceability

Change management includes tools and processes that support the organization and track the changes from the origin to the actual source code [19]. For each CR, it should be possible to see which versions of the modified files were created due to that request. Conversely, it should also be possible to answer the question, "for what reason (which CR) is this version of this file created?" (see Figure 3.6).

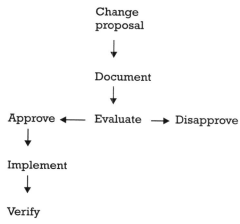

Figure 3.5   An example of a CR process.

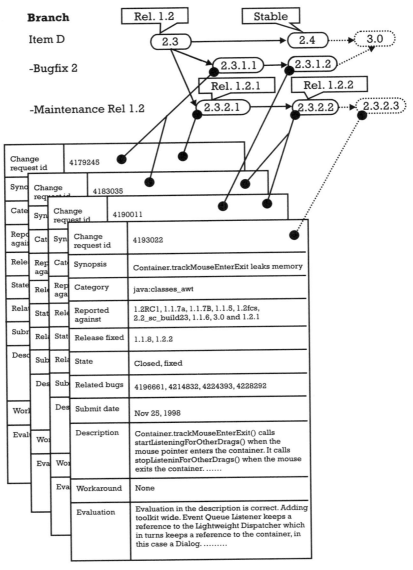

Figure 3.6 From a CR, it is easy to see which files have been changed (what version has been created) due to the CR. For a specific version of an item, it is also easy to see why this version was created, due to which CR.

Change management data can be used to provide valuable metrics about the progress of project execution [20]. From this data, it can be seen which changes have been introduced between two releases. It is also possible to check the response time between the initiation of the CR and its implementation and acceptance. Figure 3.7 depicts a part of a release document listing all CRs implemented between two releases. It also depicts one of these requests and the files changed due to this request.

Release Notes
JavaTM 2 SDK, Standard Edition
Version 1.2.2

⋮

Change Requests Fixed

CR_ID	Synopsis
4160721	AWT ScrollPane Paint Problem
4122687	AltGr keys are not working in Components (Swing, JBCL, AWT)
4148334	Button background color inheriting from frame
41t1t4073	Can't set cursor in JPanelor JComponent
4139978	Color float constructor should round (?)
4212564	Component.printAll() passes invalid Graphics object
4193022	Container.trackMouseEnterExit leaks memory
4160474	Cursor setting still not works properly
4106384	CustomCursor only shows black and white colors
4111379	DEFAULT_CURSOR has different semantic on Solaris and Win32
4119383	Deadlock between modal dialog and Container.add
4115213	Dialog.setResizable(false) does not work.
4017222	Drag Enter/Exit events not reported correctly on Solaris
4152317	FileDialog always shows English word "All Files (*.*) in all countries.

⋮

Figure 3.7 As part of the release notes, all CRs implemented between the last and the new release are listed. From these CRs, the actual changes made can be traced as depicted in Figure 3.6.

3.2.9   Integration with other tools

The first generations of commercial SCM tools, although providing sophisticated functions, often appeared to be difficult to deploy and integrate in the development process. The newer versions of SCM tools try to minimize this extra effort required by integration with tools used in the development process. Typically, some of the functions are built in integrated development environments (IDEs). For instance, operations such as check in and check out are automatically performed when a file or an item is being changed. Similarly, when building a software product or a component, all files needed in the build procedure are automatically checked out. A seamless integration of SCM with different development and engineering tools is one of the crucial factors for its attractiveness on the market.

Different SCM tools provide different integration possibilities. Many tools provide a set of line commands that can be invoked from other tools by using different trigger mechanisms that they incorporate. This is not a high level of integration, as it depends on the capability, which may be limited, of other tools to invoke the commands. A more flexible and powerful interaction can be achieved by using the application program interface (API) provided by SCM tools. An API defines a set of interfaces to the SCM functions. Development tool vendors or development organizations can build their applications using interfaces provided by SCM tools. In some cases, suppliers of IDEs specify the interface of basic SCM functions. The SCM vendors then implement these functions in accordance with the interface specification, and in this way make possible the integration of their tools with the IDEs. Users using the same IDE can select different SCM tools and use those from IDE in the same way.

The integration of SCM and other tools is far from perfect because of the different treatment of basic structures. SCM recognizes files as entities, and in some cases it is able to recognize their internal structure. This makes possible the provision of functions such as difference or merge between different versions of these entities. For instance, all SCM tools can manage ordinary text files—the differences are based on differences of lines in the files. However, SCM tools do not understand the semantics (i.e., the meaning) of the lines in a file. Development and engineering tools may have completely different structuring. In object-oriented programming, for example, a class is a basic entity. From a version-management point of view, the differences between two versions of a class are of interest. Similarly, in a relation database, tables and records are the basic entities. A comparison between two versions of a database should indicate which tables or which records are different. SCM is unable to answer this, as it does not recognize these structures.

Many SCM functions are of a general purpose and might be included in other tools. Many tools build in their own SCM functions. For example, certain word processors or CAD/CAM systems can save and manage different versions of a document. As these tools know the internal structure of such documents, they can provide difference and merge functions on a semantic level. A word processor is able to show that formatting is different in two versions of a document or that two paragraphs have changed their positions. Although in this aspect they are superior to general SCM tools, these tools can include only some basic SCM functions on an entity level. They are not able to define a configuration of a set of documents by specifying a particular version of each document. For this reason, they cannot replace SCM tools.

3.3   Related domains

3.3.1   CM

CM manages both hardware and software and is therefore more general than SCM, which, historically based on CM, is more closely focused on specific software support. CM was developed before SCM, and its original focus was on manager support rather than on developer support.

From a management perspective, CM directs and controls the development of a product by the identification of the product components and the control of their successive changes. The objective is to document the composition and status of a defined product and its components, to publish this to ensure that the correct working basis is being used, and that the product is being composed correctly. One example of a definition supporting this discipline is ISO 10 007, which states that the major objective of CM is "to document and provide full visibility of the product's present configuration and on the status of achievement of its physical and functional requirements" [18]. Many other standards [4, 18, 21–23] also define CM as consisting of four activities, or areas of responsibility. These are (according to ISO 10 007):

- *Configuration identification.* This consists of activities comprising determination of the product structure, selection of CIs, documentation of the physical and functional characteristics of the CI (including interfaces and subsequent changes), and allocation of identification characters or numbers to the CIs and their documents.

- *Configuration control.* This consists of activities comprising the control of changes to a CI after formal establishment of its configuration documents. Control includes evaluation, coordination, approval or disapproval, and implementation of changes. Implementation of changes includes engineering changes and deviations, as well as waivers with impact on the configuration.

▸ *Configuration status accounting.* This is formalized recording and reporting of the established configuration documents, the status of proposed changes, and the status of the implementation of approved changes. Status accounting should provide information on the relevant configurations and all deviations from the specified basic configurations. In this way, the tracking of changes in relation to the basic configuration is made possible.

▸ *Configuration audit.* This is an examination to determine whether a CI conforms to its configuration documents. *Functional configuration audit* is a formal evaluation to verify that a CI has achieved the performance characteristics and functions defined in its configuration documents. *Physical configuration audit* is a formal evaluation to verify the conformity between the actual produced CI and the configuration according to the configuration documents.

The problems and solutions associated with SCM are almost the same as those associated with CM. However, there are some additions, and some parts are more important when managing software than when managing other items (e.g., hardware). One difference between software and hardware may be that for software, the model used during development is almost the same as the product delivered, which is not the case for hardware (a design is not the same as the product produced following the design). Another difference is that the transition from the design phase to the production phase is less clearly defined in software development and often the same person or team is involved in both. As compared with hardware, it is easier to build the software product from the model (it is automated). Also, developers may be tempted to introduce changes close to the point of release, which may cause problems. In addition, a lexically small change may have a considerable effect on the behavior of the product. For these reasons, SCM has focused particularly on problems related to changes (e.g., version control and change management).

3.3.2 Document management

Documentation is an important part of software development. In many of the SCM procedures, documents are treated as any other item. They are under the control of version, change, and release management in the same way as source code or any other type of file. However, the processing of documentation is somewhat different from the development of software. The build process is of no interest for document management, but other parts that are specific to document management are not present in SCM tools. In SCM tools, there is no advanced search capability; comparison and merge functions usually do not work for documents because of their internal format; and Web management is not part of SCM. It is questionable whether documents should be under the control of SCM instead of, as an alternative, under document/content management tools or under a PDM system. Although many companies keep documentation separated from software, others keep the documentation under SCM control. There are several reasons for this—companies may not be able to afford the costs of additional resources or the developers may want to work in an integrated environment, with documents treated in exactly the same way as other items and available in the same place. In the latter case, it is more a question of the possibility of integrating these tools. When tools are properly integrated in a common environment (this depends on the integration capabilities of the tools and the environment), the users should not be aware of any difference when using different tools.

3.4 Trends

SCM as a discipline has achieved a level of maturity that permits its implementation in many variants. There are over 100 SCM tools currently available on the market (see Chapter 11). In addition to these stand-alone tools, many other tools have built-in SCM functionality. SCM tools are sometimes seen as too complex, too expensive, and insufficiently flexible, which results in development organizations preferring to buy or to use free SCM tools. This was not the case in the 1980s, when most of the larger organizations developed their own SCM tools. In most cases, the companies use only basic SCM functionality (i.e., versioning and baselines), while additional functionality, such as change and process management is not used. The most important requirements from industry are not sophisticated functions, but simplicity and interoperability with other tools.

During the entire SCM evolution period, SCM researchers collaborated closely with industry and have been involved in product development. Leading SCM researchers have attended software configuration management symposia in 1988 [24], 1999 [25], and 2001 [26]. These symposia have been characterized by close cooperation between researchers and SCM tool suppliers. Even SCM customers, both large and small companies, have participated and an "industrial experience" session is a normal item on the agenda. One conclusion from discussions at the most recent SCM symposium was that many of the research problems of the 1990s had been solved and the solutions implemented by the vendors. It is to be expected that new problems will be encountered in the next decade, and for this reason the SCM-10 symposium was much more research oriented.

Trends in certain areas currently emphasized by researchers and suppliers are discussed next.

3.4.1 Versioning models

The main stream of solutions today is based on the version mechanism described in Section 3.2.1, storing all versions in a repository. A trend in versioning models is to distinguish different levels of version. The main difference between two versions remains the principal question. Is it the number of different lines or different bytes, or is the difference managed on a higher, semantic, level (e.g., differences of properties of entities), or a functional change introduced in the system, or something else?

The use of change sets—logical changes introduced into the system—is one higher level of change management. The management of changes on this level gives a more distinct separation of the abstract, functional change from its implementation. This, however, can result in an enormous number of versions of configurations, many never existing before and thus never tested. In time it was realized that classical versioning and change-set versioning are complementary, and many SCM tools now use them both.

Another level on which differences can be managed is the semantic level. The *logical* differences between two items can be recognized on the semantic level. The demand to view differences on this level has increased with the complexity of software entities that cannot be mapped to files or to lines of files. Examples of such are objects in object-oriented programming, tables in a relational database, CAD models, and different type of documents. To recognize these types of differences, SCM tools must understand the semantics of the objects. As these semantics are not standardized, an SCM tool that will understand them all is an impossibility. Another possibility would be to formally specify the common, standardized version management of standard infrastructures and semantics of entities. In that perspective, XML appears promising, as it is flexible and powerful enough to be able to specify different formats that can be used by different tools. As yet, however, except in Web-distributed authoring and versioning (WebDAV) (see Section 3.4.4.2), XML has not been applied to any extent in SCM.

3.4.2 Workspace management

Workspace management is related to the what happens with a file when it is checked out from the repository to a workspace. The simpler tools leave this control to the user; the more advanced tools keep the workspace under their control. For example, ClearCase [11] can find configurations already built in workspaces and in that way speed up the build ordered in another workspace. In the research prototype COOP/Orm, the clients, instead of saving to a local workspace, continuously checkpoint changes to the server to provide developers working on the same document more complete knowledge of activities in the project [27, 28].

In all current solutions, the workspace is mapped to the file system, as the modules are usually implemented as files. However, there is a trend to require management of other types of items also, raising the question of how to manage workspaces for entities different from files (e.g., entities in development environments or databases).

3.4.3 Distributed CM

Distributed SCM has grown in importance with the tremendous increase in the development and use of software and with the globalization of software development and software marketing. Specialization and outsourcing have also influenced the development process. Finally, the Internet and World Wide Web (WWW) have dramatically improved the communication possibilities available to companies using distributed development. The requirements of distributed development are different from those of local development. An increasing number of SCM tool vendors provide support for distributed CM, and this has been a topic of research during recent years.

There are different aspects of distributed SCM. Managing the source-code level is an extension of the *local* management. There are several excellent examples of successful management in the open source domain, including Linux, KDE, and Mozilla (Netscape 7). Many of them use simple SCM tools such as concurrent versions system (CVS). In most of these cases, the central repository accessible via the Internet contains all of the relevant data in one place. Different SCM tools offer support for a more complex management in which repositories are distributed over the networks.

A detailed analysis of SCM and trends in distributed development, as well as use cases from Swedish industry, can be found in [15].

3.4.4 SCM and the Web

With the WWW explosion, the number of files to be managed has increased dramatically, and the lifetime of documents or document versions has decreased correspondingly. A new challenge for SCM appears—how is this enormous volume of items to be managed? A similar question related to dependency management arises—how is the unlimited number of hyperlinks that are being changed literally every second to be managed? Further, how can SCM benefit from the Internet and WWW?

3.4.4.1 SCM supporting WWW development process

The support of activities related to Web processes is a major problem facing SCM. The Web itself meets a number of challenges related to CM. According to [29], these include speed of change, variant explosion, dynamic content, and process support. These challenges also define the requirements for SCM. Many vendors are aware of these requirements and of the large opportunities presented. To remain competitive, they include WWW support in their SCM tools. The first three of these challenges determine somewhat different goals usually defined by SCM. Instead of emphasizing traceability, the application of an appropriate amount of work is the most important item. Artifacts with a short life (days or even just hours, such as Web pages) should be managed as simply and as quickly as possible, while more critical data should be treated in a more deliberate and thorough manner.

Most SCM tools provide support for mapping the structures of Web pages to SCM structures. Some vendors [30] speak of Web-object management, defining CIs on the higher abstraction level. In a Web application, we find different types of Web objects, including programs (Java and ActiveX typically on the client side), graphics, sound, video, links, and HTML, which usually but not always encapsulates simple text. Web objects contain these artifacts, different in form and thus differently treated by SCM (e.g., in versioning, merging, and *diffing*). One of the several books discussing support for WWW processing is [29]. In this book, the challenges, requirements, and SCM processes for managing Web pages are described in detail.

3.4.4.2 SCM and WWW—WebDAV

One example of version control utilizing WWW technology is WebDAV. WebDAV defines an extension to the hypertext transfer protocol (HTTP) permitting distributed Web authoring tools to be broadly interoperable. WebDAV also provides a network protocol for creating interoperable, collaborative applications. Major features of WebDAV are:

> ▸ *Locking and versioning (concurrency control).* Versioning support, similar to that provided by RCS, supports operations such as check out, check in, and retrieval of the history list.

> ▸ *Properties.* XML properties provide storage of arbitrary metadata (similar to PDM metadata), such as a list of authors of Web resources.

> ▸ *Namespace manipulation.* Because resources may need to be copied or moved as a Web site evolves, WebDAV supports copy and move operations. Collections, similar to file system directories, may be created and listed.

How does WebDAV support geographically dispersed teams of Web site authors and developers? Web sites typically collect information from diverse sources, often from people who are geographically separated. Using a WebDAV server, the HTML pages, images, and other information that constitutes a Web site can be directly authored by the primary sources of the information. By using WebDAV functions, the tools may work transparently on a local network or on the Internet, making it possible to show the distributed environment as a local environment.

3.4.5 Component CM

A new paradigm in the development process has been recognized in recent years, from complete in-house development to a development process focused on the use of standard and de facto standard components, outsourcing, and commercial-off-the-shelf (COTS) products. The products are not closed, monolithic systems, but are components that may be integrated with other products available on the market. Software systems based on standard components are the results of a combination of development and the integration of existing components. The requirements for conventional use of SCM remains, but new requirements related to component management appear in all phases: in the design, integration, and during run time. The integration part (i.e., configuration) and version management of the components becomes more important. New aspects of SCM arise in the run-time phase, as components usually are loosely coupled and can be replaced or updated in the run-time environment. The basic requirements of component-based systems are identification of components and their remaining under version control.

Closely related to component CM is the product line development approach. In a product line, many variations of products are built from a number of core components always present in the products and many optional components or different variations of components. In component identification, selection, and the integration process, CM plays an important role. SCM methods are yet to be established in product lines. Problems in both component management and product lines are similar and deal with identification and structures, which approaches similar problems (and maybe solutions) present in PDM.

3.4.6 SCM process

By the late 1990s, the basic problems involving version, selection, and workspace management had been solved, and support for medium-size projects had been established. Support for large-size development projects came into focus. One of the main challenges with large projects is to keep track of the project's process. Process issues also become interesting with the wide acceptance of the CMM® from industry. CMM® classifies the ability of companies to develop software on five levels. Each level identifies several crucial processes (key areas) that must function in the organization. One of the basic functions of level 2, at which the companies should be able to repeat a development project, is SCM. Many SCM vendors claim today that they support CMM® level 2 in general. By including process support, SCM has enlarged its area of operations. SCM support is focused not only on developers and tools for automation of certain actions, but also on management, planning, and project follow up. An SCM plan, including planning for resources, efforts, SCM milestones (most often baselines), and even SCM metrics, becomes a standard part of project documentation.

In the late 1990s, many organizations began to improve their processes by following CMM®. Consequently, they began using SCM tools and, more importantly, began planning for SCM activities in development projects, identifying SCM activities, and allocating resources.

3.4.7 Integrated environments

During the last decade, most SCM tools have been transformed. Once large, cumbersome, expensive, complex and user unfriendly, and, in particular, isolated from other tools, they became more user friendly, easier to deploy, and much better integrated with other engineering tools. Much remains to be done, particularly with respect to integration with other tools. As this is more a practical marketing issue, it is of primary interest for vendors rather than for researchers, among whom the widespread opinion is that in principle, the problem is solved. The main idea of integration is to conceal SCM as much as possible in the developer's everyday work. For example, many SCM tools have an API compatible with Microsoft Visual Source Safe, which makes it easier to integrate with Microsoft Visual Studio. No standardized API for SCM functions is available as yet.

3.5 Summary

This chapter presented an overview of SCM, ranging from its history to current trends. We learned that SCM was initially associated mostly with manual routines and tools only supporting versioning. However, today's SCM tools are highly automatic and really support much of the daily work of developers and at the same time provide managers with information for project management.

Nine important areas, referred to as basic functions, in which SCM normally provides support were also described:

1. *Version management*—making it possible to store, retrieve, and compare versions and variants of a document;

2. *Configuration selection*—providing functions to create and select associated versions (or branches) of different documents;

3. *Concurrent development*—controlling simultaneous access by several users, either by preventing it or by supporting it;

4. *Distributed development*—by means of which geographically dispersed developers can work concurrently on a project;

5. *Build management*—providing mechanisms for building software, preferably without unnecessary rebuilding;

6. *Release management*—packaging software in a form suitable for distribution and generating documentation to enable users and developers to keep track of changes included in the product release;

7. *Workspace management*—providing a private sandbox for each user in which the user can work in isolation, remaining under the control of the SCM tool;

8. *Change management*—keeping track of changes introduced in the product and providing support for the process of entering and implementing changes in the products;

9. *Integration with other tools*—ways that SCM tools are often integrated with the development environment and with other tools.

Two large domains related to SCM were also described briefly—document management and CM. CM is the basis of SCM, which was developed by adding specialized support for software to CM.

Finally in this chapter, certain trends were highlighted. These included the influence of WWW on SCM, how to manage all the items on the Web, and how to utilize WWW for SCM purposes.

References

[1] Feldman, S. I., "Make, A Program for Maintaining Computer Programs," *Software—Practice and Experience*, Vol. 9, No. 4, April 1979, pp. 255–265.

[2] Tichy, W. F., "RCS—A System for Version Control," *Software—Practice and Experience*, Vol. 15, No. 7, July 1985, pp. 637–654.

[3] Estublier, J., "Software Configuration Management: A Roadmap," *Proceedings of 22nd International Conference on Software Engineering, The Future of Software Engineering*, ACM Press, 2000.

[4] Paulk, M. C., et. al. (Eds.), *The Capability Maturity Model: Guidelines for Improving Software Process*, Reading, MA: Addison Wesley, 1995.

[5] Babich, W. A., *Software Configuration Management: Coordination for Team Productivity*, Reading, MA: Addison Wesley, 1986.

[6] Brad Appleton, "SCM Definitions," www.enteract.com/~bradapp/acme/scm-defs.html, 2003.

[7] Feiler, P., "Configuration Management Models in Commercial Environments," *Technical Report CMU/SEI-91-TR-7*, Software Engineering Institute, Carnegie Mellon Institute, March 1991.

[8] Brenda S., U. Manber, and R. Muth, "Compressing Differences of Executable Code," *Proceedings of ACM SIGPLAN Workshop on Compiler Support for System Software (WCSS)*, April 1999.

[9] Tichy, W. F. (Ed.), *Configuration Management*, Chichester, UK: John Wiley & Sons, 1994.

[10] Estublier J., J.-M. Favre, and P. Morat, "Toward SCM/PDM Integration?" *Proceedings of 8th International Symposium on System Configuration Management (SCM-8)*, Lecture Notes in Computer Science, No. 1439, Berlin Heidelberg, Germany: Springer Verlag, 1998, pp. 75–94.

[11] Rational, www.rational.com, 2003.

[12] Telelogic, CM Synergy, www.telelogic.com, 2003.

[13] Microsoft, www.microsoft.com, 2003.

[14] Hoek, A. V. D., et al., "Software Release Management," *Proceedings of 6th European Software Engineering Conference*, Lecture Notes in Computer Science, No. 1301, Berlin Heidelberg, Germany: Springer Verlag, 1997.

[15] Asklund, U., *Configuration Management for Distributed Development—Practice and Needs*, Licentiate Dissertation No. 10, Department of Computer Science, Lund, Sweden: Lund University, 1999.

[16] Merant, PVCS Tracker, www.merant.com/products/ECM/tracker, 2003.

[17] Elsitech, Visual Intercept, www.elsitech.com, 2003.

[18] Swedish Standards Institute, *Quality Management—Guidelines for Configuration Management*, ISO 10 007, 1995.

[19] Crnkovic, I., "Experience with Change-Oriented SCM Tools," *Proceedings of 7th Symposium on Software Configuration Management (SCM-7)*, Lecture Notes in Computer Science, Berlin Heidelberg, Germany: Springer Verlag, 1997.

[20] Crnkovic I., M. Larsson, and F. Lüders, "Software Process Measurements Using Software Configuration Management," *Proceedings of 11th European Software Control and Metrics Conference*, IEEE Computer Society, 2000.

[21] ANSI/EIA-649-1998, "National Consensus Standard for Configuration Management," American National Standards Institute, New York, 1998.

[22] MIL-STD-973, "Configuration Management," Washington, D.C.: U.S. Department of Defense, April 1992.

[23] ISO 9000-3:1997, "Guidelines for the Application of ISO 9001:1994 to the Development, Supply, Installation, and Maintenance of Computer Software," ISO, Geneva, Switzerland, www.iso.ch, 1997.

[24] Winkler, J. (ed.), *Proceedings of the International Workshop on Software Version and Configuration Control*, B. G. Teubner, Stuttgart, Germany, 1988.

[25] Estublier, J. (ed.), *Proceedings of 9th International Symposium on System Configuration Management (SCM-9)*, Lecture Notes in Computer Science, No. 1675, Springer Verlag, 1999.

[26] Hoek, A. V. D. (ed.), *10th International Workshop on Software Configuration Management (SCM-10)*, Toronto, Canada, May 2001.

[27] Asklund, U., et al., "The Unified Extensional Versioning Model," *Proceedings of 9th International Symposium on System Configuration Management (SCM-9)*, Lecture Notes in Computer Science, No. 1675, Springer Verlag, 1999.

[28] Asklund U., *Configuration Management for Distributed Development in an Integrated Environment*, Doctoral Dissertation, Department of Computer Science, Lund, Sweden: Lund University, 2002.

[29] Dart, S., *Configuration Management—The Missing Link in Web Engineering*, Norwood, MA: Artech House, 2000.

[30] Quinn, E., and R. Heiman, "Web Object Management: Bringing Order to Opportunity," white paper, www.mks.com/wom/idc_wom.htm.

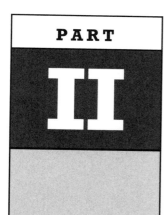

PART

II

Similarities and Differences Between PDM and SCM

CHAPTER

4

Comparison of technical principles and key functionality

The beginning of wisdom is to call things by their right names.
—Chinese proverb

Chapters 2 and 3 gave general and coherent descriptions of the PDM and SCM domains, respectively. In this chapter, we will continue discussing these domains but focus on a technical comparison. We will compare the typical functionality of tools within the two domains, both on a fundamental principle level and with respect to specific functions.

Many companies use various PDM and SCM methods and tools for similar purposes. It might seem easy to compare a PDM and an SCM tool, but this is not necessarily the case. The same or similar terminology is used in both domains but often with different meanings, and a thorough analysis of their use shows that there are significant differences. Different ranges of functionality and different user cultures are two more factors that make a comparison difficult. For example, Estublier [1] considers that although the PDM and SCM domains appear to be very similar, this is only on a principle level, as their implementations are very different.

We begin this chapter with a comparison of some fundamental principles of PDM and SCM:

• System architecture;
• Product model;

> Evolution model;
> Process model.

We then compare specific functionality important in one or both of the domains. These are:

> Version management;
> Product structure management;
> Build management;
> Change management;
> Release management;
> Workflow and process management;
> Document management;
> Concurrent development;
> Configuration/selection management;
> Workspace management.

The comparisons of principles and functionalities overlap. In the comparison of principles, we discuss differences and similarities in a more conceptual way, whereas when comparing specific functionality, we compare tool functionality.

4.1 Comparison of principles

In this section, four fundamental areas are discussed, and the implementation of each in the PDM and SCM domains, respectively, is compared.

4.1.1 System architecture

The system architecture describes the way a system is built up, its infrastructure, and ways it can be integrated with other systems. Most PDM and SCM tools use a client-server architecture, the server containing the database in which all data is stored. This data is stored following a certain data representation implementing a storage data model. To provide effective support to distributed development, many servers are needed. The architecture also includes the strategy for server use (what data is stored in which server), the client-server and server-server communication, and ways that servers are kept synchronized.

4.1.1.1 Data representation

Ways that data is stored and represented in PDM tools is fundamentally different than in SCM tools. As described in Section 2.3.1, PDM tools focus on managing product data stored in business items. This data, relating to the product, is designated metadata. The actual data (e.g., drawings produced in CAD tools) are stored in files and referred to as data items. A business item is thus an entity in a database, described by metadata, while a data item is the actual file. Most PDM tools use an object-oriented data model, in which a hierarchy of different types of business items can be created with references to related data items. Many PDM tools also use an object-oriented relational database in which to store the business items (often called the PDM database), while the data items are stored separately in file servers.

Separating the business items and data items makes it easier for a PDM system to manage heterogeneous data (i.e., different file types and objects). Very large amounts of data can be stored and managed in a PDM system. When distributing (replicating) the data in order to make it more available in a distributed setting, only the business items are replicated. See Section 4.1.1.2 for details.

Data is represented in SCM by what is more or less a file system with directories and files. The two different types of files, source (plain ASCII files) or binaries (executables), are usually treated differently. For source files SCM provides additional support, such as showing differences between different file versions or enabling interactive merging of two file versions. In general, all kinds of file types and objects represented as a file or directory may be managed and stored in the SCM tool. Metadata for a file is stored together with the file itself and not in a separate database. SCM systems usually manage large amounts of data.

The difference in data representation reflects the different histories of SCM and PDM. SCM mainly manages source files, which, together with directories, are their primary data model. It is possible to store, compare, and merge this data within the SCM tool. The need to manage metadata was only realized subsequently and was then implemented as an *add on*, using attributes. Moreover, in most cases, the user interface for managing attributes is rudimentary and is rarely used by developers (end users).

For PDM, the reverse is the case. The metadata is considered the most important. This data is stored in a well-defined (user-defined) data model that can be searched through and accessed through different views. The data items themselves, however, are treated as atomic objects, often stored by some other tool and only referred to from the business items.

There is, however, a tendency for SCM tools to also use a separate database for storing the metadata, thereby reducing this difference between PDM and SCM.

4.1.1.2 Data replication

Both PDM and SCM support distributed development by enabling replication of data (i.e., the storage of the same data on many servers where it is automatically kept synchronized and consistent)—see Sections 2.4.3 and 3.2.7. There are, however, differences.

As illustrated in Figure 4.1, a typical PDM tool has a master server (often called a corporate server). This server contains common information such as access rights for all the other servers and the locations of the other servers in the network. The replication architecture can be likened to a constellation with the master server at the center. SCM tools usually have no such master server. Instead, servers replicate data between two nodes, using a peer-to-peer protocol. Thus, any structure of servers can be built by connecting servers to each other. An example with four servers is depicted in Figure 4.2.

In PDM tools, it is often possible to decide that either both the business items and the data items or only the business items should be replicated. It is

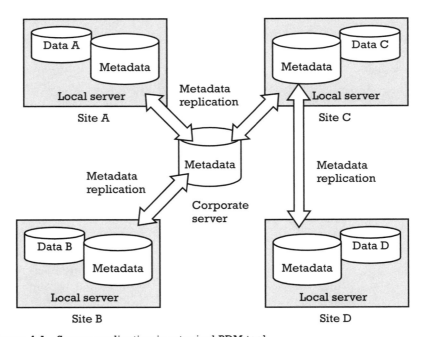

Figure 4.1 Server replication in a typical PDM tool.

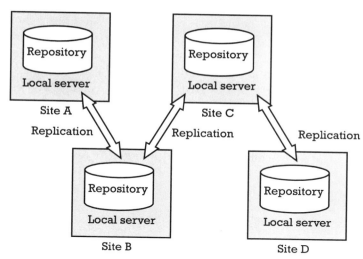

Figure 4.2 Server replication in a typical SCM tool.

most usual to replicate only the business items (the metadata), leaving all data items unreplicated, stored at their respective servers (one data item existing in one server only). In Figure 4.1, a typical example of replication of business items between four different sites is shown. At sites A, B, C, and D, the data items are stored in their respective local data repository (e.g., on a file server), here denoted Data A, Data B, etc. The business items are replicated to all servers. When a user requests a specific data item, the PDM system first searches for its business item, which, because it is replicated, can always be found on the local metadata server. The business item has a reference to the data item, pointing out the server in which the item is stored and from which it can then be requested. The local server will present the information for the user. Assuming that a user has access permission, he or she can update (check out and check in) a file and change the file itself and its metadata, irrespective of where in the network the file is located. A distributed locking mechanism controlled by the master server prevents the checking out of a file by two users at the same time. When a local server wishes to lock an item, a lock flag is sent to the master. If the item is not already locked, the server receives the lock flag and can begin modification of the item. To set a lock flag, it is thus necessary to reach the master server but not to reach all the other local servers.

In most SCM tools, the replication functionality was implemented as an add-on feature long after the standard systems were developed, and it is not possible for the SCM tool to manage metadata and files separately. The user can decide which data (typically, which files) should be replicated. Both these files and their metadata are then replicated. As stated earlier, the replication is performed between pairs of servers. Figure 4.2 depicts an example of how four servers can be connected and data are replicated by connecting the servers two by two. It is only possible to access data stored at the local server. A global lock is seldom used to avoid multiple updates. Instead most SCM tools implement replication using site ownership of the branches, as described in Section 3.2.7. This means that only one site is allowed to create new versions on a specific branch (the owner of that branch). Versions on a branch not owned by a site are read-only and cannot be updated (check out and check in) without requesting and obtaining transfer of the ownership to that site.

4.1.1.3 Application integration

A PDM system is usually integrated with various applications and builds an information infrastructure in which data from applications is gathered and exchanged. Integrations range from the simple, where the appropriate application is launched when a file is viewed, to the tighter, where the PDM system retrieves information from the applications, either through APIs or by direct access to application repositories.

The role of an SCM tool in a complete environment is somewhat different. It can be used as a stand-alone tool, or as a set of tools, and also as a set of functions offered for use by other tools. SCM tools are often designed to provide other applications with information and data (e.g., a file is checked out and sent to a compiler to be compiled). Many SCM tools are integrated in other tools. Typical examples are IDE. For this reason, many SCM tools include APIs with basic SCM functions (check in, check out, and baseline), which make them easy to encapsulate in other tools. It is also interesting to mention that many different tools incorporate certain basic SCM functions as their integral part and not as a part of an SCM tool. For example, Microsoft Word contains rudimentary version management.

The data format used for the exchange of data is also different. PDM has standards defining transfer protocols to enable the exchange of data with different formats. SCM uses plain files only.

The historical difference in the way integration with other applications is performed affects the possibility of integrating a PDM tool with an SCM tool. While PDM tools are often the central process that initiates activities in other tools, SCM tools are more passive, offering an API. Their complementary behavior makes their integration is easier (PDM encapsulating an SCM tool), but is not sufficient. To obtain a seamless and user-friendly integration, the entire processes must be integrated and the redundancy in functions must be avoided. For example, both PDM and SCM provide support for version management, but they are quite different (see Section 4.2.1).

4.1.2 Product model

A *product model* is an information model used to describe the structure (building blocks such as parts) and behavior (e.g., outputs, effects, and properties) of a product managed by the system. The extensive support for product model management in PDM and its absence from in SCM is perhaps the largest technical difference between PDM and SCM systems.

A PDM system has an explicit product model. The basic principle of product modeling in PDM is the composition relationship, which is used to form tree structures (often referred to as product structures), as described in Section 2.2.3. The product structure is not hidden in the system, but presented and edited by the user.

On the other hand, in SCM, product modeling is very weak. Even though creating a product structure is part of the identification activity in CM (see Section 3.3.1), SCM tools do not manage a product model. The differences in approach come from fundamental differences in the nature of hardware products and software products. For hardware, the product has a physical existence and consists of physical parts. For that reason the product structure can be represented by a part structure. In the software PLC, the software is transformed through different structures. The software architecture developed during the design phase determines the structure of the software system, which comprises software components, the externally visible properties of those components, and the relationships between them. The development structure used during the implementation phase includes source code and documentation related to it. It is natural that the software architecture and the development structure are similar, but in practice they are different as a result of two factors. First, the development process itself: the isolation and coordination of development activities requires a structure different from the software architecture. Second, many of the development tools used require specific structures. As a consequence, in the implementation phase, developers use a separate development structure adjusted to the development process. A completely different structure is that of the software product delivery package. It includes binary and user-documentation files and is adjusted to be most convenient for the delivery. Note also that different structures can be defined for different delivery media. This structure is derived from the development structure by a build and release activity. Moreover, we have a structure on the target system, when the software is installed. In many software systems, we recognize two different target system structures—an installation or deployment structure in which the software is saved on a medium (for example, a disk), ready to run, and a run-time structure in which the software is executed (the primary memory). Finally, we must remember that all of these structures are not physical, but virtual. The difference is very important, as they can be changed very easily. Indeed, completely different structures may be used in different versions of the same product. Because SCM tools are focused on the development phase, they usually have certain support for managing developing structures.

Different building blocks are used when creating (defining) the product model. The types of these blocks are defined in the data model, which describes not only the types of objects, but also object attributes and the relationships between objects. This data model may be changed in a PDM system to more exactly suit the particular company business model. A set of industry-specific data models is included in the STEP standard [2]. The purpose of STEP is to facilitate data transfer between various information systems within and between companies. It is a comprehensive standard, and its contents include descriptions of geometry and product structures. Several PDM systems support data transfer based on this standard, and some even have a data model based on this standard.

Only a few SCM systems include a customizable data model. Most SCM systems structure information by using the file and directory structure used in the operating system. SCM has no standard such as STEP.

4.1.3 Evolution model

The *evolution model* manages changes during the PLC and is related to version management.

PDM distinguishes three different concepts of versioning: *historical versioning*, *logical versioning*, and *domain versioning*. Historical versioning is conceptual and similar to SCM versioning, dealing with revisions/versions of a product. However, it is not possible to branch and merge. Logical versioning manages versions of parts as alternatives, possible substitutes, or options. Finally, domain versioning is not actually versioning but a presentation of further views of the product structure (e.g., as planned, as designed, and as manufactured) used by different actors during different phases in the PLC. These views are fundamental in PDM tools.

The emphasis on historical versioning in SCM, which is more advanced than PDM, arises from the differences in the natures of the products:

software may be changed more easily than hardware. Thus, SCM must manage versioning in a more sophisticated way than CM for hardware [3]. Versioning in an SCM tool almost always includes the possibility of creating and merging branches. It is also easy to present the differences between two versions because the source code is usually stored in text format. There is no logical versioning in SCM. Variants are managed—but often using branches or conditional compilation—and are not clearly visualized using the product structure. The concept of *view* exists in many SCM tools and is related to the possibility of creating configurations by the selection of consistent versions of the files included in a specific configuration. This is used both to create private workspaces and to build the product.

4.1.4   Process model

The *process models* for SCM and PDM are conceptually similar. A process is described by a set of states and rules for passing from one state to another. These states and rules can be specified by state transition diagrams (STDs). An STD describes the legal succession of states (and optionally which actions produce the transition) for a product type, and thus describes the legal way for entities of that type to evolve. The alternative way to model processes is so-called activity-centered modeling, in which the activity plays the central role, and the models express the data and control flow between activities.

PDM systems have two process-related concepts: object states and workflow. The object state defines the life cycle of an object (e.g., preliminary, approved, and frozen). Workflows are based on a description of the process, its activities, their sequence, and the relationships between them. A workflow can be used to control data management activities within or between processes and is therefore an activity-centered model.

As SCM is intended to control software product evolution, it is not surprising that many process models are based on STDs. As [4] concludes, experience shows that complex and fine-grained process models can be defined that way. Unfortunately, experience also shows that STDs do not provide a global view of a process, and that large processes are difficult to define using only STDs. The activity-based model is not used to the same extent as in PDM, but some SCM tools provide process support similar to the workflow in PDM. Most SCM tools provide triggers to implement a process. These triggers, activated on certain occasions such as check in, can be used to activate scripts implementing a workflow, running tests, or for sending notifications to other developers.

4.2 Comparison of key functionality

This section outlines some functionality important in either PDM or SCM (or both). We focus on the differences between PDM and SCM. Functionality closely related to PDM or SCM only is not treated here. Separate tools or modules within the tools, such as requirement management (RM) tools or modules, manage these.

4.2.1 Version management

Version models in PDM differ from those in SCM.

In PDM systems, the versions of a business item are denoted revisions. Revisions are organized in a flat structure (only one main branch, denoted A and B in Figure 4.3), as compared with the hierarchical structure in SCM, which allows branching and merging. A business item represents and carries metadata for both products and documents. This metadata, shown in Figure 4.3, is denoted *attributes*. Attributes are used frequently in PDM systems and are visible to the users. Only major changes of a business item are tracked by revisions (i.e., revised from revision A to B—see Figure 4.3), and this transition is performed manually by the user. The different revisions of a business item are connected by means of a *relationship*. The *revision-of* relationship is depicted in the figure, but a PDM system can contain many other relationships, which may have one or more attributes.

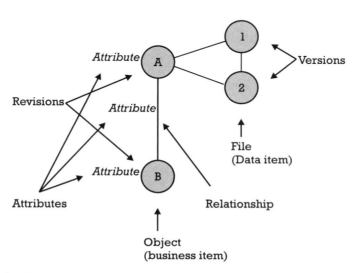

Figure 4.3 Version management in PDM.

To change a released business item or its associated data items (files), a new revision of the business item must be created. When the business item is approved, its new revision is frozen. If data items are associated with the business item, it is most often the data item that is changed. While the data item is changed, it may be checked in and out several times without creating a new revision. To manage the sequence of data items (shown as 1 and 2 in Figure 4.3), *versions* are used internally in the PDM system. These versions are normally not visible to the user.

Versions in SCM form a hierarchical structure (see Figure 4.4), in which two versions of a file can be developed simultaneously in branches, which may be merged together again if needed. Each time a file is checked out and in, a new version is created. This corresponds to a version in PDM. In SCM, however, versions are visible to the user and are used frequently. A version of a file can be marked with *attributes*, but is rarely used and normally not visible to the users. Later, a baseline is created by manually selecting the versions to be included in the configuration.

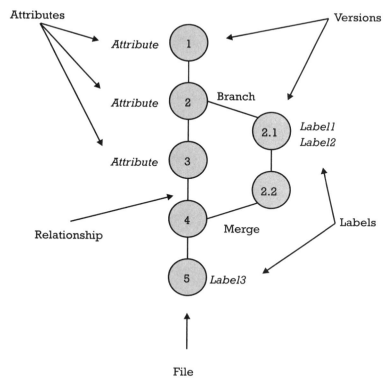

Figure 4.4   Version management in SCM.

These versions are then marked using a special attribute often called a tag or label. Labeled versions thus almost correspond to revisions in PDM.

In the following list, the concepts in Figure 4.3 and Figure 4.4 are shown in italic type. The following list shows the similarities of version management in PDM and in SCM and the differences between them:

- PDM manages *objects*. SCM manages *files* and *directories*.

- PDM uses *revisions* for major changes. SCM uses *versions* for all changes.

- SCM has *branches* and supports *merge* functionality. PDM does not.

- In SCM, several people can work on the same file at the same time using the branch facility, which is not possible in PDM.

- Both SCM and PDM tools have *attributes*. SCM has a special attribute called *label*, which is frequently used. General (user-defined) attributes are rarely used in SCM due to *restricted* usability. PDM strongly supports customized attributes through its data model.

- PDM has *relationships*, SCM does not (apart from the revision-of relationship implementing historical versioning).

- A relationship may have attributes in PDM but not in SCM.

4.2.2 Product structure management

Product structure management is a basic and fundamental functionality in a PDM system, described in detail in Section 2.2.3. The PDM system describes a configuration by arranging the parts in a structure consisting of different products or parts connected by relationships. The product structure commonly follows the same pattern as the structure of the physical product. Different kinds of structures can be defined in a PDM system by specifying different views (e.g., the view describing the parts by their business items connected by relationships). A database model supports the building of product structures. Different views of a product structure can also be used to support different roles (e.g., the manufacturing engineer needs to see the components of a product to enable him to assemble it for delivery to the customer).

SCM tools do not explicitly address and support product structures. Only rudimentary support, in the form of directories in a file system, is available for use in building a hierarchical structure, and SCM tools provide support for managing these structures during the development phase. It is not possible to see directly the relationship between these structures and the structures of the executable software. This relationship is not visible, even when some of the advanced SCM tools use relational databases for storing product metadata. Metadata is used to describe the states of CIs, which are not complex objects or components but only files or sets of files.

4.2.3   Build management

The build process is very specific to software products. It is both computation and automation intensive, but short in comparison with other phases or with the process of building hardware products. The build process includes two central types of transformations. First, the source code, legible to humans, is transformed to a binary form (also designated as machine code or executable code). Second, the product structure itself is changed. Typically, a new directory structure including the newly created binary files will be created. The transformation from source code to binary code is performed by compilers. Transformation of the structure is a part of build management.

Build is essential in SCM and supported as described briefly in Section 3.2.4. Build is in no way supported in PDM for software.

4.2.4   Change management

The basic principles of change management in PDM and SCM are similar. In PDM, add-on modules support change management. In SCM, there are specific change management tools integrated with the SCM system. Because of the nature of the software, the change process and the traceability (see Section 3.2.8) are better integrated with change management. For hardware products, the change process itself is usually outside the scope of the change management tools. The changes are either performed outside the computer system (if a physical change) or with tools (such as CAD/CAM), whose management objects (drawings) are not manageable outside these tools. This has the consequence of change management (in PDM systems) becoming a way of documenting the process, which is very similar to document management. For software producers, whose artifacts are always stored in a computer, it is easier to achieve a tight integration between the change process itself and change management. For example, a developer can access files to be modified directly from the change management tools, or a new product version can be built automatically from a particular product version or baseline with added changes. This type of support is often available in SCM tools.

4.2.5 Release management

Simple support for release management is available in SCM for pure software products (e.g., packaging of the executables, related documents, and installation program). In PDM, the support for release management is strong. The manufacturing engineer uses the BOM (the list of all parts included in the final product, as described in Section 2.2.3) to assemble the final product. The BOM is a part of the product structure. The package sent to the customer is a component in the product structure with relationships to the constituent artifacts.

4.2.6 Workflow and process management

Workflows and processes can be defined and executed in PDM systems. All processes can be changed and adapted to specific projects. Some SCM tools incorporate similar functionality or provide it using tools tightly integrated within the *tool suite*. In most SCM systems, however, there are only triggers, which can execute scripts written by the users. This is support of little value, as the result is a mess of scripts that are difficult to survey and maintain.

4.2.7 Document management

PDM has built-in document management facilities such as query, viewing, and access control, which are not available in SCM. However, as developers prefer to work in an integrated development environment with easy access to all of the artifacts being developed or used in the development process, there is a trend to store more and more documents within SCM, despite its lack of query functions and other document management capabilities.

4.2.8 Concurrent development

Both PDM and SCM provide shared databases/repositories and locking functions to prevent simultaneous updates. SCM also provides workspace management together with branch and merge, which makes it possible for developers to work concurrently on the same file (see Figure 4.4). The support of merge also makes it possible to provide optimistic check out instead of locking, as described for SCM in Section 3.2.6.

4.2.9 CM and selection management

There are usually many versions of the same file stored in an SCM system. The SCM tool provides support for selection of the correct version of each file. This is important both when retrieving versions for use in workspace and when the product is to be built. There is no functionality in PDM comparable with the selection function in SCM. Many PDM systems support configuration *effectivity*, which is a time or revision limitation (see Section 2.5.1). However, this is not selection management but more logical versioning, as described in Section 4.1.3.

4.2.10 Workspace management

In an SCM system, the user checks out all of the files to be changed and stores these in his or her workspace. The SCM system registers all files checked out, the version checked out, by whom, and in which workspace the copy is stored. If many users check out the same file (and possible the same version), these check outs are coordinated under the control of the tool in accordance with the synchronization model used. Each user can set up and change the definition (selection) of the files (versions) that are to be checked out to the workspace.

Workspace management in this form is not provided in PDM systems. PDM systems have work locations (which are private file locations), with one location defined per user (described in Section 2.4). In PDM, the user checks out one file at a time and updates it. Locking prevents more than one user from checking out the same version of the same file simultaneously (it is usually only the latest version that is checked out). When checking out the file, it will be saved in a private work location, which must be set up by the system administrator. The user need not know the physical situation of the location and has no authority to change the location.

4.2.11 Role definitions

While the role concept is an important feature of PDM tools and is integrated with the support for workflow and process management, the support provided by SCM tools is more varied. Many SCM tools distinguish users only by the user identity. A few SCM tools support roles and access rules.

4.3 Summary

The results of the discussion in this chapter are summarized in Table 4.1. PDM and SCM are compared, with respect to the availability of different functionalities. This is followed by Table 4.2 summarizing the pros and cons of PDM and SCM.

Table 4.1   Summary of Functionality of PDM and SCM

Type of Functionality	PDM	SCM
Version management	Yes	Yes, with branch and merge
Product structure management	Yes	No
Build management	No	Yes
Change management	Yes	Yes, well integrated with other processes
Release management	Yes	Yes, but weak
Workflow and process management	Yes	Yes, but weak
Document management	Yes	Partly
Concurrent development	No	Yes
Configuration/selection management	No	Yes
Workspace management	No	Yes
Roles	Yes	Yes, but weak

Table 4.2   Pros and Cons of PDM and SCM

PDM	SCM
PDM tools are strong in product modeling.	SCM tools are weak in product modeling.
PDM tools have a long tradition in standardized product evolution control know how.	SCM do not have a long tradition in product development.
Some tools use a standard to a certain degree; some do not.	There is no standard for SCM tools.
PDM tools are strong in workflow and process management.	Many SCM tools have a good support in workflow and process management.
PDM tools are strong in document management.	SCM tools are weak in document management.
PDM is strong in data representation where metadata and data are separated.	In general, SCM tools are weak in management of metadata.
PDM is strong in the data modeling where an object-oriented data model is used.	There is no data modeling in SCM. SCM tools manage files and directories effectively.
PDM tools are strong in release management.	SCM tools are weak in release management.
PDM has a weak support for concurrent engineering.	SCM tools are strong in concurrent engineering on a single file.
PDM does not support workspace management.	SCM tools are strong in workspace management.
PDM tools do not support build management.	SCM tools are strong in build management.
PDM tools do not support configuration/selection management.	SCM tools are strong in configuration/selection management.
PMD tools have simpler version management model.	SCM tools are strong in version management.

We can conclude, in comparing SCM and PDM, that SCM tools do not have the necessary functionality to support the development of a complex product during its entire life cycle and that PDM tools do not have sufficient functionality to support software management, particularly during the development phase. However, even though there is much functionality redundancy, SCM tools and PDM tools complement each other.

References

[1]   Estublier J., J.-M. Favre, and P. Morat, "Toward SCM/PDM Integration?" *Proceedings of 8th International Symposium on System Configuration Management (SCM-8)*, Lecture Notes in Computer Science, No. 1439, Springer Verlag, Berlin Heidelberg, Germany, 1998, pp. 75–94.

[2]   ISO TCI194/SC4/WG5, "STEP Part 1: Overview and Fundamental Principles," November 1991.

[3]   Westfechtel, B., and R. Conradi, "Software Configuration Management and Engineering Data Management: Differences and Similarities," *Proceedings of 8th International Symposium on System Configuration Management (SCM-8)*, Lecture Notes in Computer Science, No. 1439, Berlin Heidelberg, Germany: Springer Verlag, 1998, pp. 96–106.

[4]   Estublier, J., "Software Configuration Management: A Roadmap," *Proceedings of 22nd International Conference on Software Engineering, The Future of Software Engineering*, ACM Press, New York, 2000.

Analysis and general findings

The only difference between a problem and a solution is that people understand the solution.

— Charles F. Kettering

In Chapter 4, we saw that many functions appear in both PDM and SCM tools. In some cases, these functions are more advanced in PDM than in SCM; in others, the opposite is true. Important questions for companies are:

• Is it possible to use either a PDM tool or an SCM tool irrespective of the type of product being developed? If this is possible, in which way can the tool functions be utilized, and in particular how can functions from one domain be applied in the other? For example, can version management from PDM be used to manage versions of software, in particular source code? Or, can the SCM change management function be used to work with changes of hardware products and product parts?

• If a tool from either of the domains can be used in any development process, is it more efficient to use a PDM tool or is it preferable to use an SCM tool?

• If SCM cannot replace PDM and PDM cannot replace SCM, a new type of question arises. When should a PDM tool be used and when an SCM tool? Is it necessary to use tools of both types?

▶ If both PDM and SCM tools are to be used, do we need to integrate them? If so, what type of integration is needed?

To answer these questions about the use of PDM and SCM and their possible integration, it is first necessary to analyze the particular functions of these domains, as in Chapter 4. However this is not sufficient. We must also analyze the processes, and we must identify the data and the functions used in the processes. This is the main goal of this chapter. Beginning with the generic PLC described in Chapter 1, we shall analyze information generated and used in different phases of the process, in particular the development process. We shall analyze PLCs for pure hardware products, pure software products, and complex products that include both hardware and software components. This analysis will be exemplified by a concrete development process from industry.

The analysis will indicate the prerequisites for the use of these tools and the prerequisites for their use when integrated.

5.1 Development process and information management

In Chapter 1, we depicted a generic life cycle process model. This model is general and valid for both hardware and software development, although different subactivities are included and different priorities are allocated. In this section, we will describe the life cycle processes of both hardware and software products in more detail, to be able to determine if there are different requirements and, if so, what these are. We will focus on the phase with the most activities, the development process, and identify the PDM- and SCM-related requirements to provide support for the development activities.

5.1.1 Hardware products

In this context, a hardware product is a product containing hardware only (i.e., no software components). Most of the hardware product development consists of different descriptions of the product in many different documents (e.g., drawings and manufacturing specifications, which describe the product itself and the components included in it). The most important PDM-related requirement for hardware development is the ability to manage these documents and the product structures.

A more detailed description of the most common requirements related to information assets (documentation and other type of data) that are created, changed, and used is given next.

▸ Customer demands are translated into system requirements. These requirements are combined with internal requirements from stakeholders, such as production factors (e.g., low production costs, compatibility with existing production processes, and low assembly costs) and maintenance requirements. It must be possible for requirements engineers to access all information needed to identify the requirements for the particular products and to specify the requirements that will be used later in the development process.

▸ The mechanical and electronics designers need to manage the documents, which they create using CAD/CAM and other tools or directly by means of a PDM system.

▸ The developers must be able to version control their parts (components in the product structure) and related documents. Normally, concurrent work on the same document or part is not allowed, but locking mechanism is used. However, some CAD systems allow developers to divide a part into *zones*, each zone being checked out separately, instead of the part as a whole. The manufacturing and purchasing departments must be able to purchase and manufacture components, assemble the product, and deliver it to a customer. They need a BOM to prepare forecasts to perform purchasing and production line planning, tool ordering, and assembly. Drawings and other documents are used to specify how to build manufacturing tools and to manufacture parts.

▸ The documents and the product structure must be available for writers of user manuals. They need to know the product's functionality, design, requirements met, and so on.

▸ Information about the product must be available to other stakeholders, such as advertising and sales people.

▸ All information assets must be stored in archives. All components and their documents must be available in up-to-date versions for maintenance purposes and for future releases of the product.

▸ To establish a baseline or a release, it is necessary to freeze all relevant products and documents. Beyond the baseline point, formal change management is required to manage changes. In hardware development, late changes can be very expensive, due to the probable costs of redesigning manufacturing tools and the production process.

Let us study the development process from Chapter 1 to determine in which parts of the process each information asset is actually generated and used. The process contains five steps, as shown in Figure 5.1. It begins with the collection and analysis of detailed requirements and a conceptual development phase, in which the needs of the market are investigated and the overall requirements defined, followed by the generation of product concepts. In the system-level design phase, the architecture of the product is decided. This includes the identification of subsystems, components, and the interfaces between them. The design of the components is further developed during the detailed design phase. The testing and refinement phase includes the building of product prototypes used to test both the product and the production system. During the production ramp up, the production system is used for serial production of the product, beginning at a low rate and then increasing to full production capacity. The figure also shows the types of information used to describe the product. The bars show approximately in which of the phases information evolves and in which it is used.

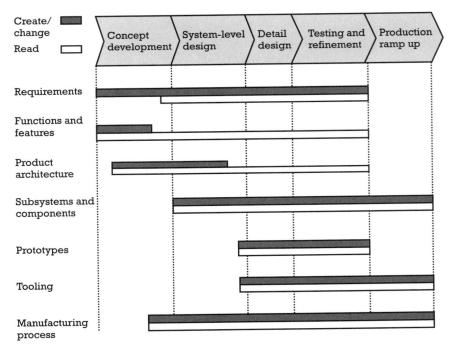

Figure 5.1 Hardware development process and information usage.

In the early phases, the product is described by functions and possibly also in terms of geometric layouts. The architecture is not an information object in itself, but is presented as geometric layouts, system structures, and preliminary product (component) structures. During the detail design, the product structures become more detailed, components are identified and designed, work on the prototype development is begun, and documents related to the manufacturing process and tooling are prepared. In the final stage, preparations for production are concluded, and the final release of the product documentation is prepared. From Figure 5.1, we can also see that most of the information is used during the entire process.

5.1.2 Software products

During software product development, it is most important for developers to be able to manage documents and a huge amount of source code. An SCM tool is usually used to manage software structures and the relationships between components, which mostly exist in source code form. Documents are most often stored together with the source code in the SCM tool. This product category contains no hardware of any kind, and there is no apparent need for a PDM system.

The requirements related to the management of information assets, created, changed, and used in the development of software are summarized next:

- The customer demands are translated to system requirements, in the same way as for hardware products. As one of the main characteristics of software is that it is easy to change, many requirements address the improvement of existing products, which is a part of the maintenance process.

- The system designers prepare overall and subsequently detailed design documents. These documents may include textual information but also other types of information (e.g., diagrams or formal specifications) that can be used for the generation of templates for source code.

- During the development phase, developers use different tools for writing and generating source code and for building executable code. Software systems are built from large numbers of source code files. To concurrently develop such systems, software development needs a support for detailed version control (using revisions, branches, and merges). There are many more versions of software files and databases than there are of hardware.

> • A baseline, with frozen documentation and source code files, must be established. As it is relatively easy to build executables from source code, they are usually not versioned in the same way as the source code because they can be reproduced.[1] When the baseline is verified, the developer may release the product for further testing or delivery to the customer.

> • To deliver the product to a customer, the manufacturing department must be able to produce product packages suitable for delivery (e.g., the product can be burned on media or published on the Web). The manufacturer must also retrieve relevant documents.

> • For marketing and sales, the product information (e.g., brochures, release notes, list of known problems, and product descriptions) must be available for communication to customers.

> • All information (documentation, source code, and deliverables) must be stored in archives. All components and their documents must be available in the right revisions for maintenance purposes and for future releases of the product.

> • Technically, changes are easy to introduce in software products, which enables a more flexible development process. However, if the change process is not under strict control, enormous overhead in the time and costs can appear. An uncontrolled change process is one of the largest problems in software development. For this reason, when the software product is released, or even when the first baseline of software is created, the formal change management must be performed.

The software development process [1] follows a schema similar to that for hardware development. During the requirements analysis phase, the system's services, constraints, and goals are established in the system specification. In the next phase, software design, an overall system architecture is established in which the fundamental software systems abstractions and their relationships are identified and described. The implementation phase comprises formalization of the design by creating source code or using pre-existing code or packages. The implemented units of software are created and tested. In the integration phase, the software units are integrated in

---

1. Automatic reproduction of executables is often a cause of many problems, as it is based on the principle that the executables can be reproduced in exactly the same way each time. While it is easy to identify source code used to build executables, it is almost impossible to reproduce the entire context in which the executables are created. For this reason, more sophisticated SCM tools are able to keep the executables under version control.

a software system. The integration phase corresponds to the production of hardware. During the test phase, the system is verified and validated. Finally, the system is released and delivered to a customer.

The phases of the development process are shown in Figure 5.2. This sequential model is a well-known waterfall model. We can, however, see that the information flow is not sequential, but rather follows a V shape. Indeed, there is a development model called the V model [2], which provides support for exchanging information between the different phases of the process. The V model indicates the reuse of information. The requirements specification is used in the later phases (e.g., during the test and release process). The test process itself is divided into a validation phase, in which the implemented functions are tested, and a verification phase, in which the product is tested with respect to the specified requirements.[2] The requirements may be modified during the design phase and even later

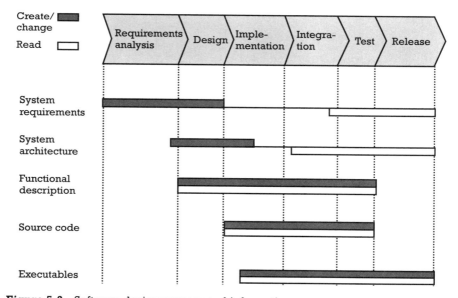

Figure 5.2   Software design process and information usage.

---

2. Validation and verification are terms that can be easily confused, although there is a clear distinction between them. Verification is a process that checks if the system meets its specified functional and nonfunctional requirements. A validation process should ensure that the system meets the customer's expectation. Or, as expressively described by Boehm [3]:

   • Validation: Are we building the right product?

   • Verification: Are we building the product right?

during the implementation. Overall design documents specify the product overall structure, main classes and objects, functions, and interfaces between different parts. This information is frequently used during the specification of the detailed design, which includes descriptions of objects and functions to be implemented. The detailed design, created in the next phase and most likely modified during the implementation phase, is used later in the test (validation) phase. The source code created in the implementation phase is later used when building the product and in the test (validation) phase for review and debugging purposes. Finally, the executable code, which is compiled from the source code and different libraries in binary form, is used during the test and delivered to the customer. Project management plays the same role as for hardware products. An efficient and accurate project management is of as great importance as change management. The need for a tight integration of information through the entire process is similar to that for hardware products.

5.1.3 Remarks

Analyzing these hardware and software processes, we can derive the following conclusions:

› The development processes for hardware and software products are similar, but the terminology differs, and the activities and type of information managed may be very different.

› In both cases, it was shown that information integration during the process is very important. Most of the information is used and often updated during the entire process.

› Neither PDM nor SCM provide full support for the whole development process. An indicative example is requirements management and its relation to implementation and test. One of the main functions of PDM and SCM is to assure traceability, and yet these tools provide only rudimentary traceability from implementation or test to the requirements. An SCM tool often can include CRs and connect them to changes made in the source code, but how the relations between CRs and requirements are obtained is not clear. Similarly, with PDM, it is not possible to trace which CR is related to a change implemented in a CAD/CAM drawing. To provide full support, other tools are needed and even then a problem with their interoperability remains.

› Because of the importance of information integration, it is necessary to integrate the different tools used in the entire development environment. This is not only so for PDM or SCM tools, but is also the case for other tools used in the process.

In the analysis, we have focused on the development process (and to a degree on maintenance), not on the entire product life cycle. The development phase in which there is the largest overlap of SCM- and PDM-related functions is the most complex. The results from the analysis can be extended to the entire PLC.

5.2   A case study—Information management and PLC

The PLC model described in the previous section describes the development and maintenance processes in general terms. In practice, companies have their own process models, which are usually a variation of the generic model. Companies frequently use their own vocabulary to emphasize particular activities or the overall goals of the development process. In this section, we will show activities and the information flow in the development process of the PLC model used by the telecommunication company Ericsson [4], which develops complex products consisting of both software and hardware.

5.2.1   Development and maintenance of a hardware-based product

Figure 5.3 shows a development process[3] and the information created during different phases. In the subprocess *business opportunity,* the product manager identifies customer needs that cannot be satisfied by existing products in the product portfolio, or different opportunities to increase performance, or to obtain a competitive advantage by providing a new product, or new technologies and standards that customers require. This builds the scope for the new product. The business case is stored in the PDM system. In the subprocess *define product content,* the prestudy is initiated, and system engineers, designers, the CM manager, and the project manager begin to define the implementation proposals, CM plans, and project specifications. The requirements are written in requirement documents and stored within the RM tools. All other documents are stored in the PDM tool. A design base

---

3. To emphasize the importance of time-to-market constraints, Ericsson designated this model as the *time-to-market process.*

including this information is defined, either created or taken from an existing base. The design base will be found in the CAD/CAM or the design archive. After the identification of requirements, a detailed content of the product is specified. The system architecture, an initial product structure, interface specifications, and function specifications will be written and fed into the PDM tool. The requirements will be redefined and refined if necessary. A product implementation description will be developed from the requirements and product content specifications. Information from the design will be imported into the CAD/CAM tool. If a requirement must be changed or added, a CR must be performed. The CR will be documented and analyzed, and the CCB will decide whether or not to introduce the change in the product. The CR will be managed in the CR tool. When the detailed specification is ready, the subprocesses *design* and *implement* and after that *verify product* will begin. The product structure will be refined, the design of hardware documents obtained net lists generated, test cases written, and test cases performed. For example, to verify a printed circuit board (PCB), a manufacturing team designs the PCB, tests the design, and produces a new prototype of the PCB. This procedure may be repeated several times until the PCB is tested and found to function satisfactorily. Before full-scale production begins, the manufacturing team will perform a prerelease of the PCB to check the production machinery. Before beginning production, a verification of the entire system will be performed (a test in which the system requirements will be tested against its performance, and the characteristics and performance of the system will be measured). During the development phase, CRs and trouble reports (TRs) will be managed in the TR tool. The CCB decides whether CRs and TRs are to be managed at weekly project meetings. Information will accumulate in the PDM system, in the design archive, and in CAD/CAM tools. The subprocess *exhibit product in operation* follows the product verification. The delivery structure is then defined, product revision information written, and the TR process initiated. Marketing activities will begin. Product catalogs, brochures, and other marketing documents will be written on the basis of the description of the new product. Product portfolio plans will be prepared in accordance with the company's business strategies. All of these documents will be stored within the PDM system.

The product information is managed by different tools (e.g., requirements will be stored in a database used by the RM tools, error reports and requests for changes in CR and TR tools, and product structures and BOM in the PDM system or in the CAD/CAM tools). Marketing documents will be stored in the PDM system.

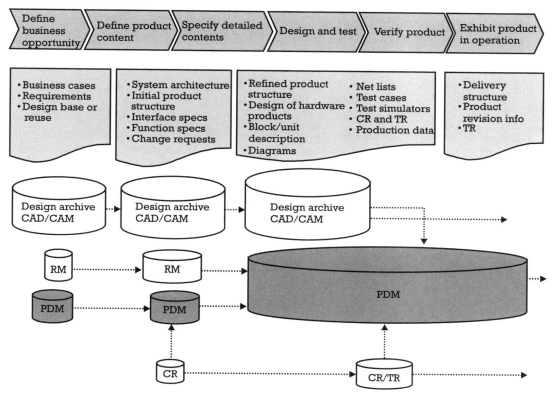

Figure 5.3   An example of processes and information storage for hardware development.

Figure 5.3 depicts the process, activities, information, and use of different types of databases. We can see from the figure that a PDM system has a central role.

5.2.2   Development and maintenance of a software-based product

Ericsson uses the same development process model for its software products. The particular procedures and information are, however, different. Figure 5.4 shows a development process for software products. The subprocess business opportunity is the same as for hardware products. Similarly, the overall functionality for this new product will be defined in the subprocess *define product content*. The requirements are written in requirement documents and stored within the RM tools, and the design base is defined. The design base will be created in the design archive and saved in a PDM system, and the design-related information will be added into the SCM tool. If a requirement must be changed or added, this must be done under change management. A CR will be created and analyzed and the CCB will decide whether to introduce the change. The CR will be managed by the CR tool. When a detailed specification is ready, the subprocesses *design and implement* and *verify product* will begin. Use cases, source codes, detailed design descriptions, test cases, and user documentation will be written, executable files generated, and test cases performed. During the development phase, CR will be managed in the CR tool. Later during the product maintenance TRs will be used for reporting errors and introducing changes into existing products. As CRs and TRs are very similar, they will be processed by the same tool (e.g., the TR tool). The CCB makes decisions about CRs and TRs in weekly project meetings. The subprocess *exhibit product in operation* includes activities similar to those for hardware products. However, there are two significant differences: no production machinery is used, and the product manufacturing will most often be performed by the same team (i.e., the development team). The product information needed for sales and service will be saved in the PDM system.

We can observe from Figure 5.4 that the activities are similar (or the same), but tools are used differently. The development is SCM centric (i.e., information is concentrated around SCM). We can also see that PDM tools are used also for software development.

5.3   Complex products

5.3.1   Structures of complex products

Most relevant products consist of many components and are developed as complex systems. A complex system consists, per definition, of many parts (called subsystems or components), and to cope with this complexity its development process is performed by different teams. The teams use different technologies and procedures to develop their specific type of documents and components. The result from each team is assembled on the system level to give a final product ready for production or delivery. Common to all product development activities is the necessity to manage data on the system level, between the teams, and within the teams.

On the system level, in addition to information about components, information about the contents of the products, customers, vendors, suppliers, baselines, releases, prices, and markets are needed. The project manager must know if the project is following the time schedule. The CM

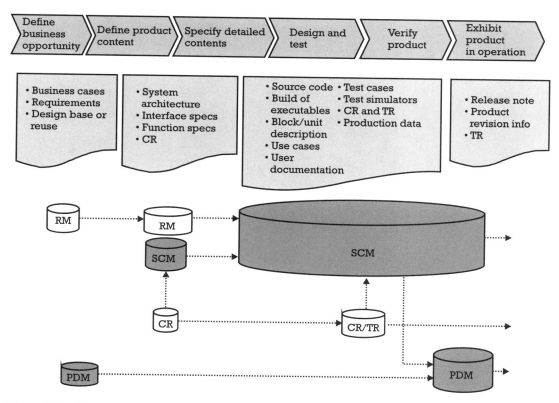

Figure 5.4 An example of processes and information storage for software development.

manager needs to know the current product configuration and its status, as well as related documents for the entire system and for all components (subsystems) included in the system. The designer must have access to requirements documents, project specification, and all information related to the product to be developed. The production engineer needs to find all documents related to a product ready for manufacturing. The sales person needs to find information about the product to present to a customer. There are many different roles within the company that need access to the right information about the right product at the right time. All of this data, created by different subsystems, must be available on a system level.

Figure 5.5 shows examples of systems and subsystems of different kinds of products. Figure 5.5(a) shows a system containing three different subsystems developing—mechanical, ASIC, and electronic. Products developed from the different subsystems will be integrated and tested on a system level

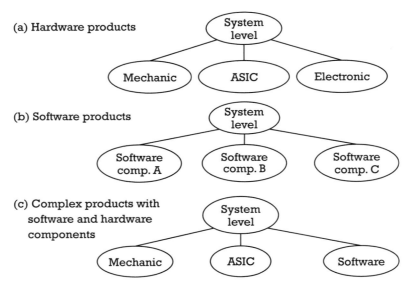

Figure 5.5 Product development configurations.

before the product will be manufactured and shipped to customers. Figure 5.5(b) shows a pure software product in which all subsystems develop different parts (components)[4] of the software. The software will then be integrated and tested on the system level before it will be available for delivery to customers. While the required support at the subsystem level is strongly software related, at the system level the support required is more similar to the support for hardware products. On the system level, mostly data about the products (i.e., metadata) is used, rather than direct product data. Figure 5.5(c) shows an example of a complex product that includes both software and hardware components. Once again, the procedures, technologies, and hence the support required are specific at the subsystem level, but common at the system level. At the system level, the differences between the subsystems are disregarded and each subsystem is treated in the same way, irrespective of whether it is a software or a hardware component.

4. There is a difference between subsystems and components. A subsystem is an integral part of the system, while a component can be a part that is independent of the system. A component can be used in different systems, developed independently of the systems, and easily replaced. Most of the hardware products are developed from components. This is also a noticeable trend in software development, although many concepts of component-based development of software systems are not yet precisely defined and established in practice.

5.3.2 Information flow

The information flow is not directed only from the subsystem level to the system level. In the beginning of the development process, much of the information that will be used at the subsystem level is generated at the system level. A development process begins at the system level in which the overall goals, constraints, and requirements are identified, and an overall design of the system is prepared. Further, the system is developed by a successive division into subsystems, which can be developed in parallel, followed by their integration. This process is shown in Figure 5.6, in which we distinguish processes from life cycle models. A process consists of activities, while a life cycle is characterized by states and milestones. A system or a component is in a state during the performance of particular activities. The activities are concluded when their goals, which are indicated by milestones, are achieved. The entire process can be divided into three parts—a *common* part in which activities related to the system are performed and information needed later in all subprocesses is obtained, an *independent* part in which the subprocesses are progressed in parallel and the information in each subsystem is generated independently of other subprocesses, and finally an *integrated* part in which the information from all processes must be accessible and integrated in common information.

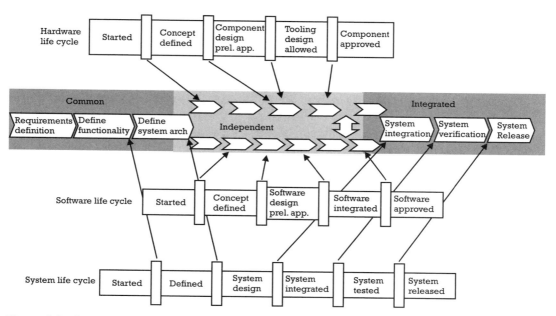

Figure 5.6 Complex PLC.

In Figure 5.6 we can also see when, at certain points in the development life cycle, common activities are divided into separate activities and when they are merged together again. At these points, it is important that all system-related information is easily accessible and that it is possible to import this information into the tools used in the activities in the subsystems. Figure 5.1 and Figure 5.2 show the information flow through the phases of the parallel subprocesses. From these figures, we can summarize that we need the information flow of the following assets:

- From common activities to the parallel hardware and software activities, we need requirements, CRs, and overall system design (defined partly by a product structure). We also need information related to the project management.

- From the parallel activities to the integration phase, we need the refined requirements, final detailed design, and final deliverables (executable code for software, prototype specifications for hardware, and documentation for both).

From this, we can conclude that both hardware and software development processes should follow common procedures for product structure management, RM, change management, and document management in general.

5.3.3 Integration

PDM tools deal with metadata and have advanced functions for data retrieval, data classification, and product structure management. This implies that PDM tools are suitable for managing the system level. For development of hardware products, PDM includes or is well integrated with many development tools (e.g., CAD/CAM). In this way, PDM supports procedures at the subsystem levels. However, there is no, or inadequate, integration of PDM tools with software development environments. This means that for a product configuration shown in Figure 5.5(a), a PDM tool can be used successfully, while this is impossible for products of the types shown in Figure 5.5(b, c).

SCM tools are, of course, not integrated with hardware development environments and therefore do not support product configurations as shown in Figures 5.5(a) (pure hardware) and 5.5(c) (hardware and software). The question is whether SCM can support pure software products. SCM tools do not provide complete support on the system level. As a product becomes increasingly complex, many activities at the system level are not strictly related to the pure software domain, and the efficiency of SCM support then becomes much less than at a subsystem (development) level.

5.4   Integration requirements and constraints

5.4.1   Integration needs

For the cases shown in the previous sections, we can conclude that for an efficient development, tight integration of information is needed during the entire development process at all structure levels. All of the different development groups need support for their daily routines, especially during the intensely active development phase. In practice, this means that tight integration with development tools, such as those for mechanical design and graphical viewing and for electrical design and test, are required. It should be observed that information could be provided in very different forms, not only as documentation legible to humans. Information can include CAD/CAM diagrams, lists, and any other type of presentations of components or specification of functional interfaces. Much information is frequently used by different tools, so the interoperability between the tools that are used in the development process is of considerable importance.

The demands of tool and data integration can be a significant obstacle to the use of a specific tool from PDM and SCM in any type of process, or to their simultaneous use. From the efficiency point of view, it would be preferable to use tools dedicated to particular functions in a particular type of process. However, using many tools increases the problem of interoperability between the tools. Even in a specific domain (pure software or pure hardware development), the major problems are related to inadequate interoperability. We can expect even more problems if we use a tool that is a part of one domain in a process that mostly uses tools from another domain.

5.4.2   Overlapping functions and redundant data

In complex software development environments, we can meet two types of redundancy that make the development process difficult, inefficient, and inaccurate. The first type of redundancy is functional redundancy—when two or several functions provide the same or a similar service. Functions may provide the same service on a general level (e.g., generate a status report), but in particular cases they may give different results as they use different types of objects or data or have slightly different behavior. In such a case, functional redundancy is acceptable, although it is preferable for the interfaces and the behaviors of these functions to be the same or at least compatible. If the functions operate on the same or similar data and provide the same service, the redundancy is functionally superfluous and an unnecessary cost. The second type of redundancy is data redundancy, which means that the same data is saved at several places. There are many types of redundancy used to increase the safety of systems (e.g., backup data or dual databases). If the redundancy is incidental and not the goal itself, it might cause many problems. The same data must be updated at all places when it is changed, and if there is no systematic way to do this, the system may enter an inconsistent state with unpredictable consequences. A typical situation of unwanted data redundancy occurs in complex systems with many (independently developed) functions operating on the same data and keeping them in their internal repositories.

Many functions overlap in PDM and SCM. Figure 5.7 depicts the most important functions from both domains. As the figure shows, many functions support the same or similar processes. In the overlap between the two domains are common activities. They are often referred to as a part of CM. However, even for these common activities, different tools and different processes are used. In addition to these overlaps, we must take into

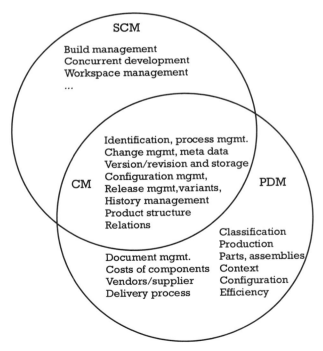

Figure 5.7   Function overlap in PDM and SCM.

consideration other tools that might have redundant functions or use redundant data (e.g., requirements management tools or trouble report tools).

5.4.3   Cultural differences

Interoperability is not the only challenge when using PDM and SCM tools. The cultural differences between software and hardware development groups play an important role, which unfortunately often introduces many problems, misunderstandings, and even disregard. Some of the typical problems that occur are:

▶ Users of both domains believe that the system they use can manage all situations and do not understand the specific requirements of the other domain. Many software developers believe that SCM tools can manage data at the system level as effectively as PDM systems. PDM users, on the other hand, often believe that software consists of binaries only, as easily controlled by a PDM system as any other component. One reason for these beliefs may be the large overlap of functionality and the similar terminology.

▶ Different terminology is used for the same concepts (e.g., configuration control is the definition and management of product configurations for PDM, as compared with the control of changes to a CI after formal establishment of its configuration documents for SCM).

▶ The same terminology is used for different behavior. An example is version management, whereby the same terms are used, but the behavior in a PDM context is different from its behavior in an SCM context.

▶ PDM and SCM users are often located at different departments within the company, and their geographical separation can increase the gap in their understanding of the other group.

These differences increase the difficulties of using tools from the other domain.

5.4.4   Choice between PDM and SCM

The characteristics of the PDM and SCM systems emerge from the nature of the products developed. In the PLC, PDM is focused more on the system design phase, hardware development, and subsequently the production and maintenance/support phase. PDM is less concerned with the software development phase. It is rather the final results of the software development that is controlled by PDM. On the contrary, in the software PLC, the development phase is usually the most intensive part (despite the intention of software engineering to move more activities to the beginning of the PLC). Consequently, the tools bring into focus the support for the corresponding processes.

This means that PDM cannot replace SCM, and SCM cannot provide the functionality provided by PDM. PDM cannot be used for the development of software products, and SCM cannot be used for the development of hardware products.

When developing a product consisting of both hardware and software, the hardware and software subprojects are developed concurrently, and it is particularly advantageous to manage these together. To manage these types of products, we need to have access to all product data in a collected form on system level. For access to all product data in a collected form, we need to have all metadata relating to the product and collected in a single system with connections to all subsystems.

Figure 5.6, in which we can recognize common and parallel (independent) activities, shows the processes during the PLC. Hardware developers use their development tools in the parallel subprocesses. These tools are more or less tightly integrated with the PDM system, and they send information automatically to PDM. Software developers work in their tools and do not gain any benefits from using the PDM system until the product is ready for integration and verification or customer use. At this point, PDM needs information provided by SCM tools. From a purely functional point of view, the PDM and SCM tools fit together and completely cover the entire PLC, which gives attractive predisposition for their integration. To obtain full support for managing development and product assets (items), we cannot use one of the systems alone. Neither PDM nor SCM can give the full, integrated support required during the entire PLC. We need the functions of both systems.

Hence, for the development of complex products, especially those that consist of both hardware and software parts, the need to use both PDM and SCM tools is evident. Further, it is essential that a seamless integration between these tools is obtained.

5.5 Summary

In previous chapters, we learned about the basic characteristics of PDM and SCM systems, and we pointed out the differences and similarities in their functions. In this chapter, we analyzed how these tools are used and how they can and cannot be used. PDM systems are historically used in the development and maintenance of hardware products. SCM tools are used in the development and maintenance of software products. However, SCM does not support all activities in a PLC, and for complex software products there is a need for the supporting functions that PDM provides. Products that consist of both software and hardware need support from both PDM and SCM. Software parts cannot be supported by PDM, and hardware parts cannot make use of SCM. On the system level, where hardware and software parts are used as components of products, PDM systems provide the support needed. Further, for an efficient development, PDM and SCM tools must be integrated in a way that makes it easy to exchange information and remove functional and data redundancy. Before beginning to discuss integration (the subject of the next chapter), we have become aware of the many difficulties in achieving an efficient interoperability between the tools of these domains—not only for technological reasons, but also because of cultural differences between developers accustomed to using only one or the other of these two domains.

References

[1]   Sommerville, I., *Software Engineering*, Sixth Edition, Harlow, UK: Addison-Wesley, 2001.

[2]   Stevens, R., et al., *Systems Engineering—Coping with Complexity*, Hertfordshire, UK: Prentice Hall, 1998.

[3]   Boehm, B., "COCOMO II Model Definition Manual," Computer Science Department, University of Southern California, 1997.

[4]   Telefonaktiebolaget LM Ericsson, worldwide telecom company, www.ericsson.se, 2003.

PART

III

Integration and Deployment

CHAPTER

6

Contents

PDM and SCM integration

The whole is more than the sum of its parts.
—Aristotle, Metaphysica

The purpose of PDM and SCM tools is to provide an infrastructure and support for many activities during a PLC. Many other tools are available that provide services with the same purpose, but these are most often focused on one particular activity in the life cycle. From the stakeholders' point of view (i.e., from the perspective of developers, managers, and salesmen), it is important that the use of many different tools does not introduce new complexity into the entire process and that the information and services must be accessible in a smooth and uniform way. For this reason, integration issues are a very important factor for the successful and efficient utilization of these tools, and not only for PDM and SCM. Most PDM and SCM tools provide a certain support for integration. As we saw in Chapter 4, there is a tendency for other tools to be integrated into PDM tools, whereas SCM tools are often used as components in other tools (e.g., in integrated development environments). In this chapter, we shall concentrate on an analysis of the integration of PDM and SCM. This integration might be complicated, as PDM and SCM cover many activities in the PLC and provide support using similar, but not necessarily identical, data and process models. We shall first analyze integration alternatives, then consider several scenarios in which PMD or SCM tools are used in an integrated environment, and finally show two cases of integration of commercial PDM and SCM tools.

133

6.1 Possible integrations

In general, there are three possibilities for achieving PDM and SCM interoperability:

> By obtaining a full integration of PDM and SCM tools, developing a common package with all functions using the same common structures and data, common user interfaces, and common APIs.

> By obtaining a loose integration in which each tool has its own functions, independent of the other, but in which there are mechanisms for exchanging information and providing services automatically without additional effort by the users.

> By obtaining no integration, but by using certain import/export functions; in this case, manual procedures, which enable information exchange, must be identified and introduced in the processes of the PLC.

6.1.1 Full integration

Figure 6.1 shows an ideal full integration model, which includes APIs of PDM, SCM, and other engineering tools, which provide a common information model and a common user interface, transparent to the tools. The tools are integrated in a common layered architecture; the layers are not encapsulated within particular tools, but common to all functions. The lowest layer is a repository (data) layer, which includes repositories such as databases and file systems and a common information model that defines the internal data structures, such as product and project structures, configurations, and versions. The middle layer includes business logic and consists of different tools providing different services. The tools use a standardized API for connection to the common information model. The business layer is connected to the upper layer via the common user interface using standardized API in a similar way. The main function of the upper layer, human application interaction, is as far as possible independent of particular tools. Recent technologies, in particular Web- and Internet-based technologies, make it possible to achieve the desired uniformity.

This model enables easy integration of new tools and functions that use standardized data types and standardized API.[1]

---

1. Implementation of new tools might be somewhat more complex because the tools must conform to the standards of the common information model. On the other hand, when standards are used, the development of tools using these standards may be facilitated by different development tools, which automatically generate standard parts of the tools.

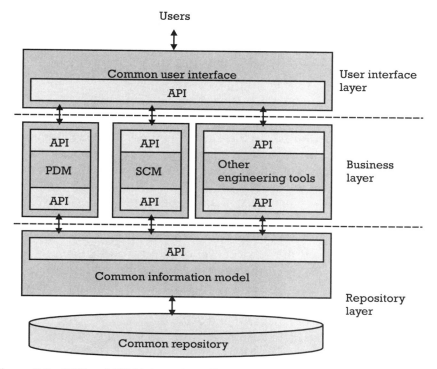

Figure 6.1   PDM and SCM integration—Common API and common repositories.

Unfortunately, it is difficult to implement this model using the tools available on the market today. The tools have their own specific API, and the functionality of many of these APIs does not completely match the functionality of the tool. The repository layers are tightly integrated with the business layers, and it is therefore impossible to build a common repository using the repositories of the tools. PDM and SCM may have the same basic type of repository (e.g., a relational database and a file system), but without a common information model, the level of abstraction is too low to be appropriate for integration. The main disadvantage of this model is the lack of a standardized information model. For the same reason, the interoperability of PDM and SCM tools with other engineering tools is not easily achieved. Despite these difficulties, work is in progress to obtain full integration of different engineering tools in some PDM systems. In such cases, the PDM tool consists of a larger number of different functions integrated directly in PDM or added as options to the basic package. The weakness of this approach is the proprietary nature of the information model, which is not readily acceptable to other PDM tool vendors. This increases the difficulty of developing and maintaining new tools. The PDM system is expanding and becoming increasingly expensive and complex.

6.1.2 Loose integration

In a loose integration, the tools operate more independently of each other and store data in their own repository. Although their repositories may be of the same type for different tools (e.g., relational database), the information models are different and accessible only from the particular tools. Different layers are visible within the particular tools. Information is exchanged through additional interoperability functions, which may be either separate applications or functions integrated within the PDM or SCM tools. The interoperability functions communicate with these tools either via their APIs on the service level or directly on the data level. The data exchange may be started in different ways—triggered from specific tools or initiated by the users. Loose integration system architecture is shown in Figure 6.2. The figure does not show integration with other tools, but the same principle applies as for PDM and SCM.

The main advantage of this approach is the omission of the requirement of a common information model, which makes it more possible to use existing tools. Instead of using a common information model (experience

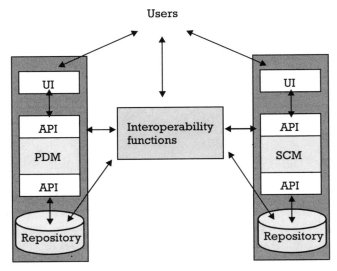

Figure 6.2 PDM and SCM loose integration.

has shown that it is extremely difficult to agree on a common information model), it is sufficient to have a common data model (i.e., structure specification on a lower level and conversion rules between different data types). The main disadvantage is the necessity to build additional interoperability functions. Each addition of a new tool will require the development of new interoperability functions between the new tool and other tools. It may also require changes in existing functions. The number of interoperability functions may increase very quickly and it is not clear who is to be responsible for developing these functions, the PDM vendors, the SCM vendors, or the customers themselves.

Because data is encapsulated within particular tools in a loose integration, it may happen that the same information is stored in several places. This means that there will always be a risk that data in only one of the several repositories is updated, thereby introducing an inconsistent state. To avoid such an inconsistency, synchronization of the tools and monitoring of the repositories to detect inconsistency must be performed periodically or on an interrupt/trigger basis.

Another aspect of this problem is that there may be constraints on the workflow between tools, because while it may be possible to synchronize changes in tool A with tool B, the reverse may not be true. The problem arises when changes in a *downstream* process (in tool B) demand changes in an *upstream* process (in tool A). It may not be logically possible for the downstream process to create data to automatically populate the upstream process. A relationship between requirements management tools and software development environments is an example.

6.1.2.1 Loose integration and the component-based approach

As different tools provide different APIs, new interoperability functions must be built for every new tool introduced, for both the business and the communication parts. Modern development technologies based on component-based development [1] make use of mechanisms that provide support for many standard functions, such as communication between the components (often designated as middleware) or integration of components in distributed applications. When using these technologies (e.g., CORBA, COM/DCOM, .NET, and JavaBeans), development efforts can be significantly reduced, with the interoperability functions including only the business logic while all of the other parts required for the operation are added automatically. Modern tools including SCM and PDM tools use these technologies today. Figure 6.3 shows the architecture of a loose integration that uses a middleware facility.

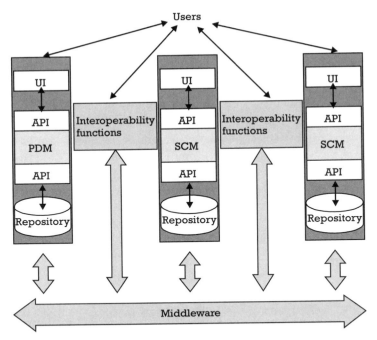

Figure 6.3 A loose integration using middleware technology.

6.1.2.2 PDM-centric integration

As PDM covers a larger part of the total PLC and as PDM deals with meta-data (i.e., description and structuring of data), it is natural that, as far as possible, communication with the user is via PDM. However, there will remain tools and users that interact directly with SCM tools. SCM tools can be integrated with PDM tools in the same way that they are integrated with other engineering tools (such as IDE tools); PDM tools use the API from SCM. Users communicate only via PDM, which is responsible for updating information for both PDM and SCM data. This model provides better control of the consistency of duplicated data. However, similar problems remain. For example, there are many existing integrations of different development tools with SCM tools, and it is unrealistic to assume that such integrations will not be used independently of the PDM integration.

6.1.2.3 Integration points

The complexity of managing system consistency depends on the development process, which identifies data and stages in the process in which data is exchanged or copied (see Figure 5.6). For this reason, it is important to identify these stages. The fewer the number of these points and the less the frequency of information exchange, the simpler the model will be—but the benefits of the integration will be lower.

The freezing of a product version is an important integration point in the development process, and the minimal data integration then required is on the product version and configuration level. As PDM does not provide support for the branching and merging that is important in software development, it is suitable for software file versioning to be under the control of the SCM tool. From a PDM point of view, it is more interesting to keep information about specific versions of files, but not all versions of files, created in the software development process collected in a specific configuration or in a baseline. This means that a list of files of a baseline containing the pointers to the actual files can be saved in the PDM system, as shown in Figure 6.4.

6.1.3 No integration

If no integration is obtained between the tools, manual intervention is required, and there is a great risk of inconsistencies being introduced into the system. It is therefore important to precisely identify and describe the manual routines for data updating and to strictly follow these routines. The routines will typically include import/export functions between the systems.

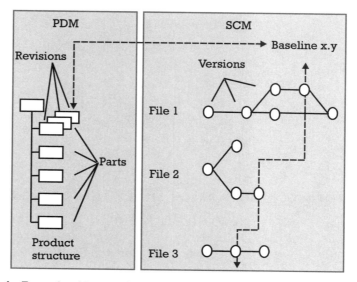

Figure 6.4 Example of integration of software items.

6.1.4 Conclusion

For many good reasons, the integration of PDM and SCM is advantageous. In practice, there exist many problems. First, the integration requires the sharing or exchange of data between different tools from the same domain (PDM or SCM) but from different phases. Neither PDM nor SCM has yet solved this problem completely. A more serious problem arises when data must be shared or exchanged between tools from these two domains. The second problem is the choice of the tools and methods from the overlapping areas. Even if a particular tool provides excellent support within one domain, that does not mean that it is suitable or well integrated within the other.

To achieve a full integration of PDM and SCM, we must define and implement a common product model, common evolution model, and common process model as described in [2]. A common support for the process model can be used with the present tools to some extent, but other models with today's functionality differ too much to be of use as common models. A full integration would require enormous efforts from PDM and SCM vendors and from users of the existing tools. It is not likely that the vendors can or wish to take this step.

We can conclude that the realistic solution for system integration is a loose integration, with relatively independent tools and well-defined interfaces between them. To obtain an efficient and useful integration we must have:

› APIs of PDM and SCM tools;

› Easy-to-use and accurate interoperability functions between PDM and SCM;

› Synchronization monitors, which can resolve inconsistency between the systems;

› The possibility of using PDM and SCM tools directly without running into an inconsistent state.

6.2 Different scenarios in an integrated environment

For a loose integration, it is necessary to solve problems related to function and data redundancy. It must also be decided which data each system should manage, where the different data should be archived, and which functions from which systems should be used. Dependent on how we make these decisions, we end up with different integrations and with different requirements of the interoperability functions. Data stored in PDM and SCM can be classified according to how it is exchanged (see Figure 6.5):

1. *Information managed exclusively by PDM.* Certain types of data will be stored and used only in the PDM system. Documents strictly related to products, hardware components, sales information, or similar are one type of such data. Information in PDM is stored in a standard way as business and data items, shown in Figure 6.5 as metadata and data.

2. *Information managed exclusively by SCM.* Source code and certain internal files strictly related to the development of software components are saved and managed only in SCM. They are of no interest to PDM. In addition to the data itself (under version control), SCM saves different attributes of data (such as state, lock flag, and user information), which to some extent correspond to metadata in PDM.

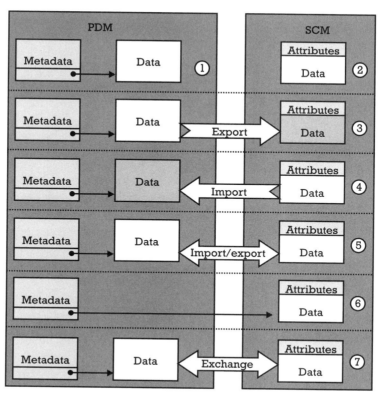

Figure 6.5   Saving and exchanging data.

3. *Information exported from PDM to SCM.* This data will be managed in PDM, exported to SCM, and used in SCM for reading only, without it being possible to modify its contents. For this type of data, it is important that the export function is performed each time data in PDM has been changed, preferably automatically but at least at specified integration points in the development process. When data is exported, the attributes in SCM must also be defined to relate properly with metadata in PDM. Examples of such data are requirements specifications or project plans and overall designs.

4. *Information imported to PDM from SCM.* Data that is created and updated in SCM can only be used in PDM without the possibility of change. However, it must be possible to change metadata in PDM. Examples of this type of data include different documents related to software binary files (executables and libraries), particular source code, which are built in SCM systems.

5. *Import/export data.* Certain types of data may be created in one system, say PDM, then exported to SCM at an integration point, and set as frozen in PDM. Data is then changed under SCM control and imported back to PDM. There are many examples of information that is related in this way, such as detailed designs of software components and product error reports when errors are corrected in software.

6. *Common data.* Data itself (i.e., a data item) is stored in SCM, but metadata (business items) is stored in PDM. There is a reference from metadata to the data saved in SCM. This type of reference is not a reference to data directly (such as a file path), but a specification of an action to be performed in SCM in order to retrieve data. This could be, for example, a "file check out" command. It is required that users of both PDM and SCM should be able to update this data. Many types of documents are in this category. Consistency of data as seen from both PDM and SCM is important here.

7. *Redundant data.* This is a variant of the *common data and import/export* type of data. Redundant data is saved at two places and can be updated from the two systems. This type of data is very likely to cause the state of the system to become inconsistent. For example, data in PDM can be updated but remain unchanged in SCM. To maintain consistency, a means of automatically updating data at both sites must be provided.

An important requirement of an integrated environment is uniformity of user interface, irrespective of where data is stored. A PDM user should be able to independently access a document stored in either the PDM system or an SCM system. Similarly, an SCM user should not perform any additional action when a document stored in the SCM system is related to metadata in the PDM system.

6.2.1 Integration prerequisites

We shall discuss here an example of an integrated environment and identify the resulting requirements. First, we define the basic assumptions for the integration and decide where to store data. We then follow two scenarios containing several use cases. One scenario describes cases for a PDM user, and the other one for an SCM user.

The integrated system has the following characteristics:

▸ The PDM system is the *umbrella tool* and will also manage certain metadata for the software information.

▸ The PDM system will manage the product structure and the revisions of all products included.

▸ The SCM system is the archive for all software information (i.e., all software files—source code and binary files built from them—will be stored in SCM).

▸ Documents related to software are stored in the SCM system, and related metadata is stored in the PDM system in the corresponding business items. The business items will be related to the specific product in the product structure.

▸ The items, stored in the SCM system with corresponding metadata in the PDM system, are marked with specific attributes, used to avoid changes being made asynchronously in SCM and PDM.

▸ When data stored in SCM with corresponding metadata stored in PDM is changed, SCM automatically sends particular information to PDM (e.g., information about documents—status and other business-related attributes, such as a new version of the document, document number, document name, and author—when they are checked out in SCM).

▸ The PDM manages metadata of the delivered products, including its components (i.e., libraries and executables).

▸ SCM saves information about all software parts, and the same software parts are included in the BOM.

6.2.2 Scenario A: PDM—User interaction

In this section, we analyze certain scenarios related to users of the PDM system and files stored in the SCM system (i.e., the cases 6 and 7 in Figure 6.5). All functions required by a user are initiated by the PDM system. The use cases show the kind of information the PDM user requires from SCM and how the two systems exchange the information.

Let us study the following use cases:

• *Query for a document.* The PDM system must (1) search for the document in the SCM system and (2) present a list of all found documents that match the search criteria.

• *Get a document.* The PDM system must (1) look up the actual file or files in SCM, (2) make a copy of it, and (3) present the actual document to the user. This is needed when a consumer is to assemble a product.

• *Check out a document.* The PDM system must (1) check out the document from SCM, (2) copy the document in the WIP vault in the PDM system, and (3) set all attributes required to synchronize the states of PDM and SCM (e.g., user identity and status). The user may now update the document (see Figure 6.6).

• *Check in a document.* The PDM system must (1) check in the file in SCM, (2) set all attributes required to synchronize the states of PDM and SCM, and (3) update the version of the file in PDM.

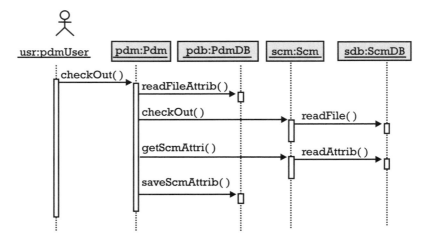

Figure 6.6 Check out sequence from PDM into SCM.

- *Delete a document.* The PDM system must (1) check if the user has the access rights and is allowed to delete the specified document, and (2) check if the document is included in a frozen product or not. If the document is not included in a frozen product, (3) search for the document in SCM, (4) delete it in SCM, (5) delete attributes in SCM, and (6) delete all metadata and relationships in PDM.

- *Import a document into PDM.* A document existing in SCM is copied to the PDM (case 4 in Figure 6.5). PDM (1) issues a query for the document and reads it, and (2) checks it in in PDM. If the document does not exist in PDM, it must be registered first and then checked in. Certain attributes (3) must be updated in metadata (for example a read-only state of the document).

- *Export a document from PDM.* A PDM user wants to copy a document from PDM to SCM. PDM (1) checks in the document into the SCM system. The appropriate attributes (2) are set in PDM and SCM.

Figure 6.6 shows a sequence diagram of a check out of a document where the metadata is managed in the PDM system and the actual document is archived in the SCM system (case 6 in Figure 6.5). The figure shows how the PDM system communicates with the SCM system by reading the metadata in the PDM database and forwarding the metadata to the SCM system. The SCM system retrieves the actual file from its database and returns the file to the PDM system.

6.2.3   Scenario B: SCM—User interaction

In this scenario, a user uses only an SCM system, not a PDM system. However, information generated in the SCM system must be automatically updated in the PDM system. The use cases show the kind of information the SCM user requires from the PDM and how the two systems should manage the information correctly. In an ideal situation, all information necessary for further work in SCM will be created in SCM, but in practice there will be cases in which SCM users will wish to create data that belongs in the PDM system. To avoid the use of a PDM system, SCM users can be provided with certain functions for more flexible working procedures. Examples of these functions are registering a new product or registering a new document.

We have identified the following use cases:

- *Register a new product or product revision.* A user from SCM registers a new product in the PDM system. The SCM (1) creates a new product item, (2) specifies all of the necessary attributes of the products (such as owner and parent product), and (3) receives the product identity, which may be used in SCM for a different purpose (e.g., for creating a baseline or a new working structure).

‣ *Register a product revision.* The SCM system must know the identity of the next revision of the product. (1) SCM sends an inquiry to PDM for the next revision of the specific product, (2) PDM allocates the product revision, (3) PDM sets appropriate attributes (such as work-in-progress state), and (4) PDM delivers the new product revision identity to SCM.

‣ *Register a new document.* One or several files stored in the SCM system are registered as new items in the PDM system. SCM must provide PDM with (1) the full path to the files and (2) attributes with relevant metadata (for example document status and document revision). SCM must also provide PDM with (3) the identity of the product to which the information belongs. When registering a library or an executable in PDM, (4) the reference to all included software source code files (e.g., the path and configuration specification) is also registered.

‣ *Import a document into PDM.* A document existing in SCM is copied to the PDM (case 4 in Figure 6.5). If the document does not exist, it must be registered first and then copied. Certain attributes must be updated in metadata (e.g., a read-only state of the document).

‣ *Check out.* The file is already registered in PDM and may be frozen. (1) SCM checks if the file has already been checked out. If the file is not checked out, (2) SCM checks out the file in SCM. If there is already an existing copy of the file in the PDM system, it is (3) checked out also in PDM. (4) All attributes required to synchronize the states of PDM and SCM (e.g., user identity and status) are set. The user may now make the changes in the file, as described in Figure 6.7.

‣ *Check in.* First, SCM (1) will perform a check in of the file, (2) check in in PDM, in cases in which the file is saved in both PDM and SCM (case 7 in Figure 6.5), and (3) set all attributes required to synchronize the states of PDM and SCM (e.g., user identity and status).

‣ *Uncheck out.* SCM unlocks the file lock and changes the status in PDM.

‣ *Update product status.* SCM sets appropriate attributes in PDM, depending on the company-specific development process.

‣ *Delete document.* (1) SCM uses the document number label and searches for the document in PDM. (2) If the document is not included in a frozen product, SCM will delete the document in PDM and (3) in the SCM

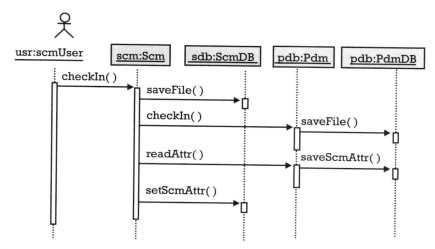

Figure 6.7 Check out sequence from SCM into PDM.

system, including all labels and attributes. (4) If the document is used in a frozen product, an error message is returned to the user and no document is deleted.

- *Query regarding product revision.* SCM will use the product number label and ask PDM for the current revision of this product. The result will be presented to the user.

- *Query regarding a product structure.* SCM will use the product number label and request PDM to retrieve the full product structure in which the actual product is included. The result will be presented in SCM to the user.

- *Query regarding documents.* An SCM user searches for the documents placed in PDM only (case 1 in Figure 6.5). SCM will (1) use a search key and perform a query in PDM to retrieve the actual document. The result (2) will be presented to the user.

- *Export documents from PDM.* An SCM user wants to copy a document from PDM to SCM. SCM (1) issues a query for the documents to the PDM system and accesses them, (2) checks it in the SCM system, and (3) sets the appropriate attributes in PDM and SCM.

The sequence diagram in Figure 6.7 shows a similar complexity of check out activity for an SCM user, as Figure 6.6 shows for a PDM user.

6.3   Examples of integrations

More advanced PDM and SCM tools provide support for integration through their APIs, integration languages and commands, Web-based services, and components. These facilities make it possible for end users to perform integration. The integration process is very complex, and it often requires considerable knowledge of both systems and different technologies. For this reason, many end users are not capable of performing the integration alone and need the assistance of the vendors or consultant companies providing such service.

This section gives an overview of two integrations: the integration of the SCM system ClearCase [3] and PDM tool eMatrix [4] developed by an end user, and the integration of ClearCase and the PDM systems Metaphase [5] performed by the vendors and available as a commercial product.

6.3.1   Case study: Integration of eMatrix and ClearCase

The research and development department of the Ericsson Company realized that the SCM tool used (ClearCase, adjusted to the Ericsson environment) did not fully support the entire development process. More concretely, it was found that even for pure software development (i.e., no hardware involved), there is a need to manage much metadata, or additional information, connected to the software items. In many SCM tools, including ClearCase, metadata management is provided through different attributes connected to the versioned items. These attributes are user defined and can be used to store all kinds of metadata. In practice, attributes are seldom used for this purpose due to poor usability in this context; the use of many and complex attributes during software development has been found to be impractical. Even for the CM group that manages software products and requires a support similar to that which PDM systems provide, the utilization of attributes alone was insufficient for providing the support required. For this reason, it was decided to use a PDM tool to handle metadata and implement the development process, using the SCM tool to store and retrieve the source code and other software items. A PDM tool eMatrix was selected for integration with ClearCase.

6.3.1.1   User functionality

The idea of using both a PDM and an SCM tool is to provide better support for the management of metadata related to the source code being developed. This provides project managers and developers with additional support. The users obtain improved support within at least three important activities—configuration identification, baseline handling, and configuration control including change request handling.

6.3.1.2 Configuration identification

Configuration identification is intended to give each CI a unique identity (see definition in Section 3.3.1), which is required in several different environments. For example, eMatrix uses a triple *name, type,* and *revision* to identify a CI. ClearCase uses version extended pathname. Mappings between these identities are performed in the interface product, MxCC, by which the product identity was converted to ClearCase attributes. It is also possible to define the entire business model (information model) within eMatrix. The type hierarchy attributes and their relationships can be modeled. It is also possible to define the states and the life cycle of all defined types of objects.

6.3.1.3 Baseline handling

An important type of object stored in eMatrix is the baseline object (BL object). All data connected to this object, including its processes, is also stored within it. Important data referred to from a BL object are the source code files included in the baseline. These files are represented as CI objects in eMatrix. A CI object contains only metadata and a reference (called link) to the real storage in ClearCase (using a *foreign vault* facility in eMatrix).

A baseline process may vary in different projects, but some core functionality is provided by the integration to cope with the most common procedures. The project management is benefited principally by being able to work entirely within the PDM tool. Metadata from the source code can now be stored and managed together with the other project data. Support for software developers is also improved. A BL object has a status flag, which is initially set to "preliminary." When the status flag is set to "approved," a baseline label is set in ClearCase. All CI objects referred to by the BL object are labeled (i.e., the specific version referred to is labeled). The developers can thus be aware of baselines being set in the PDM system by the managers. This makes it possible to select versions from any branch to define a baseline and to be able to freeze the specified version of each variant separately. This also provides support for different types of development processes and generation deliverables (such as feature based or incremental).

6.3.1.4 Configuration control

An important part of configuration control is the management of changes. The change management is usually realized via change requests, which are stored in eMatrix as CR objects. The project management benefits mostly CR objects, being able to manage data uniformly and independently of which type of change is concerned, but the integration also provides a communication link between the management and the developers used during the process. A CR object also has a status flag. When set to "approved," this information is propagated to ClearCase by updating attributes for all related files. This provides certain support in the form of warnings and process guidance:

▸ When a developer checks out a file he or she is informed of all CRs registered on that branch, including CRs merged from other branches. This makes it possible to check the satisfaction of the requirement that the CR he or she is to work on is registered.

▸ When the file is checked in, the system prompts the developer to mark the CR as implemented, if all changes related to it are completed. When a CR is marked as implemented, this is automatically registered in ClearCase and, after certain manual communication, also in eMatrix.

▸ According to the CR process, all CI objects referred to from a CR object must also be included in a baseline (i.e., referred to from a BL object). This can be checked both in eMatrix, where the same physical CI object is referred to, and in ClearCase, where the developer is warned if a version has a baseline label name but the CR is not registered in the attributes.

Figure 6.8 shows the architecture of the two tools and their integration. In eMatrix, a BL object, BL1, is stored and refers to three CI objects. A CI object is a link to a specific version of a file stored in ClearCase. A CR object is also stored in eMatrix, referring to the two CI objects implementing the CR.

Baseline establishment is always initiated from eMatrix. When a baseline item is approved by a CCB, each ClearCase CI in this baseline item is uniquely identified with a baseline item label. This label is sent from eMatrix when the CM manager approves the baseline item in eMatrix. When the designer in ClearCase checks out a baseline item, he or she will be informed (warned) if there is no approved CR connected to that CI version.

CRs are managed from eMatrix. CRs can only be written against an approved baseline (i.e., CRs can only refer to CIs that are also referred to by a BL object). When a CR is approved by the CCB, which affects a ClearCase CI,

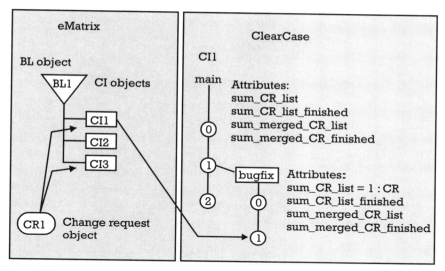

Figure 6.8 Relationship between CIs in eMatrix and ClearCase.

the CR number is forwarded to ClearCase and applied on the actual CI version. When the ClearCase designer checks out the actual CI, he or she will be informed that a CR is approved on that CI. When the designer implements the CR, he or she then inputs the implemented CR number. Metadata from ClearCase CIs is forwarded to eMatrix.

In ClearCase, each branch has its own set of attributes. CRs are registered in ClearCase using four attributes: sum_CR_list, sum_CR_finished, sum_merged_CR_list, and sum_merged_CR_finished. These list all CRs—all implemented CRs for that branch and CRs from branches merged into that branch, respectively. Each attribute has a value consisting of a list of CRs following the syntax in CC: of CR (e.g., 2:CR4 2:CR7 4:CR8—see Figure 6.8). When a CR is registered, it is appended to the attribute sum_CR_list. Note that attributes to all files referred to from the CR object are affected. When the CR is implemented, the same procedure is followed for the attribute sum_CR_finished.

Attributes in ClearCase are connected to a branch. This means that when a new branch is created, a new set of attributes is also created. CRs are not copied or moved when a new branch is created, but the new attributes are empty. When a branch (e.g., a branch designated bugfix) is merged (e.g., with the branch main), all CRs registered in the bugfix branch are copied to the merged lists in the main branch. When a developer checks out or checks in a file, the system presents all CRs registered for that branch and CRs from the merged branches.

6.3.1.5 Roles and information exchange

Software developers normally work in ClearCase. Some updates in eMatrix also result in ClearCase being updated. Information imported from eMatrix can be used to keep developers informed about up-to-date states in the project and to initiate the activities required. However, information flow from SCM to PDM is not obtained automatically. When a developer reaches a phase where metadata stored in eMatrix should be updated, he or she will send a notification to the project management using some other tool (e.g., e-mail).

The project management (e.g., project leader or configuration manager) normally works only in eMatrix. The configuration manager creates CRs in eMatrix. A CCB, which consists of a project leader, configuration manager, and, if necessary, developers, analyzes the impact of new CRs and creates the structure in eMatrix and the links to the correct versions in ClearCase.

6.3.1.6 Integration architecture

Figure 6.9 shows the integration architecture. Note that the two types of users, the configuration manager and the ClearCase manager, work with their respective tools.

The interface MxCC uses the standard Adaplet™ to access ClearCase from eMatrix. In addition to links, the interface consists of attributes mapped between the tools and ClearCase commands executed from eMatrix. The Adaplet™ provides a dynamic view of ClearCase information and is used for searching, displaying, and updating ClearCase information from eMatrix clients. For example, a user working within eMatrix can retrieve all information about a file stored in ClearCase. Metadata stored in eMatrix cannot be retrieved from within ClearCase. The interface is partly event driven. Certain operations in eMatrix also result in actions within Clear-Case. The reverse, however, is entirely manual. All modifications to data stored in eMatrix are made through the eMatrix standard interface and are not the result of operations in ClearCase. CIs may be stored in both Clear-Case and eMatrix and are updated as required by the process. Updates initiated in ClearCase are displayed on demand (manually) by a *refresh* function in eMatrix related to CRs and baseline items. Customizations in eMatrix are performed using standard eMatrix scripting (MQL/Tcl), and the ClearCase scripts are built using Perl.

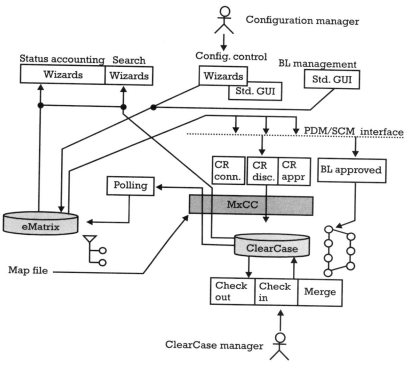

Figure 6.9   Architecture ClearCase and eMatrix interoperability.

6.3.1.7   Client-server and server-server architecture

The eMatrix server and the ClearCase server do not communicate with each other directly. Instead the eMatrix client uses a local ClearCase client to set the dynamic view and to communicate with the ClearCase server. The ClearCase designer works with the standard ClearCase client and can thus only reach information stored in the ClearCase server (i.e., the integration is asymmetric). Figure 6.10 shows an example of client-server architecture. Two types of PDM clients exist. A thick client includes business logic and the integration part between eMatrix and ClearCase. The thick PDM client communicates with the ClearCase server through the built-in ClearCase client working as a proxy. The ClearCase client makes it possible to define ClearCase settings (such as views) locally. A thin client is encapsulated in a Web browser, and it communicates only with the PDM server. The PDM server consists of the eMatrix server and the integration software with ClearCase. The integration part is implemented in the same way as for the thick PDM client. The ClearCase client is used for assessing information from the

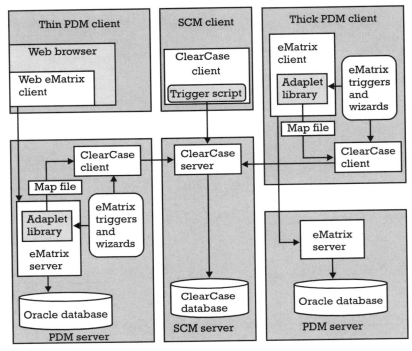

Figure 6.10   eMatrix and ClearCase client-server architecture.

ClearCase server. In this solution, users cannot set up the ClearCase setting locally, but the same settings are valid for all clients.

Figure 6.11 shows a solution for distributed development. As described in Chapters 3 and 4, SCM tools often provide replication of data in many distributed servers. ClearCase, for example, has its MultiSite synchronizing two servers. However, PDM tools such as eMatrix do not provide this support, and thus clients at different sites must be connected to the same server.

6.3.1.8   Conclusion

Both tools are used where they are most effective and use information from other tools, thus producing a synergistic effect. There are, however, some solutions that could be improved:

> ‣ Manual update from ClearCase to eMatrix is potentially problematic. Apart from slowing down the process, it may lead to data being inconsistent in eMatrix and ClearCase when a change in ClearCase has not yet been registered in eMatrix. It should be possible to implement an

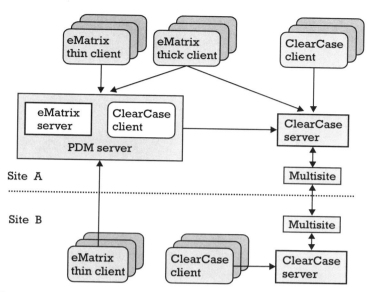

Figure 6.11   Architecture of distributed systems.

event-driven interface from ClearCase to eMatrix also. An automatic update of eMatrix through polling has been tested but significantly decreased the performance of the process.

▸ The developers are noticed/warned by the system at check out and check in (i.e., at late stages in the process). The information stored could be made available to the developers earlier to enable them to take positive action on their own initiative, instead of being informed of their errors by the system or prompted when considered necessary by the system.

▸ When a CI object is created in eMatrix, it refers to a specific version of a file stored in ClearCase. There is support that simplifies finding the correct version, as an alternative to only presenting the version graph of a selected file. The support for searching for files that belong to a specific configuration or baseline is very limited.

6.3.2   Integration of Metaphase and ClearCase

Integration of Metaphase and ClearCase exists in the form of a product, and a more detailed description can be found in [6]. The goal of this integration is to make it possible to retrieve data from ClearCase into the Metaphase

environment. Data imported from ClearCase is treated as software components that are managed in the PDM system, along with all of the hardware
components within the same product structure and within the delivery
structure to the customer. Later releases will cover the import of information from Metaphase in ClearCase. The interface is built on a data exchange
facility, in which Metaphase runs ClearCase commands with arguments
through Perl scripts. The results from ClearCase are stored in an XML file.
Figure 6.12 shows how the exchange is performed.

Because the ClearCase system manages files and directories as seen
through different views and Metaphase objects, the integration functionality focuses on operations to provide access to the managed files and directories in a manner consistent with the Metaphase look and feel. To access any
ClearCase data, a view is required; therefore, the Metaphase/ClearCase integration requires views from ClearCase to provide access to the contents. In
Metaphase, access to directories is available on two levels: access to the file
system followed by access to a directory location. In the case of the Meta-
phase/ClearCase integration, this model maps naturally to the two levels
associated with accessing ClearCase views. The top-level directory containing the views maps directly to a file system in Metaphase. The views under
the top-level directory map directly to Metaphase Work or Vault Locations.
To obtain full information from ClearCase, the ClearCase items must be registered as objects in Metaphase. There are two different ways of accessing
data from ClearCase—through the ClearCase way of describing the actual
version, or through a static view defined in Metaphase. This view is not the
same as a ClearCase view. A third way of finding data in ClearCase is by
using the configuration specification rule files, but this function will not be
available until later releases.

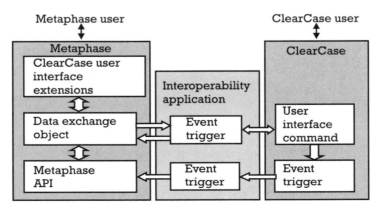

Figure 6.12 Data exchange architecture.

The following conditions are assumed to be satisfied to obtain a successful integration.

- The file system managed by ClearCase must be defined in Metaphase first.
- A particular ClearCase view must be set up before being used in Metaphase.
- A ClearCase view must exist before it is possible to register in Metaphase.
- The owner of the Metaphase installation software must be the owner of the ClearCase VOB mount point.
- A view in ClearCase cannot be updated from Metaphase.
- Only metadata of one file is available at one time in ClearCase; concurrent transfer of metadata of a number of files is not possible.
- A software product, built in ClearCase, managed in Metaphase, must be registered in the PDM system. This means that the product will be placed under version control in both systems.
- A software product managed in Metaphase is stored within ClearCase, but metadata is placed in both systems.

These requirements indicate the complexity of the integration. The end user must have an in-depth technical knowledge of both systems to understand how to use the interface and to understand the mixed terminology within the manuals and the interface. To reach a mutual understanding, the terminology must be common to the two systems or a translation table must be available.

6.4 Summary

In Chapter 5, we concluded that such integration is necessary to cope with the demands of both the system level and all components (subsystems) during the entire life cycle. In this chapter, we have concentrated on the analysis of PDM and SCM integration.

We can identify three levels of integration:

1. *Full integration:* Building one homogenous system containing both the SCM and PDM system. Unfortunately this is very difficult to implement—especially a common repository with a common information model.

2. *Loose integration:* The systems communicating with each other to keep data stored locally and accessible from both systems. The main challenge in this type of integration is to keep data consistent in the entire system. Several possible implementation solutions exist with different trade-offs.

3. *No integration:* Currently perhaps the most common solution, but it requires a lot of manual intervention, which is slow and carries a big risk of introducing inconsistencies into the system.

Concluding that a loose integration is the most (if not the only) realistic solution, the data managed by the total system were divided into seven categories depending on where it should be stored and how it should be accessed from the two systems integrated. Setting up integration prerequisites based on the analysis, two scenarios of user interaction were examined, resulting in detailed sequence diagrams of required operations for all APIs involved.

This chapter ends with two concrete examples of integration actually being developed, one by the end user and one by the vendors of the systems integrated. These examples show that integration on this level is possible and promising, but also that this is the first faltering step, with a lot still left undone.

References

[1] Crnkovic, I., and M. Larsson, *Building Reliable Component-Based Systems,* Norwood, MA: Artech House, 2002.

[2] Estublier J., J.-M. Favre, and P. Morat, "Toward SCM/PDM Integration?" *Proceedings of 8th International Symposium on System Configuration Management (SCM-8),* Lecture Notes in Computer Science, No. 1439, Berlin Heidelberg, Germany: Springer Verlag, 1998, pp. 75–94.

[3] Rational, Clear Case, www.rational.com/products/clearcase, 2003.

[4] MatrixOne, Inc., www.matrixone.com, 2003.

[5] SRDC, Metaphase, www.eds.com/products/plm/teamcenter/enterprise.shtml, 2003.

[6] Methaphase, Methapahse ® enterprise^{TM} 3—ClearCase Integration, User's Guide, Publication Number MT00334.B.

Evaluation and deployment

*Don't wait for something big to occur. Start where you are, with what you
have, and that will always lead you into something greater.*

—Mary Manin Morrisse

Traditionally, many companies have developed their own
PDM and SCM tools. The commercial tools available on the
market have been too expensive, difficult to use, inflexible, and
of inadequate functionality. This situation changed during the
1990s as new PDM and particularly SCM tools appeared on the
market with more acceptable prices and improved functions.
Today, most companies using SCM tools have not developed
these tools themselves, and many companies are replacing or are
considering replacing internally built PDM tools with commercial ones. However, this does not mean that they have started to
use these tools directly. PDM and SCM systems support many
different activities during the entire PLC, and they are seldom
implemented in one single tool with a precisely recognized
purpose. Often additional support, adjusted to the particular
processes of the company, must be provided. This can be done by
using tools in a particular way and by tailoring them. The PDM
and SCM support is provided in the form of a collection of different tools (this is especially true for PDM) that are rather different. The tools in such a collection are used by different categories
of users, are different in size, and manage different types of data.
The heterogeneous characteristics of these systems and the
involvement of many different roles in their use make them
complex. In spite of significant improvements in recent years,

159

they remain difficult to introduce into the development process, difficult to maintain and upgrade, difficult to understand, and especially difficult to replace. Finally, they are expensive. As the result of all of this, PDM and SCM tools belong in a category of tools that are very seldom replaced. For this reason, the process of integrating such a system into an organization is extremely important. If not managed in a systematic way with clear goals, and if the tool is not well understood, the process may result in a financial disaster with decreased development and production efficiency, frustrated employees, and delayed and low quality products.

The integration process can be divided in two phases:

1. Tool evaluation—to find and select the most appropriate tool;

2. Tool deployment—to introduce the tool in the everyday process.

Both phases include many activities and may require much effort. This chapter describes these in detail. Most of the procedures described apply generally to all complex tools. In addition to these general descriptions, the chapter includes descriptions of particular activities specific to PDM and SCM evaluation and deployment.

7.1   Evaluation and deployment of complex systems

The deployment process must be carefully planned, prepared, and executed. In large organizations, the deployment process can take a long time, perhaps even several years, and it may happen that the results of the deployment are not directly visible. Before the tool is deployed, it must be selected. Large investments require a thorough evaluation process in which the most suitable tool is selected, with the selection based on clearly identified requirements and expected results.

Very often, personnel working on deployment are focused on tool features and neglect other aspects of changes caused by the introduction of a new tool. The deployment of a tool involves much more than beginning to use it. The organization introducing a new complex tool must also consider the following facts:

▸ It may be necessary to change the company development, maintenance, and production procedures. New roles and activities might be introduced, relationships between procedures and data might be changed, the types of data to be processed might change, and it may even be necessary to replace certain other tools affected.

- There is often a general resistance to learning something new, which is correlated with an initial reduction in productivity and with psychological barriers when leaving a known area and entering the unknown. Some may also lose their positions as experts and be required to learn a complex new system from the beginning.

- Personal return on investment may vary. PDM and SCM are administrative systems introducing an overhead to many of the users. To many of these users, getting an increased administrative overhead is no problem because they can also see the benefits. However, to some, all extra work is only a burden without any gain in return. Because no chain is stronger than its weakest link, it is crucial for a successful deployment to motivate the entire organization. Only a few people/roles neglecting to use a new model/tool will greatly reduce its positive influence. Machines can be ordered to do whatever we want, while humans have to be motivated, engaged, and committed. Preferably all people involved should benefit from using a new model or tool themselves; every person should have a positive personal return on investment.

- Education and training will be necessary. To understand why the new and often extra procedures have to be performed is necessary—especially if there is a low personal return of investment. Knowing that the extra work put into the system actually is good or even necessary for the project as a whole can motivate a person to do it without personal gain. It is also important to minimize the extra work invested without decreasing the positive effects. Training—learning to use a new tool effectively—is therefore a good investment. In some cases it not only reduces the time it takes to perform a certain action, the action would not otherwise actually be performed at all.

- Inexperience in the use of new tools and misunderstanding their functions may lead to poorer performance or errors, which have a negative impact on productivity and the final result.

- Administration activities will increase during the transition period. When a complex new tool is introduced, it most often replaces an obsolete tool or some manual procedure. Replacement of an old tool with a new one requires concurrent execution of both tools during the transition period as well as dealing with undefined and even inconsistent states.

- Conversion of data and its import into the new system might be required. This conversion can be complex, and it can require the use of, or even development of, certain conversion tools.

▸ The maintenance of old products may become questionable. The conversion of all data and the maintenance process as whole can be very expensive, and in many cases its cost is unacceptable. An example of such a situation could be the use of a new SCM tool running on a certain computer platform, but with the product development and maintenance environments located on another platform, probably an old version, on which it is not possible to install the new SCM tool. An alternative is to retain the old environment for old products (this being a requirement in many cases, for example, for safety-critical systems) and to use new tools only for new products. This solution also might become very expensive due to the cost of maintenance of old hardware and software, and the availability of knowledge of the use of the old environment would probably decline.

▸ Complex tools cannot be used directly, but must frequently be adjusted to the processes in the organization. SCM and PDM tools are typical examples of tools by which the processes are implemented.

▸ Using a new complex tool with new functions requires continuous support. The more functionality it provides, the more administration support it will require. Introducing a new tool will not necessarily decrease the administration costs. It is more likely that the administration and support costs will remain the same, if not increase. The return on investment hoped for will instead be increased by the new functionality resulting in increased productivity, higher quality, and a shorter time to market.

▸ Introduction of a new tool may require changes in the organization on temporary and permanent bases. For example, a new support and training team may be required.

7.1.1   The organization of the evaluation and deployment process

As the introduction of a complex tool can require considerable effort and time, it is most appropriate is to perform the introduction as a project. Using the project form has many advantages: the process is planned as a standard project, resources are allocated, costs are calculated, time frames are determined, and the project goals are identified.

The entire process includes several phases:

1.   Preparation phase includes the activity:

▸ Identification of needs of a new tool.

2.   Evaluation and tool selection phase includes the activities:

   ‣ Planning of the deployment process;

   ‣ Identification of requirements for the new tool;

   ‣ Tool evaluation and selection.

3.   Deployment phase include the activities:

   ‣ Tool deployment;

   ‣ Analysis of the deployment process.

4.   Full use of new tool phase includes the activity:

   ‣ Verification of the requirements in full use of the tool.

For this reason, it is reasonable to divide the process into several projects: an evaluation project and one or even several deployment projects.

The evaluation project should deal with requirements specifications for the tool and its selection. The deployment project (or several projects) will deal with the deployment of the selected tool in the organization. This phase can take a considerably longer time than the evaluation phase. Figure 7.1 shows the entire process divided in several phases and the deliverables.

7.1.1.1   Identification of needs of a new tool

A need for a new tool need grows as the development and production processes become more complex. Examples of such situations are when a company developing hardware devices begins the development of software embedded in their products, the development moves from one place to several places, the demands for shorter time to market increase dramatically, new customers and new forms of placing the product on the market appear, or new technology is used in the products or in the product development. In many cases, this need is not recognized in the organization. Instead, temporary compensation for the need for a new tool may be provided by alternative measures, such as optimization in the process, a decrease of the profit margin, or an unawareness of the new tools needed. In due course, the need for a specific tool may be recognized. Selecting the wrong tool (a tool not needed or not appropriate for the particular processes in the organization) may be as unfortunate as not selecting a tool at all. For this reason, it is important to identify the main requirements of the procedures in the PLC. These requirements are the result of an analysis of the procedures and business goals. The analysis should identify any bottlenecks in the procedures, the main problems, and the possibilities for improvements. The analysis

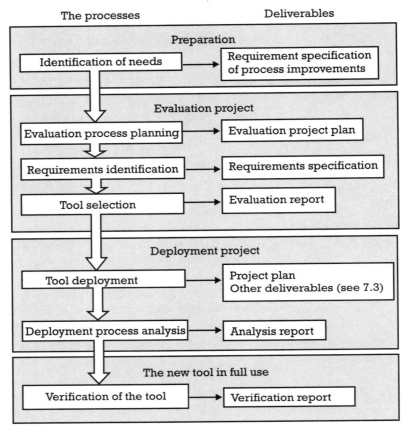

Figure 7.1   The entire process divided in several phases with documentation delivered.

should also identify the main purpose of the new tool, the main benefits, and the expectation of the return on investment. Possible risks of unsuccessful deployment of the tool and the possible consequences should also be considered.

7.1.1.2   Planning of the deployment process

Deployment process planning is similar to planning of a development project. The analysis of the need for new tools is used as input to the project. A project plan document, similarly to a development project plan, should include the following elements:

- *The project organization, the project members, and to whom the project will be reported.* The project members may change, depending on the project phases. It is important that relevant representatives of potential users, administration, and support personnel are involved in the process. The management must be involved in the process to be able to make as correct a decision as possible.

- *Project activities, time schedule, and milestones.* The entire project may occupy a relatively long period of time and the possibility of dividing the entire project into several projects should be considered.

- *Deliverables.* The deliverables from the first part of the project are a requirements specification for the tool to be selected, and an analysis report about the tools proposed for the selection. This report should include a recommendation for a tool, the bases for the recommendation, and an overview of possible scenarios of the tool deployment. The result of the second phase, or later projects, should be the integration of the tools and their acquirement by the users.

- *Costs.* As any project plan, this project should list the project costs. The costs will include costs of the use of internal resources, possible costs of the evaluation licenses, consultant help, and training of the project participants. For the deployment phase, the costs will be significantly larger than for the tool selection phase.

- *Risk analysis.* The main risk in such a project is that the conclusion drawn from the tool evaluation is incorrect due to inadequate analysis. Typical risks could be a misunderstanding of the organization's processes and a misinterpretation of the tool's characteristics. There is also a risk if the tool's behavior in a complex environment cannot be properly tested and evaluated. Such risks should be analyzed, and measures to reduce their effects should be taken.

7.1.1.3   Identification of requirements for the new tool

The requirements for the tools should be derived from the process requirements and the business goals of the organization. They can be classified as functional and nonfunctional requirements. The functional requirements describe the demands on the functionality of the tool. The nonfunctional requirements cover a large spectrum of features related to the tool and activities that cannot be expressed as functions but are important for a smooth and effective functionality.

Examples of nonfunctional features are performance, usability, portability, robustness, and reliability. Other types of features include the ability to maintain and improve the tool. Some of these features are modifiability, maintainability, modularity, and flexibility.

Moreover, requirements of the tool vendors are also important in evaluating their ability to ensure the quality of the products as required, to provide support and to maintain the product, to be able to continue with the tool development, and to have a recognized position on the market. In the long run, these requirements may be even more important than the functional requirements.

The requirements should be prioritized. It is certain that not all requirements will be met. The prioritization of the requirements indicates those that must be fulfilled unconditionally, those that are important, and those that are desirable.

7.1.1.4 Tool evaluation and selection

Selecting a tool is a multistep process that begins in parallel with or after the completion of the requirements specification. During the first phase, information about many tools is gathered. The goal of this phase is to select the most interesting candidates for the final selection. Many references available on the market can be used in this process of evaluation (see Chapters 9 and 10 for references of PDM and SCM tools). The experiences of other companies, available through news groups, other sources on the Internet, or through direct contacts, are very valuable.

The result of the investigation is a list with a limited number of tools (between five and 10 candidates). The process can continue through several iterations with deeper analysis until the two or three most interesting tools are selected. The final step is an extensive comparative analysis of the short list of final candidates. Different types of analysis should be provided:

- Quantization of the tool features related to the requirement specification;
- Demonstrations of the tools;
- Tool test in an experimental environment similar to the real environment in the organization;
- Vendor's position on the market and its capacity to further develop the tool;
- Cost analysis and estimation of return on investments.

The result of this phase is an analysis report describing the different alternative tools, their advantages and disadvantages, and finally one tool recommended for selection. The final decision should be left to management and a decision group that was not directly involved in the evaluation process.

The entire evaluation process is described in more detail in Section 7.2.

7.1.1.5   Tool deployment

Tool deployment is a separate phase, most probably performed as a separate project. The final goal of this phase is a successful use of the tool in everyday work. The procedure may be executed in very different ways, depending on the type of tool, the organization, or the processes in which the tool will be used. Most often, there is a strong requirement that development and production efficiency are not prejudiced during this phase. This requires a gradual introduction of the tool and a systematic training of its users. Stepwise integration is intended to increase the number of people in stages using the tool, the number of new functions used, and finally the interoperability between the new and other tools. As the organization deploying a new tool is usually not familiar with this tool, it might consider including some advice on using consultants to assist in the selection or deployment processes. However, the use of consultants can be a double-edged sword; on one hand they can provide much-needed expertise, while on the other hand they can add cost and inhibit the team from finding its own way forward. All of the tool companies will offer support for the deployment of their tool, and some guidance would be useful.

7.1.1.6   Analysis of the deployment process

An analysis of the project itself is included as a standard part of a project. For example, the project efforts, costs, and results should be analyzed. The experience of the deployment of a complex tool is very valuable to an organization; the experience is related not only to the tool, but also to the organization and to its procedures.

7.1.1.7   Verification of the requirements in full use of the tool

Many tools may appear to work perfectly in a simple, experimental environment but are not able to provide the same services in a large-scale industrial environment. The scalability is one the most frequent pitfalls of the evaluation process. Another pitfall is the inadequate communication and misunderstanding between customers and users. The customers buy the products, but in large organizations they are not necessarily the users—and they may have different criteria for the acceptance of the tool (e.g., the price, the vendor market position, and long-term goals) than normal end users (to whom the most important factor is usability). As a consequence, the final result, the utilization of the tool in the everyday process, may be different from that envisaged during the evaluation and deployment procedures. To avoid the creation of an incorrect impression of the tool (this is especially important for the management), the tool's performance in its full use should be verified. In the verification process, the everyday users of the tools should be involved and their experience should be compared with the initial requirements. The result of the process is a verification document, which can be used for possible negotiations with the tool's vendor and as input to other tool evaluation and deployment projects.

7.2   Evaluation

The most appropriate form of the evaluation process is a project that identifies the resources, the requirements, the constraints, the activities, the deliverables, and the time planning.

7.2.1   Evaluation team

As different categories of people work with PDM and SCM tools, either as pure users, as developers, or as support and administration staff, it is important that representatives of these groups should be involved in the evaluation process. On the other hand, it is counterproductive to build a group too large. The best solution is to form a core operational group that will work continuously in the project, while other representatives can be co-opted for particular activities. A typical core operational group would consist of the following representatives:

  ‣ Administration staff will deal with software administration. Typically, they are concerned with the resources that the tool may require (e.g., primary and secondary memory, CPU and network loading, and network and node configurations).

  ‣ Supporting staff will be responsible for the administration and support of the particular tool. They will analyze the possibilities of tool configuration, the requirements of its administration, and security issues.

▶ Experts will be concerned with the functional features of the tool. Which requirements can the tool meet? What is its potential (i.e., the possibilities of extending its functionality or of adjusting it to the processes involved)?

▶ Developers and other users of the tool will be focused on the tool's behavior in everyday use. They will be concerned with its usability, its interoperability with other tools, its possibilities of adjustment to the local environment, its usability, and its performance.

▶ Quality assurance and process improvement groups will be concerned with processes in which the tool will be used. The new tool may have a significant impact on the processes, requiring extensive changes.

7.2.2 Evaluation project activities and milestones

The main project activities and milestones are similar for both PDM and SCM tools. They were already mentioned in Section 7.1, and are now presented in Table 7.1. The particular activity flows are described in detail in the following sections.

Table 7.1 Activities and Milestones of the Evaluation Project

Activity	Milestone/Deliverable
Specify requirements for the tools to be evaluated	Requirements specification approved
Investigate the market and find the most appropriate tools	Market investigation report approved
	The main candidates selected
Collect experiences of using specific tools from other companies and other sources	
Evaluate the most interesting tools:	A comparative analysis report
Evaluate their functional features	A tool is recommended
Evaluate the vendors' positions on the market	
Estimate the initial and the total costs of the tool deployment	
Estimate return on investment	
Propose the deployment process	
Analyze the finding from the reports	A tool is selected

7.2.3   Cost analysis

There is a large variety of PDM and SCM tools on the market—more than 100 different SCM tools (see Chapter 9) and many PDM tools. The costs of SCM tools vary considerably, from free software to expensive products that can only be afforded by large companies. Most PDM tools are expensive. License costs, however, are not the total costs, and an analysis of the total costs should be performed in order to compare the alternatives. The following types of costs should be considered:

> • Product/license costs, including the licensing model;
> • Maintenance costs, including the conditions and terms for upgrades;
> • General support costs, including costs for consulting and system customization services;
> • Training costs;
> • Deployment costs;
> • Hardware costs;
> • Costs for additional internal development;
> • Costs for additional software required.

It should be stressed that the costs for consulting and training tend to dominate over the license costs. In some cases, the vendor can supply an estimate of the total cost of ownership, which includes all costs for upgrades and maintenance as well.

The costs are of two kinds—external, with costs for the external support paid by the company, and internal, the costs for internal activities. The external costs are visible, while internal costs can be hidden and often underestimated. The costs should also be analyzed in a time frame: the initial costs and annual costs. Advanced and complex tools usually have large initial costs that discourage potential purchasers. Figure 7.2 shows an example (based on [1]) of the initial and maintenance costs of two tools during 2 successive years.

Examples of two different categories of tools are shown. Tool A is an expensive tool that requires a large investment in licenses, equipment, and training. The external costs are considerably higher, especially for maintenance. Tool B is an inexpensive tool with low license fees but also providing a low level of functionality. To achieve a better functionality, additional functions must probably be developed internally, which increases the internal costs. The maintenance of internally developed functions may require more effort than the maintenance of the more expensive tool.

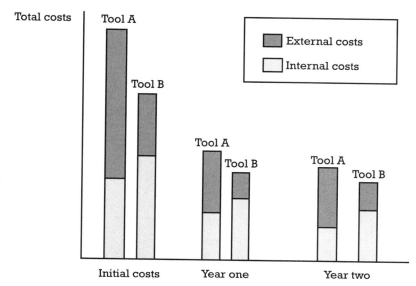

Figure 7.2 Distribution of internal and external costs.

7.2.4 Return on investment

The total cost is not the only information needed to make the correct decision about the deployment of a tool, and, likewise, only calculating the total benefits of the use of the new tool is an insufficient basis for making a decision. The difference between the benefits and the costs is the main factor to be considered. This difference is designated as return on investment. It can be expressed in an absolute value or as a relative value renormalized to the investment. In the second case, the total benefit is divided by the total costs and expressed as a percentage. The investment is justified if the return on investment is greater than one (100%). The costs (especially the external costs) are easier to estimate. The benefits should include all savings and improvements that are the result of the use of the tool. This is difficult to estimate. A detailed analysis of all activities affected by the new tool should be made. In addition, reports of similar analyses and experience reports should be used. It is also useful to perform a further analysis of the return on investment when the tool is integrated and used in normal production, and compare the results with the estimated values.

Return on investment is not a static value but varies over time. Most often the initial investment is much higher, especially for large investments. Figure 7.3 shows an example analysis of three different tools. Tool A is a more advanced tool, and its deployment requires higher direct costs initially

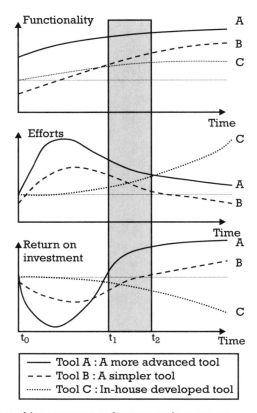

Figure 7.3 Estimated investments and return on investment.

(for product licenses, change in the infrastructure, and training). Tool B has lower licenses costs but requires more adjustments and internal improvements of the tool. The tool costs, direct and indirect, may be consistently lower, but the functionality and the return on the investment can never reach the same level as for the advanced tool. Tool C is an example of an internally developed tool. There are no license costs, but the costs of the tool development and its maintenance are high and will increase, while it will be more and more difficult to achieve the desired functionality and return on investment in the future. Deciding when the internally developed PDM or SCM tool should be replaced with one of those available on the market depends on when the return on the investment for the new tool will exceed the return on the investment of the internally developed tool (t_0 in Figure 7.3), and when the total cost of using a new tool will be less than the cost of the development and maintenance of the old tool (t_1 in Figure 7.3).

7.2.5 Evaluation of the tool vendor

It is also important to evaluate the tool vendor for the assurance of the future use of the tool and for the negotiation strategy. Because the choice of a system is a long-term decision, the financial status of the vendor is of interest. A vendor with poor finances might be bought by another vendor, which might merge the development of the acquired vendor's tool to the purchasing company's tool or simply stop further development. As experienced over the last 8 years by the Ericsson sourcing community, in a period of 2 years about 20% of the existing companies were merged with or bought by other companies.

To improve the cooperation and increase the quality of a service, some companies (mostly large companies) may choose to start a partnership with tool vendors. If the consumer company is enough large and strategically important, the vendor company will also be interested in a partnership. Such partnership in principle makes it easier to acquire the tool and integrate it with other tools. Other companies may want to sign a special agreement with the vendor company. Also, in this case, a mutual business interest must exist to make this happen. In most of the cases, however, the customer company cannot directly influence the vendor. In any case, independent of any type of cooperation, an evaluation of the vendor should be a mandatory part of the tool evaluation.

The following points are some examples of what should be studied more closely:

‣ The market position of the vendor and of the tool;

‣ The vendor's financial statement;

‣ The vendor's internal organization, including the experiences of persons making up the board of directors and the management team;

‣ The present core business of the vendor and relationship of the tool to the core business;

‣ The vision and strategy of the vendor—the technology roadmap;

‣ Strategic alliance of the vendor to their customers and suppliers;

‣ Customer list and reference users;

‣ The vendor's competitive advantages and disadvantages;

‣ The ownership of the tool.

Many SCM tools exist as free products, some of them largely widespread (for details, see Chapter 10). Most of them belong to a category of simpler tools, which may be either used directly for simpler development processes or as a basis on which additional support can be built. There are no free PDM tools, but parts of them are free. Document management and content management tools (see Chapter 11), underlying databases, and implementation of certain middleware products are available and used for further building of PDM functions. How should companies acquiring free products treat them? The answer is simple: for the end user and for the company, the result should be the same, independent of whether the tool is commercially available or free of charge. This means that it must provide a customer support and maintenance support. This can be obtained either directly by the company itself or by a consultant company. In any case, all criteria discussed in the previous sections should be applied when evaluating this type of software. The ownership of the free tools and free software is often not precisely defined. Different types of free software exist (see Chapter 10), and the company using this software should be aware of these differences.

7.2.6 SCM evaluation example

The concrete requirements for the tool should be a result of an analysis of the organization's business goal, development, and other processes. There are no unique requirements, and no one tool is the best choice for all cases.

The requirements can be classified according to the main SCM functions, and then other requirements related to integration, flexibility, and the possibilities of modification and adding new functions can be added. Table 7.2 includes an example of such a classification.

The evaluation is performed as follows. The features are tested and graded (for example, from 0 to 10). The tests should be performed in different ways, as mentioned before, by different groups that will set grades independently. An average value, or the value defined by the consensus between the groups, should be set as the final grade. The grades can be graphically presented for all tools tested, for example as shown in Figure 7.4. The figure shows three different tools and their characteristics. The inner thick circle in the figure defines the minimum grade required. From the figure, it is apparent that only one tool meets all of the requirements (which still does not mean that this tool will be selected).

7.2.7 PDM evaluation example

Choosing a PDM system involves more than choosing a technical solution. It is therefore recommended that the vendor, commercial system information, general system information, and the PDM functionality of the system should be studied to obtain a complete picture.

Table 7.2   Classification of SCM Requirements

Classification	Feature
Version management	Check in/check out process
	CIs history information
	CIs version attributes
	Configuration and baseline process
Configuration management	Possibility of finding differences between two baselines
	Possibility of merging differences between two baselines
Build management	Build support (tools such as Make)
	Possibility of reproducing the build procedure with exactly the same results
	Possibility of obtaining information on how the build was performed
Workspace management	Relationship between repositories and workspace
	Flexibility in changing workspace
	Cooperation between workspaces of different developers
Change management	Mapping CRs to the changes made in the code
	Finding changes (CRs) implemented in a baseline
	Propagating changes from one baseline to another
	Providing measurements and statistics related to changes and efforts
Release management	Automation level in generating a product release
	Automatic generation of release documentation
	Possibility of showing differences between two releases
Parallel development	Team support (awareness)
	Merging possibilities
Distributed development	Data synchronization and replication
	Merging possibilities, export/import functions
Integration	Integration and interoperability possibilities
Administration	Installation efforts required (for servers and for clients)
	Ability to convert current data to format required by the tool
	Efforts required for everyday administration
Usability	Graphical user interface
	Simple use
General	Tool quality and tool reliability
	Requirements on resources
	Performance

Similar to the example for SCM tools, a list of functional requirements for PDM tools should be prepared. It is recommended that the evaluation of the PDM functionality should be based on a broadly accepted terminology to avoid confusion of terms. The required functionality differs between companies. It is therefore recommended that the required functionality

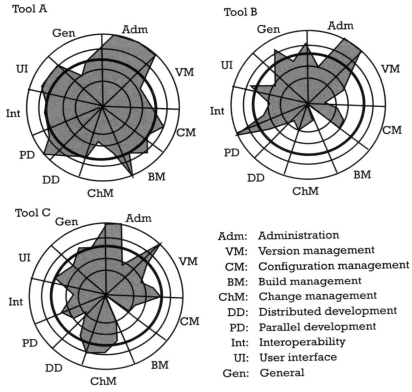

Figure 7.4 Graphical presentation of the fulfillment of functional requirements.

should be grouped according to, for example, CIMData's classification [2] of PDM functionalities:

- ‣ Data vault and document management;
- ‣ Workflow and process management;
- ‣ Product structure management;
- ‣ Program management;
- ‣ Classification management.

In addition to the PDM functionality of the system, its general properties should be investigated:

- ‣ User friendliness;
- ‣ Scalability;

> • Possibility of integration with other systems and tools;
> • Flexibility.

User friendliness includes such characteristics as the user interface and response times. Scalability means that the system will retain its performance as it expands (e.g., with the number of users, the number of sites, and the volume of data managed). Flexibility is a measure of how easy it is to customize the system.

7.3 Deployment

The introduction of a tool or integration of two tools into the everyday process of an organization is referred to as the deployment of the tool. Different ways to gradually deploy complex tools are described in this section. The section also includes thorough, more specific descriptions of PDM deployment and SCM deployment.

7.3.1 Deployment process

The deployment of a large complex tool, perhaps replacing another complex tool, is difficult to perform in one large step. There are several reasons for this. The new tool may not immediately function 100% at the organization's environment. The problems that may appear in the beginning should not affect the entire organization; they should be processed by smaller groups first. The new tool may require education and training of the personnel concerned, often best performed in smaller groups. A deployment group is often used to help developers using the tool for the first time, and this help is more efficient and under control if the numbers of beginners is kept small. It is therefore often wise to train users, and deploy the new tool gradually. What follows is a series of examples of how such incremental deployment can be performed.

> • *Imitate the old tool.* All users involved are assumed to be familiar with the old tool. Using first all of the functionality of the old tool that is incorporated in the new tool simplifies the deployment of the new tool. The new functionality in the new tool can then be introduced gradually. When the new functionality has been introduced, the redundant functionality can be removed. The disadvantage of this method is that it may lead to overlap between old and new

functionalities during the transition phase. There is also a risk that users will avoid using the new functionality but will continue to use the old and remain unprepared when the old functionality is finally removed.

‣ *Utilizing organization structure.* Within a company, a product is often developed by several more or less independent teams, with each team responsible for their part of the product. The deployment process can utilize this organizational structure by letting only one of these teams first use the tool in order to make it work effectively in the company environment, before deploying it to the rest of the company.

‣ *Pilot project.* If the development is project driven, a common strategy is to execute a pilot project. When the pilot project is completed successfully and all of the lessons from this are learned, full deployment can be accomplished. A considerable advantage of this method is that a pilot group often consists of enthusiastic experts, those interested in testing new tools, those most eager to learn the latest developments, and those most likely to make the project successful. Such a project group will generate positive feedback, engaging and inspiring others in the organization after the successful pilot project and assisting with their education and training. Unfortunately, it is not always the case that such a group is available, as their capabilities are needed in all sections of the organization.

‣ *Dividing the data managed.* It is possible to deploy a tool to process only a portion of the data or certain types of data and continue to use the old tool for all other types of data. In this way a large number of users can learn the new tool at their own pace without jeopardizing the production. For example, a new PDM tool can be used to process nonproduct data initially, and when all users have learned the new tool, its use can be extended to the processing of product data.

‣ *Deploy the new tool on a new mainstream project.* This can work well in a project-based organization. A decision is made to commence deployment on the next available project. The deployment project works closely with the mainstream project to ensure that the mainstream project is not compromised by problems with the new tool. This approach has the advantage that there is a realistic environment to establish the new tool, and the deployment can naturally work through the various project stages. When the mainstream project team members get deployed on to other projects, they take the experience of the new tool with them. The risk is that is if there are major problems with the deployment, then the mainstream project may be jeopardized.

7.3.2 PDM deployment

PDM system deployment involves both process and infrastructure changes. The main purpose of a successful deployment is a smooth transition from older business processes to newer, improved processes utilizing the new and improved functions provided by PDM. However, due to the extensive changes in the infrastructure involved, the initial step of a PDM deployment requires large efforts. For example, PDM and database servers and the PDM software must be installed. Before the installation, the infrastructure must be specified: the network topology to be used, the capacity of the corporate server and of the other servers, and ways that the network can be expanded in the future. The entire network will probably not initially be built, and the full capacity of the nodes will not be achieved. As the PDM system will be integrated in new processes, the network and the capacity will also increase. In addition, changes in the system infrastructure and the information architecture (information model, data structures, databases, and vaults) must be specified, and the migration of data from older systems must be performed.

Apart from what is described in general for the evaluation and deployment of a complex system in Section 7.1, and cultural differences described in Section 7.3.4, additional areas must be taken into consideration to shorten the time and decrease the difficulty of deploying a PDM system:

> ‣ *Administration and performance tuning.* A PDM system should be customized in a test system separate from that which is in production (i.e., where the system users store, retrieve, and update product data). The newly implemented functions can be tested in the test system without disturbing the users. Later, all of the adjustments done in the test system will be exported into the production environment. The migration of existing data from an old system to the deployed PDM system must be planned; programs for automatic data conversion written, tests performed, routines and procedures for the migration written, and original data migrated into the new PDM system. The administrators must install client software, perform general administration of the PDM system, supervise database transactions, and install new servers, including software. Further, close cooperation with system and network administrators, system performance tuning, and timing of hardware upgrades must be taken into consideration. Before the deployed system can be used in a production environment,

a system acceptance test must be performed to verify that the new system will function correctly with the migrated data and fulfill customer requirements.

▸ *Training.* Planning for training and user support are essential factors in a successful deployment plan. Middle managers, users, and administrators should be prepared before system usage. Key users will play a critical role in mentoring and supporting other users. The training must emphasize the process tasks and not only tool functions. A broad-based training plan will help minimize the obstacles caused by enforced cultural changes. Training for new users (e.g., new employees) and retraining of users moving between projects must be provided on site.

▸ *User support.* PDM tools are usually large and complex, and they require a lot of efforts in the beginning when users do not understand all of the concepts. PDM tools require a permanent support from experts.

▸ *New groups.* Deployment of PDM requires the involvement of new groups. For a successful deployment, several groups must be formed. Examples of such groups are an enterprise deployment team, a core team, and a training team. These groups must be closely coordinated for a successful deployment of the PDM system into a production environment.

The main task of the core team is to define the new processes used in the PDM system (see Figure 7.5). To implement these new processes, the core team forms a project group; specifies the project goals, all activities (e.g., new functions to be implemented or servers to be used), and a time

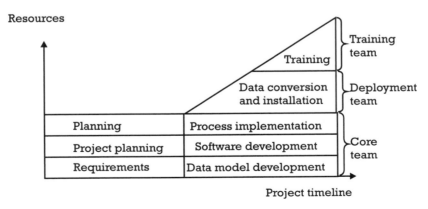

Figure 7.5 Deployment project resources and activities.

schedule in a project plan; defines necessary additional requirements from other systems; and defines requirements for system administration and operation and support. The team then specifies how existing systems will map into the PDM system. Further, additional requirements related to the data model, working process procedures, the user interface, system information, infrastructure, and system administration must be identified and implemented. One type of change will be implemented by specification or modification of the data model. The new data model will define new work processes, new objects, new attributes, and new relationships to be implemented in the database. Another type of change will require writing additional software.

An enterprise deployment team should be formed early in the project (i.e., when all requirements and planning for the project are finalized). The team's responsibility is the deployment execution. The enterprise deployment team should be focused on the enterprise view of the system deployment. It should consist of persons responsible for business-focused functions and persons responsible for communication with support people of the local sites (the site support teams). The enterprise deployment team will also need to establish user-support teams and identify key users. Key users will act as mentors and in some cases as backup for the first line support (i.e., they will answer questions from end users and managers). The responsibility of the site support team is to focus on local administration and end-user support issues (i.e., to ensure that servers are up and running, to supervise clients' installations and upgrades, and to supervise databases and software upgrades on the PDM server). The team must also prepare a training team with start time, users to be educated, and location.

The training team includes technical writers and teachers. Their tasks are to write training material and train different end users at different locations, depending on information given by the project plan of the enterprise deployment teams.

7.3.3 SCM deployment

The efforts and time spent in the deployment of an SCM tool can vary considerably, depending on the software development process and the SCM policy of the organization. For small development teams, SCM support should be simple. For large projects and large teams, or distributed development, the requirements for SCM support are much greater. This calls for a more advanced SCM tool, which requires considerably more effort for deployment and subsequently for providing support and maintenance. The SCM policy will determine which type of tool will be selected and in which way it will be deployed and used. For this reason, organizations usually have an SCM policy, which identifies the purpose of SCM and the main directions of its use in the organization.

In the same way as PDM, SCM supports the infrastructure (i.e., makes it easier to organize the work and makes it possible to accurately maintain the old products), but it does not provide direct support for development as many other tools are used in the development environment (e.g., language-sensitive editors, wizards, debuggers). Many developers therefore do not see the direct benefits of SCM, and, on the contrary, they may feel that its use slows down their development work. In many cases, there are psychological barriers, but there are also SCM tools that are not user friendly and that require much additional work for the developers and the administration. This is especially the case if the tools are not properly integrated in the development process. To overcome these obstacles, the SCM tool must be adjusted to the development process to be used as smoothly as possible, and all SCM users must be well prepared for its use. This is the main goal of the deployment.

The goal, the results, and the deployment activities should be identified and specified in the deployment project plan. Depending on the complexity and size of the development process, different deployment groups can be involved in the deployment procedures. An SCM group (which will also exist during the full exploitation of the SCM tool) will be responsible for building the SCM infrastructure, the administration group will be responsible for defining the SCM system topology (the network of servers and clients), and a training group will train the SCM users. The building of the infrastructure and the integration of the tool in the development environment may require the development of additional software that can automate certain activities (such as automatic check in and check out), so that it may be necessary to build a development team. Such a team may be a part of the SCM group. Many of these activities may require expertise that the organization does not have. This expertise can be obtained by special training of the deployment groups or as assistance from external experts, often offered by the vendor.

SCM procedures should be integrated in the development process smoothly (i.e., as much as possible stepwise, both with respect to the functionality and the coverage of the development projects). If possible, each new function should be deployed in a particular project and then successively distributed through the organization.

To illustrate the deployment process, let us look at an example of a deployment scenario divided into several steps.

7.3.3.1 SCM process planning

As the benefit from SCM tools is only gained by their use in a development process context, it is necessary to specify the entire SCM process. This can be done on several levels of abstraction. We have already mentioned the SCM policy, which explains the overall goals of SCM. An SCM plan gives more details of particular activities that should be performed in development projects. In addition to such a general SCM plan, each project should have its project SCM plan that will describe the SCM activities in detail. Such a plan should state the following:

- The SCM structure that will be used;
- The tools (SCM and all other tools) and development environment that will be utilized;
- The software entities that will be changed;
- The baselines and configurations that will be created;
- Who will make the SCM decisions and how;
- Ways that the change management will be performed.

For the deployment process, a set of documents that are normally a part of any project should be created. These documents include deployment requirements specification, deployment project plan, project reports, quality assurance report, and final project report.

7.3.3.2 Tool installation

The SCM tool must be installed and the resources (i.e., servers and storage devices) for its installation must be obtained. The simpler SCM tools usually operate on the file system and do not require any considerable space. More advanced SCM tools usually use a database that might require a large storage media and additional software (e.g., database servers). The client parts of the tool must be installed on developers' workstations. SCM tool installation is a task for the administration group.

7.3.3.3 SCM infrastructure

The basic infrastructure of an SCM tool includes a repository and workspace. The repository, which manages versions of CIs (such as files and folders), has an internal structure. It is usually a hierarchical structure representing a file system. A workspace might either be a part of the repository or placed in the file system. During the deployment, the organization should decide on the repository model—if there will be one common repository to include all development (and other) projects or if several repositories are to be created. Similarly, the overall structure of the workspace should be defined, where the developers will have their workspaces—in their private directories, on local clients, or on a common users' server. The SCM group is responsible for the design of the SCM infrastructure.

7.3.3.4 Version management and concurrent development

We saw in Chapter 3 that there are different approaches to version management. The organization or the project groups should decide which model is to be used in the development projects. Should a concurrent check in and check out be allowed? Will it be possible to work on different variants? What is the merge policy? Different models are the bases for different types of development in which different goals are emphasized. For example, for a flexible and less firmly controlled development, a full concurrency will be allowed, while in a more strict process, only the strict lock mechanism and sequential version will be permitted. To facilitate the developers' everyday work, the parameters defining the default behavior of the version management can be set up centrally.

7.3.3.5 Configuration selection

In the same way as for version management, the default selection criteria can be set up by the SCM group.

7.3.3.6 Build management

SCM tools usually provide basic support for building software in the form of a particular tool (for example, a program named Make). A single tool alone is not sufficient for an efficient build procedure. The developers must often define how the building will be performed, and this specification is often time consuming and error prone. The SCM group can provide the developers with programs that automatically create the build procedures.

7.3.3.7 Release management

Most SCM tools do not provide direct support for release management, but many small supporting functions and data are available to be used in the release management process. The minimum support that the SCM group should provide is a guideline for creating a new product release, indicating which tools can be used and how. Better support is provided when the release management process is performed automatically. Such support requires additional software, including functions from the SCM tool, such as that for generating a list of items included in the product and a list of all changes implemented (new functions and error corrections). This software can be rather simple (e.g., a set of scripts that execute particular SCM functions). More advanced support will include a reach user interface, which makes it easy to understand and to use different options that might be required for different types of projects.

7.3.3.8 Integration with other tools

To avoid distracting the developers with administration tasks, the entire SCM process should performed as smoothly as possible and should not disturb the developers more than necessary. This may be achieved by integrating the SCM functions in other tools and by adding new functions that use the SCM tool. For example, when a developer begins work in a project, all tools and all data used in the project (i.e., source code, libraries, and documentation) should be automatically available. Another example is automatic check out and check in of the files that the developers wish to modify. Many SCM tools provide such functions or functions that can be executed via line commands or via API. This makes it possible to build new applications that will automate different procedures in everyday work. These applications or the SCM functions can be triggered directly from other tools. The SCM development team (and the SCM group) must develop these applications and must integrate them in other tools. This work can require much effort, especially if a simpler SCM tool has been selected.

Integration with other tools should be performed stepwise. The basic functions, which are easiest to implement and which have the largest impact in the everyday work, should be implemented first (e.g., the automatic check-out/check-in sequence). More advanced procedures can be developed later and successively replace the guidelines.

7.3.3.9 Change management

Many SCM tools incorporate support for change management. Some do not, and for this case external change management tools are available. Change management is one of the more advanced activities and will usually be included in the process when the basic SCM functions are already established. Different levels of integration of basic SCM functions and change management can be achieved. In a nonintegrated solution, the tools are separate and the developers are those who do the integration job by manually updating documentation (e.g., entering changed file names in "change requests"). In a fully integrated solution, every change made in software or documentation is automatically related to change requests. Additional functions related to change management are functions that provide the statistical results [3] of the change process. This type of function is one of the more advanced support functions that only organizations with a mature development process require.

7.3.3.10 Distributed development

A distributed development is considerably more complicated than a local development. The basic principles must be clearly specified before the distributed development is begun. Examples of questions considered by these rules are [4, 5]: Who is responsible for which part of the system? In which way is the data replication achieved? How is awareness of each other's activities between different groups supported?

Different SCM tools provide different support for distributed development. When using simpler tools, the development of additional software may be required. Even if sufficient support exists, the distributed infrastructure must be defined and built. The introduction of distributed development is a costly process, and it should usually be introduced in the organization in the form of a separate project.

7.3.4 Deployment of the PDM and SCM integrated environment

We can observe a large difference between deploying a tightly coupled integration and deploying a loosely coupled integration (see Chapter 4). A tightly coupled integration becomes like a completely new tool, with new functionality and with a new user interface. With a loosely coupled integration, on the other hand, it is possible for the users to continue working with their old tool. The integration then also provides additional functionality, which can be deployed according to the examples in Section 7.3.1. Two different, complementary issues should be taken into consideration: the integration and deployment of the tools and a common environment, and the integration of people that will work in the common environment and that must understand the entire process.

7.3.4.1 PDM and SCM tools integration and deployment—Different scenarios

We can distinguish three basic cases for obtaining a PDM and SCM integrated environment. The first case is applicable to companies developing hardware products and beginning with software development or including software components in their products. Together with software development, a new SCM tool will probably be introduced. Companies that traditionally develop hardware products tend to see the software components as hardware components. On the system level, this is a good approach, and it should be reflected in the use of PDM and SCM tools. The software deliverables (binary code and documentation) should be exported from SCM to PDM, while the software development should be performed in the framework of SCM. The deployment phase will include the deployment of the SCM tool itself and development of the import/export procedures. The second case applies to software (or dominantly software) companies that need PDM for managing final products outside the scope of SCM. The deployment will include deployment of the selected PDM system and the development of import/export functions between PDM and SCM. The third case comprises a situation in which a company develops both hardware and software components (and systems), and uses both PDM and SCM, but in separate processes. This case is in a sense simpler, as the users are familiar with both tools and the integration can be achieved faster and with less effort. However, it can happen that the process goes with much more difficulties if the users of these tools do not understand each other. For this reason the human and social aspects are very important.

7.3.4.2 Integrating people—Human aspects

Assuming a loosely coupled integration has been implemented, the PDM and SCM users can continue to work within their respective tool with particular additional functions related to the integrated environment. The next step is to:

- Get the users to begin to use the new functionality. This is similar to the introduction of any new tool and is not specific to PDM/SCM integration. It may also happen that some of the old functions will be replaced with new functions.

- Get the users to begin to talk with each other (with users from the other domain) and collaborate in order to understand the common process.

This collaboration must, in fact, begin during the requirement phase of the integration process:

1. Together decide upon the requirements of the integration;

2. Together decide how to collaborate using common parts. Even though it is always preferable for all the users involved to receive a positive personal return on their investment of effort, there is always a risk that some persons may be required to perform extra work to be able to provide others (from the other domain) with information. Within a group this might be acceptable, but the less people know of each other, the less knowledge they have of the needs of others, and the greater the risk of failure. It is thus even more important to ensure a positive personal return on investment for all when directing people from two domains to work together.

7.3.4.3 Cultural differences

Unfortunately, our experience is that PDM and SCM users seldom collaborate or even communicate with each other. The reasons for this may be several:

• Persons from both domains rarely meet each other. PDM users and SCM users work in different groups in different departments of the company and software developers have little contact with hardware developers.

• They usually have different backgrounds, interests, and goals (technicians versus nontechnicians). For example, SCM users work closely with developers, and often it is software developers who also have the role of configuration managers. These persons tend only to see the software and not the entire product. PDM users, on the other hand, are often located closer to the product managers (who may even be nontechnicians, with economy more their primary goal).

• The terminology used is not consistent. Some common terms are interpreted differently by PDM and SCM users. An example is *configuration control*, which is the definition and management of product configurations for PDM users and the control of changes to a CI after formal establishment of its configuration documents for SCM users. Closer understanding across the domain boundaries is complicated by such differences in the use of terminology.

As a result, the two groups tend to confront each other rather than try to develop a collaboration. The impression gained is that both believe that their methods and tools are superior and that problems in the other domain can be solved easily by using their tools! Persons working in each domain do not understand the requirements of the other domain. Many software developers believe that SCM tools can manage data at the system level. PDM people, on the other hand, often appear to believe that software is a set of binary components only, as easy to put under the control of a PDM system as any other component. For vendors, also, the cultural differences are a difficult subject when discussing PDM and SCM with customers.

7.3.4.4 Building bridges

What can be done to make integration successful despite the cultural differences? Information is probably most important. Information can be directed to both groups to make them understand the benefits and needs of the other domain. Because it often is possible to continue to work within the same old tool after integration, it is quite easy to gradually introduce new functionality. Incremental deployment and a personal return on invested time will keep all involved positive to the change.

7.4 Summary

This chapter described the final step to be taken before beginning to use PDM or SCM, or both tools together, in an organization—the deployment process. The deployment process is not just the installation of the tool, but also includes a thorough evaluation of the tools available to permit the selection of the most appropriate to use.

Much of the procedures for PDM and SCM deployment are the same as that for any other complex tool. The evaluation and deployment process is divided into several phases, each analyzed in detail. One important observation is that the analysis of tool functionality is only a (small) part of the entire evaluation. Examples of equally important factors are the total cost of the deployment and use of the tool, the return on investment, the vision and strategy of the vendor, and its competitive advantages and financial situation. Figure 7.3 and Figure 7.4 are examples of the graphic presentation of evaluation results, depicting the estimated investments and return on investment and the functional distribution of requirements fulfillment respectively.

The deployment process for both PDM and SCM is analyzed in great detail. We found that the execution of a pilot project is a good practice; the pilot team tests the new tool, identifies any need for adjustment that might be required, and often makes such adjustments before the tool is released for use in production by the organization. Such a pilot project has many advantages. Typically, the members of the project team are interested in experimenting with new tools and are engaged and enthusiastic. As a result of their usually successful work, they generate positive feedback to the organization, which results in faster acceptance of the tool in the company environment, making the full-scale deployment more likely to succeed.

In addition to general principles, more specific aspects of the integration of PDM and SCM are presented. Because both domains are to a degree of an administrative nature, the engagement and motivation of the users can be of vital importance.

Finally, the deployment of an integration of PDM and SCM is discussed. Technically, the implementation of a loosely coupled integration means that most users can continue to work comfortably with the tool to which they have become accustomed while gradually becoming familiar with the new tool in the integration as a whole. However, due to human nature, it is often difficult to integrate persons from the two different domains. They must be given increased knowledge and understanding of the requirements and needs of the other domain to be able to collaborate and reconcile the different demands of the integration.

References

[1]   Crnkovic, I., "Why Do Some Mature Organizations Not Use Mature CM?" *Proceedings of 9th International Symposium on System Configuration Management (SCM-9)*, Lecture Notes in Computer Science, No. 1675, Berlin Heidelberg, Germany: Springer Verlag, 1999.

[2]   CIM-Data, www.cim-data.com, 2003.

[3]   Crnkovic, I., and P. Willför, "Change Measurements in an SCM Process," *Proceedings 9th International Symposium on System Configuration Management (SCM-9)*, Lecture Notes in Computer Science, Berlin Heidleberg, Germany: Springer Verlag, 1998.

[4]   Asklund, U., *Configuration Management for Distributed Development—Practice and Needs*, Licentiate Dissertation, Department of Computer Science, Lund University, Lund, Sweden, 1999.

[5]   Asklund, U., *Configuration Management for Distributed Development in an Integrated Environment*, Doctoral Dissertation, Department of Computer Science, Lund University, Lund, Sweden, 2002.

PART

IV

Case Studies

CHAPTER

8

Contents

Case studies

As a rule, software systems do not work well until they have been used, and have failed repeatedly, in real applications.

—Dave Parnas

8.1 Introduction

In this chapter, six case studies from international companies based in the United States, England, Switzerland, and Sweden are presented. They serve as practical examples of how PDM and SCM are actually managed and thus complement the more theoretical part in earlier chapters. The products developed and manufactured by the companies described range from pure software products to mixed products containing both hardware and software. Also the issues discussed vary from development processes and PLCs to a description of the tool sets used to support these processes from an information flow perspective.

The information presented was acquired through interviews and discussions with one or many persons in the companies who had responsibility for or experience using their PDM or SCM solutions. The case studies focus on particular topics and do not have ambitions to describe the companies in general. Furthermore, the cases do not follow the same pattern or format and cannot be used for any type of benchmarking. Each case study focuses on some important issues from the company, ranging from technical descriptions of tool interfaces to descriptions of the development process. At the end of each case study, there are cross references to chapters in the book that discuss these issues further and more generally than in the specific case. The case studies are not official statements from the respective organizations. For each case, some of the terminology used within the company was used, and in some cases this differs from terminology used in the rest of the book. Because both PDM and SCM are under continuous development and change within the companies, all of the studies represent a snapshot from when the interviews were conducted.

Here are short outlines of the cases described in this chapter:

> *Sun Microsystems, Inc.* The case study describes Sun's PLC, which is one of its core business processes. The four key process elements—structured process, product approval committees, product teams, and phase completion reviews—are explained. Also, a short description of the tools supporting PLC and how they have been deployed is given.

> *Mentor Graphics Corporation.* The description of the case is focused on the development process and PLC at one division at Mentor Graphics Corporation. The requirements management, development process, and change management are discussed. Currently, a simple tool support during the development phase is implemented, but the company is in a phase of deploying a new SCM tool enabling better support for distributed development and traceability.

> *Ericsson Radio Systems AB.* Operational PDM/SCM concept from a concrete project is described. The process supporting the PLC is well defined. However, due to lack of integration between the tools, many procedures must be manually performed, transferring data between the many tools.

> *Ericsson Mobile Communications AB.* The study discusses the importance of the PDM tool acceptance among developers. The development of a new, more user-friendly Web interface on top of one of the existing PDM tools is described. The development and the deployment are divided in two phases; in the first phase only nonproduct data is managed, and in the second phase the support is enlarged to also include product data.

> *ABB Automation Technology Products.* The case discusses the management of hardware and firmware—how the product structure is designed to efficiently manage different product variants that are realized in different ways, depending on the manufacturing volume. The advantage in flexibility and limitations in traceability are discussed.

> ▸ *SaabTech Electronics AB.* A case is described in which there exists a need to replace the current PDM system. A specification of the new planned process and the architecture of the new PDM system are discussed.

8.2 Sun Microsystems, Inc.

Sun Microsystems, Inc., sells network servers, data storage systems, engineering workstations, and information appliances for use in a wide range of markets, including telecommunications, financial services, government, manufacturing, education, retail, life sciences, media and entertainment, and health care. Their product line stretches from ultrathin, rack-mountable servers priced under $1,000 to massive, high-integrity systems in configurations costing $10 million or more.

Sun recognizes that business today is all about services—within the enterprise and between enterprises, with and without wires. The Sun-Open Net Environment™ (Sun ONE)™ provides the software products—from developer tools to an industrial-strength operating environment—needed to create, assemble, deploy, and manage services on demand. The Sun ONE™ software stack includes identity management, security, integration, Web, application, portal, and messaging solutions.

Sun's rapidly growing service organization helps customers architect and support their network computing environments. The focus of consulting, education, and support services is on maximizing uptime, increasing productivity, and controlling costs.

Sun's primary markets are the Global 2000 companies. Specific product growth subsegments include servers, storage, services, and software infrastructure products. Within the Global 2000, Sun targets specific environments and user types. At the highest level, their target environments are enterprise data centers and service provider data centers/telecommunications. In terms of user types, they focus on CXOs,[1] developers, information technology managers, and global sales partners. In terms of priority, the target vertical industries include government, education, financial services, telecommunications, automotive, healthcare, media/entertainment, eManufacturing, retail, life sciences, and transportation. Key customer applications such as ERP, data warehousing, server consolidation, and

---

1. CXO is an acronym for a member of top-level management. The "X" is a variable so the term can stand for chief information officer (CIO), chief financial officer (CFO), chief executive officer (CEO), and so on.

customer/partner relationship management (CRM/PRM) run across all of these segments.

All levels of service are provided, from warranty only to service packages including consulting, maintenance, and configuration. Sun creates and sells approximately 300 products per year, which are developed both on order basis and as standard products. For the most part, products are configured and shipped to order. The products have many variants and versions, which are constantly being updated and improved. The company sells hardware products independently from software products, and vice versa. Software is shipped via a fulfillment site (manufacturing) when it involves physical media and documents, or on-line via virtual distribution. Software products are also shipped bundled with hardware products.

8.2.1 Development process and PLC

Sun's PLC process is one of its core business processes. It consists of four key process elements: structured process, product approval committees, product teams, and phase completion reviews. The PLC process governs cross-organizational and cross-functional product development and PLC management activities. It also provides checklists that assure strong customer focus with increased product reliability and program execution predictability. The process is realized as a set of dedicated processes on top of a vault. It is integrated with many of the development tools, although it is not yet fully integrated.

The structured process element of the Sun PLC process spans the entire PLC, from product concept to customer acceptance, and from product deployment to product retirement. It is articulated in eight distinct phases, which contain activities with associated deliverables and tasks that are used to clarify each activity. This process element provides guidelines for developing and sustaining products and enables consistent terminology and effective cross-functional and cross-organizational linkages. The structured process is divided in a sequence of eight phases, as shown in Figure 8.1.

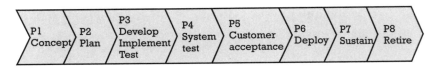

Figure 8.1 The eight phases of Sun's structured process.

The objectives of each phase are:

1. *Concept.* Explain the concept and key customer needs (e.g., critical to quality parameters), evaluate the market opportunity, assess product feasibility, and assess fit with company strategy.

2. *Plan.* Clearly define the product, develop technical approach and strategy, and plan the product development activities.

3. *Develop/integrate and test.* Develop and/or integrate product components, verify component performance, develop company's and critical partners' production processes, and prepare comprehensive plans for introduction, service, and support.

4. *System test.* Qualify the product functionality and performance and qualify production and supplier processes.

5. *Customer acceptance.* Confirm product functionality in planned customer environments and execute introduction and support plans.

6. *Deploy.* Launch the product. Stabilize operational, service, and support processes.

7. *Sustain.* Manage product profitability and growth, provide customer support and defect tracking, and plan product retirement.

8. *Retire.* Retire product and manage customer transitions.

A product approval committee (PAC) (see Figure 8.2) is a cross-functional decision-making body within the process. Each PAC assures effective resource allocation and manages all development activities within a product line throughout the PLC process. At each phase completion, PAC makes go/no-go or redirect decisions.

Product teams are small, cross-functional teams representing the entire product program. Members of product teams assure effective communication and coordination and have program focus with clearly defined responsibility and authority to execute within the product plan (i.e., the contract). Each product team is lead by a product program manager whose rank is proportionate to the size/complexity of the program.

Product approval committee chair							
Marketing	Dev. eng.	Operations	Service/ support	Sales	Finance	CTO	CA

Figure 8.2 Product approval committees.

Phase completion reviews are event-driven reviews, conducted by PACs, which help maintain an effective pipeline of new products. These reviews are decision based (go—proceed, no go—terminate the program, and redirect—repeat the previous phase), as shown in Figure 8.3.

Key benefits of phase completion reviews are:

▸ Provide a mechanism for early interventions that help reduce the unnecessary research and development spending;

▸ Enable pipeline pruning, which is critical for optimizing the product portfolio;

▸ Contribute to improved performance to plans because of frequent information exchanges;

▸ Provide forum for cross-organizational resource management to minimize project delays;

▸ Drive risk assessments and mitigations to increase probability of product successes.

In addition to the phase completion review, Sun uses program reviews during each phase to keep stakeholders informed about the progress within the PLC process.

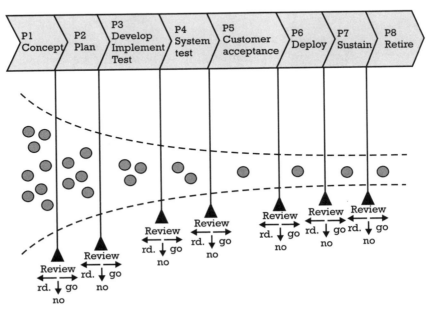

Figure 8.3 Phase completion reviews.

Sun has designed its processes to be scalable both in terms of programs scope (i.e., program size) and program content type (i.e., systems products, software products, and hardware products). At the top process level, Sun treats all development programs the same, regardless of their program content type. Process differences that appear at the third and the fourth level of the process are dictated by specific needs of different product types or program scope.

8.2.1.1 Distributed development

There are many situations in which parts of products are designed and built in different locations. Distributed development is organized around the PLC process, its infrastructure, and its requirements. A key contribution of the PLC process to the effectiveness of the company is its overall architecture, which manifests itself in defined team structure, review requirements, management structure, and roles and responsibilities. For example, the PLC structured process requirements allow diverse geographic locations to have a common base upon which to standardize and operate consistently.

Internal deliveries of products or parts between geographically dispersed teams are done with the help of different tools. All of Sun's employees have access to the same PLC information (as per a need-to-know basis) through applications available on the company network. For example, the Sun PLC process support application contains critical product information accessible by any team member at any location at any time. Also, conferencing tools enable team members anywhere to collaborate and work in a virtual team environment.

Sun utilizes a distributed development model for all product types. Because many of Sun's products and components are shared by higher level products, part of Sun's technical review structure is geared toward identifying economies of scale inherent in the reuse and sharing of components across products and product lines. Sun has developed processes that enable effective execution in such an environment. The software development subprocess specifically enables predictable product release schedules by virtue of identifying stable interfaces to which all components within products must comply at all times, regardless of their origin (i.e., either they are developed internally or externally). For example, in the event that a particular component undergoing changes suffers a schedule slip, the higher level release can still use the prior version of the component and will pick up the new component if it is ready on the next release cycle. This system allows Sun to maintain a fixed software release schedule at all times.

8.2.1.2   Change management

Product changes that result from customer-identified issues are categorized (e.g., bugs/defects and feature requests) and scheduled for action according to level of severity. Sun regularly releases patches and product upgrades to address such issues. In addition, new feature work is integrated into a development planning process so that it can be delivered within an established release schedule.

One of Sun's major achievements is a complete backward binary compatibility of its microprocessors and operating system. They were able to achieve this because of good component interface management and management of product architecture.

8.2.1.3   Tool support for the development process

As mentioned earlier, Sun currently manages the PLC process through a dedicated process support application. All product development teams are required to use this application regardless of the product type. In general, product teams manage and archive through this application the PLC process specified deliverables, such as market requirements documents, product requirement documents, product concept documents, functional specifications, product plans, product boundary and summary, design schematics, and software code. Sun also uses intranet tools to manage financial data, BOMs, factory-level execution, inventory controls, part number registry, ECM process, and document management. In addition, Sun's product development organizations use numerous CAD and other eEngineering tools.

Mostly Sun uses the same tools within development and manufacturing processes, although a few gaps remain. Currently, Sun is evaluating the cost and benefit of integrating several applications, such as portfolio management, requirements management, collaboration, PDM, and materials sourcing in an integrated PLM system, which is aimed to assure complete integration of product development information and systems across the enterprise.

In addition to the PLC process tools, software development is managed through SCM tools. General requirements on software management include support for concurrent development (such as branch and merge), version management, build management, workspace management, and history management.

Although Sun can monitor progress of all product devolvement using the PLC process support tool, they recognize an overlap between the information in the different process support tools (e.g., PLC, PDM, and SCM). In fact, this is one of the drivers behind the initiative to deploy an integrated PLM system.

8.2.2   Deployment of tools

Sun usually develops and/or updates key processes first and subsequently deploys process support tools to the user base. For example, the PLC process support application was deployed companywide together with the rollout of the PLC process improvements. Sun experienced some difficulties with the acceptance of these tools, which is typical for the introduction of complex tools (see Chapter 6). To assure success, Sun dedicates a substantial amount of effort to manage required cultural changes. Cultural change management is an integral part of any large initiative, and Sun has gained a substantial experience doing that both with PLC and Six Sigma deployment, which they call Sun™ Sigma.

8.2.3   Conclusion

Sun sees the following four areas as key advantages of using PLM, PDM, SCM, and document management tools:

‣ Automation provides huge opportunity for improved transactional efficiency.

‣ Common data and search functionality enables more effective reuse of design knowledge.

‣ Effective architectural, technical, and phase completion reviews assure better utilization of resources and guarantee lower cost of quality.

‣ Overall increased efficiency yields better time to market, which in turns enables the capture of higher revenue and assures better margins.

More about hardware and software PLC processes and the importance of information integration during these processes can be found in Chapter 5.

8.3   Mentor Graphics Corporation

Mentor Graphics Corporation supplies software and hardware design solutions that enable companies to send better electronic products to market faster and more cost effectively. The company offers innovative products and solutions that help engineers overcome the challenges they face in   the increasingly complex world of board and chip design—in which deep submicron (DSM) technology and system-on-chip (SoC) design multiply the challenges of establishing promising product ideas on the market [1].

The Mentor Graphics Corporation business unit (BU) we interviewed has a wide range of customers in the electronics field, from small to very large companies. It supplies out-of-the-box software products, with thousands of licenses for their use sold to the electronics design automation (EDA) industry annually. This BU markets different packages of software, four or five in each family, usually two main releases per year plus revisions in the form of patches when necessary.

This case study is focused on the Hardware Description Languages (HDL) Design Entry BU of the HDL division, one of the product divisions of the Mentor Graphics Corporation. The HDL Design Entry BU designs and supplies two different kinds of software products: the HDL Designer Series, a family of software tools to capture, analyze, and manage register transfer level (RTL) designs using HDL, and Field Programmable Gate Array (FPGA) Advantage, a suite of tools for the design, verification and implementation of FPGA.

The HDL division markets only software, unlike some of the other Mentor divisions. Software products for the U.S. market are shipped from Wilsonville, Oregon (the location of corporate headquarters), and for the international market, products are shipped from the division's facility in Ireland.

Mentor Graphics Corporation has developed an extensive support organization in United States and abroad, in both Europe and Asia. It also has a consulting organization available for customization of the tools it markets or to help customers with their design flow. Customers who have entered into a maintenance agreement with Mentor Graphics Corporation can enter a call log and submit a defect report (DR) or an enhancement request (ER) through the call centers. The status of the call log is monitored by an automatic system.

8.3.1   Development process and PLC

8.3.1.1   Requirements management

Requirements are assembled in different ways—through interviews, customers meetings, sales presentations, and partnerships with universities. In the HDL Design Entry BU, the chief scientist and product architect are responsible for issuing a marketing requirement document (MRD). The engineering group then produces a technical specification on the basis of the MRD. The engineering group, the marketing organization, and the management group decide in agreement what functionality should be developed for each particular release. The quality assurance department collaborates with the engineering department in planning and assuring testing procedures. Similarly, the customer documentation department plans the customer documentation with the engineering department. Customers with a maintenance agreement are entitled to upgrades of the releases.

8.3.1.2 Development process

The HDL Design Entry BU is one of the few groups in the Mentor Graphics Corporation that use an off-the-shelf library as a basis for the implementation of its products. In this case, it is a standard library from the French company ILOG. This library is developed for different platforms and provides the ability to develop single source code applications across multiple platforms. A specific product variant is built using conditional compilation. Graphical user interface and C++ libraries (C++ View from SCL, Ltd) are used in addition to the ILOG standard library.

A daily build procedure is performed for software using standard Make files. The HDL division develops and releases software but does not manufacture the final products, which are delivered on CDs.

The HDL Design Entry BU develops software in the United Kingdom, the United States, and Egypt, with the different engineering teams working in close cooperation. Today, RCS is used as the SCM tool, but the unit is moving to a Rational ClearCase environment. The main reasons for changing the SCM tool are: geographically dispersed development teams, concurrent development (managing multiple branching and merging) features, and demands for improvement of the traceability of changes. SNIFF+ from Wind River Systems will be used on top of ClearCase. This tool already has an interface to both ClearCase and RCS. This enables SNIFF+ to use the RCS repositories and ClearCase database and also both standard Make files and ClearCase Make files. This gives the ability to smoothly transition from one tool to another and to keep a transparent interface during the transition process (see Figure 8.4).

From time to time, the division outsources the development of software components. This is always done in a very controlled way; only very well-defined, independent, and self-contained pieces of software are outsourced. The companies developing the outsourced components have a development

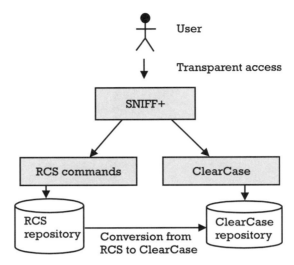

Figure 8.4 A transparent interface to SCM tools.

process similar to that of the HDL Design Entry BU. For example, they also use MRDs, technical specifications, and test plans. The original source code will always be delivered to the division. The main Mentor engineering team is always responsible for the integration of the outsourced software components.

8.3.1.3 CM and change management

The HDL division uses a simple SCM process supporting basic versioning, baseline, and change management. All baselines are managed manually on the fileserver. All metadata (e.g., information regarding releases and baselines) are stored on this fileserver. Versions of baselines are managed manually by creating and updating a directory structure based on the software release number.

All changes identified are placed in MRDs. Customer support can influence the change process through the report from ERs and DRs from customers. All changes in the source code are managed in the SCM tool (i.e., stored in the RCS repository). Changes are connected to a BL using comments in RCS. There is no traceability from a CR to the actual changes made implementing the request.

There are plans to introduce ClearCase Unified Change Management (UCM) to ClearQuest to improve the management of changes.

8.3.2   Document management

The HDL Design Entry BU has no large volume of documentation and therefore no need for a traditional document management tool. The documents are placed in the server's file system and the file system and the RCS repository are used for managing the access to documents. Requirement documents are mainly written with the Microsoft Office tool suite. Software documentation and customer documentation is written in FrameMaker. Complex documents (i.e., documents that may consist of several files) are managed by FrameMaker's book support. All customer documentation is shipped in PDF format, either by publishing it on the Web or on a CD. Some documentation is also converted to hypertext markup language (HTML) format and made available on the Web.

8.3.3   Conclusion

The main advantage to the HDL Design Entry BU of using an SCM tool is the ability it provides to manage the handling of thousands of files and classes developed by many users at different locations. It would, in fact, be very difficult for them to manage and create their tools without SCM tools.

The HDL Design Entry BU development environment has been in place for several years and is being improved in parallel with product development. The improvement process is not trivial. It requires dedicated resources from both the information technology and engineering points of view and is usually expensive. As the SCM tool used currently is a very simple tool providing only basic support, the need for more advanced support is recognized and the division has therefore begun with the replacement of RCS with ClearCase.

As a pure software development organization, the division does not feel any need for support from PDM, and a possible use of PDM has not been considered.

This case illustrates a situation in which many software companies are today. The complexity of software development constantly increases, and this requires new investment in software development support. Simple SCM tools such as RCS have proven to be very efficient and flexible to date, but they now demonstrate limitations in managing complex processes. New investments can be made in the development of internal additions to the basic SCM tools or by buying new, more advanced tools. Pure software companies with a relatively simple production process feel no need for product management tools.

Further reading about concurrent development and distributed development of software can be found in Sections 3.2.6 and 3.2.7, respectively. The specific tools mentioned, RCS and ClearCase, are shortly described in Chapter 10.

8.4 Ericsson Radio Systems AB

Ericsson Radio Systems AB is a company within Ericsson AB. Ericsson AB is a supplier of a complete range of solutions for telecommunication systems and applications to services and core technology for mobile handsets. With the establishment of Sony Ericsson, the company is also a leading supplier of complete mobile multimedia products. Ericsson supplies operators and service providers around the world with end-to-end solutions in mobile and broadband Internet. The company supplies solutions for all existing mobile systems and future third generation mobile systems, in addition to broadband multiservice networks and broadband access. The solutions include network infrastructure, access equipment and terminals, application enablers, and global services to support both business and private communication.

This section contains two separate case studies from Ericsson, one from Ericsson AB (formerly Ericsson Radio Systems) and one from Sony Ericsson (formerly Ericsson Communication Systems).

8.4.1 The case study

This case study describes a project designated "Phase 10," in which a product for the standard personal digital cellular (PDC) was developed at the Ericsson subsidiary Ericsson Radio Systems AB. The Phase 10 project was a large development project performed at design centers in Sweden, Germany, and Japan. This project has been finalized, and the product has been delivered to the customer. The complex product that was developed (further called the PDC system) consists of a large number of subproducts, both hardware and software. The main project management group of 32 persons directed the work of hundreds of project members. The main objective of the Phase 10 project was to develop a packet data solution for the Japanese market, known as packet data PDC (PPDC).

This case study discusses the CM methods, the processes utilized in the project, and the support provided by PDM and SCM systems covering the PLC from customer requirements until delivery to the customer.

8.4.2   The PDC system

Figure 8.5 schematically depicts the PDC system and the subproducts implementing the PPDC product. The figure depicts how the public switched telephone network (PSTN) and data networks (ISDN) are connected to the existing switched network communicating via the gateway exchange (GMSC). Two more exchanges, a voice mobile switching center (VMSC) and a packet mobile switching center (PMSC), are the main constituents of PDC systems. Depending on the nature of the incoming input, voice, or data, the GMSC switches either to the VMSC or to the short message center (SMS-C). Mobile phones are connected to the base stations (BSs). The packet data nodes use IP communication. The nodes are connected to the IP backbone. Operation and support system (OSS)/network operational centre (NOC) integration is the integration between existing and new operational support. The packet data traffic and signaling toward the mobiles and BS from the PMSC are carried in timeslots over T1 communication links connected to the VMSC and further connected to the BS.

Most products in a PDC system consist of both hardware and software.

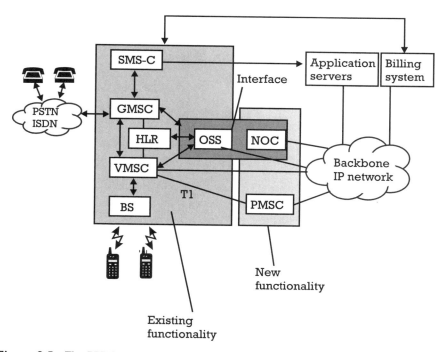

Figure 8.5   The PPDC network architecture.

8.4.2.1   Product structures

To manage products and subproducts, Ericsson Radio Systems uses a standard way for identifying and describing them. Each product has a unique identity and a list of product revisions. The particular document versions are connected to a particular product revision. To fully describe a product, four different views are used, called *product structures*. The structures are hierarchical and comprise different aspects of product information during its life cycles. Each product revision is described by a separate set of the tree structures. The five structures are:

1. *Functional structure.* Functional structure is the specification of product functions. The structure points to the functional subproducts at the level below and can also point to implementation products (e.g., hardware or software).

2. *Realization structure.* A realization structure describes a realization product with all of its realization components. Realization products implement the functions described in the functional part of the structure. This structure includes BOM, all documentation of a particular product revision, and manufacturing structure for particular products, such as a printed board assembly, magazine, and cables.

3. *Project structure.* This structure specifies the document structure, which lists all directive documents for the project (e.g., project specification, time schedule, configuration management plan, verification plan, and delivery plan). This structure can be linked to the level of the functional structure.

4. *Sales structure or commercial structure.* This structure contains all product packages (i.e., all products to be placed on the market).

5. *Delivery structure.* This structure gathers the product packages, defined in the commercial structure, depending on the specific order from the customer.

Figure 8.6 depicts an example of the five Ericsson structures and how they relate to each other.

Three of these five structures (functional, realization, and commercial) are used for the PDC system. The product structures are registered in a product information management (PRIM) system, which is developed internally. PRIM contains product structures and document identities. Documents themselves are archived in a document archive system designated general

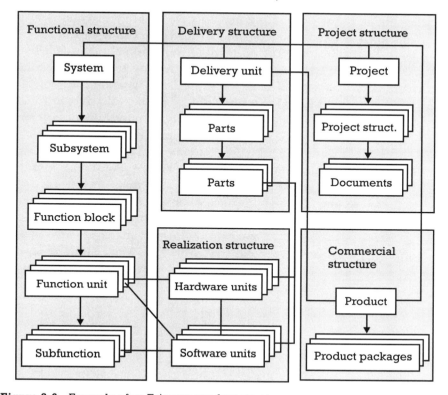

Figure 8.6   Example of an Ericsson product structure.

archive system for communication (GASK). PRIM and GASK are described in Section 8.4.5.

Besides the functional structure, mechanical assemblies (e.g., processor, telephone, and packet data) are included in a structure separate from the basic function modules. This is done to reduce the size of the functional structure. Mechanical assemblies have no direct connection to system functions. Furthermore, products such as batteries, special cables, and antennas at customer sites are not included in this overall product structure.

8.4.3   Project organization

A project organization at Ericsson Radio Systems is a temporary organization, separate from the regular company organization, and established to execute a particular project. The project organization is grouped according to three organizational functions: a project steering function, a project management function, and a project executing function. Several groups realize each function with different responsibilities, as depicted in Figure 8.7.

The groups realizing the steering function consist of managers in the organization with the authority to provide the project with management support and the resources needed for successful project completion exercise. A special member of the steering group is the project sponsor, who is commercially responsible for the project. He or she decides what is to be delivered, when and why, and what will be the development and maintenance budget. The sponsor has the main responsibility to initiate the project. In large projects, there may be more than one sponsor. The project steering group is usually formed when the decision is made to execute the project and is dissolved when the project has been concluded.

The groups realizing the project management function are responsible for managing the project toward its goal. These groups are established on the initiation of the project, when the responsibility for planning and

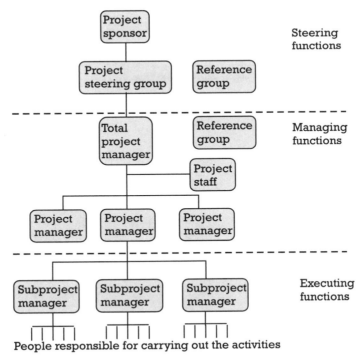

Figure 8.7   Generic project organization and roles in a large project.

executing the project is formally handed over to the project manager. The authority granted is limited to the lifetime of the project. The manager of large projects may appoint one or more project staff members as deputies. Depending on the scope of the project, these can be project managers on different levels: total project manager, project managers, and subproject managers. The project managers' tasks are the same, independent of the magnitude of the project, but the size of the project, its complexity, and strategic importance naturally put different demands on the project manager's competence and skills.

The groups realizing the project executing function are responsible for executing the project in accordance with the specifications developed by the project management function and for ensuring that the processes, methods, and standards of the organization in which the project is executed are adhered to. These groups are composed of personnel from the line organizations. Having performed the work required of them, they return to their respective line organizations. The purpose of establishing a project organization, in which the relevant stakeholders are identified, involved, and integrated, is to ensure that the authority and competence needed for the successful execution of the project are available for and contribute to the project. The Phase 10 main project is organized in the manner described earlier, as depicted in Figure 8.8.

The group members in "Project Staff" are responsible for general project support and are involved with the persons responsible for carrying out project activities (e.g., designers, CM managers, and system test managers work with designers, developers, and testers). This demonstrates the importance of integrated information systems providing accurate up-to-date information. The subprojects were geographically dispersed. Subprojects in the project organization of particular interest include:

- Test configuration management (TCM), responsible for supplying other design subprojects with test beds for function test;
- System integration and test (SIT), responsible for the integration of other network products and the packet data.

The very first release of the final customer product is delivered directly from the project to the customer. This delivery is called first office application (FOA). Other supply services are managed through the deployment project (not included in the development project).

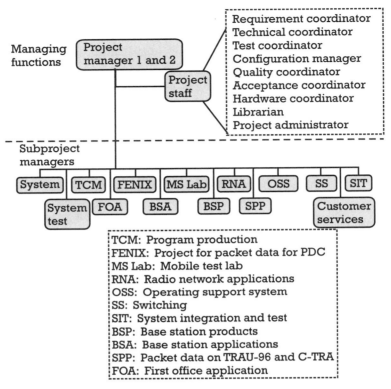

Figure 8.8 Example of project organization from the PPDC product line.

8.4.4 PLC process

The PLC process used in Ericsson Radio Systems is divided in three sub-processes: time to market (TTM), time to customer (TTC), and maintenance and support. These processes are illustrated in Figure 8.9.

TTM spans from customer input (several other inputs may also exist) to the delivery of the product design. It contains product management, design, and marketing processes. Marketing activities and the design process are normally concurrent activities during TTM. In the Phase 10 project, however, the situation was different, as there was one single customer (i.e., the input to the project was one single contract). The TTC flow is the manufacturing process from the final design to the delivery of the final product. The maintenance and support flows are parallel with TTC. These activities start up before the actual product is delivered. This is done to prepare and educate the help desk and repair center before any customer enquiries exist or

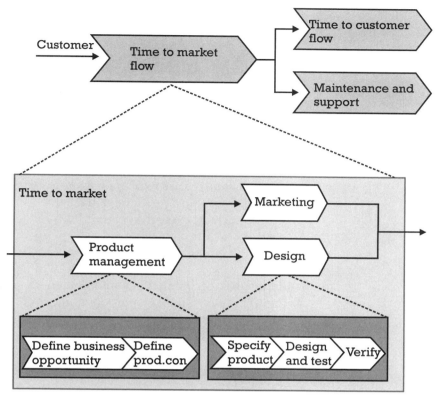

Figure 8.9   Time-to-market flow for PDC systems.

products need to be repaired. This PLC is well understood within the project, which is an advantage for implementing system support.

8.4.4.1   Maintenance

After product release, the product is handed over to the local Ericsson Company for service (first-line support). Second-line support (support of first-line support and coordination with maintenance) is normally managed within the design and maintenance organizations. Development, maintenance, and second-line support are located within the same organization. Product corrections are all delivered through ongoing development projects and therefore no separate fault correction releases need be managed.

8.4.5 The most important tools

Within Ericsson, hundreds of different tools are used during the products' life cycles. Certain tools are used over the entire company. Also, some tools are used more often, especially in distributed development environments. Such tools manage product data, archives, and requirements management. They are described next.

8.4.5.1 PRIM

The PRIM is the central Ericsson product catalog, in which all released products and related documents are registered. Although other systems are used locally elsewhere, only PRIM provides global access to the unique number of every product. This is the only comprehensive product register within the Ericsson group. PRIM has four different subsystems that contain different kinds of basic information. These four subsystems are (see also Figure 8.10):

1. Product data providing basic information about products, such as product name, number, revision number, function designation, design responsibility, revision state, design status, release status, and production status;

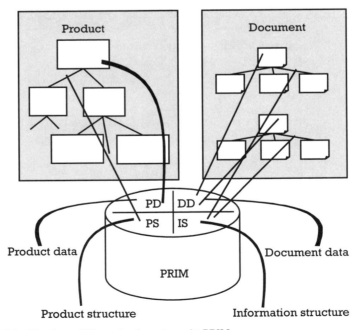

Figure 8.10 The four different subsystems in PRIM.

2.   Product structures providing present and historical information about the product structures through the delivery level, down to raw material and components;

3.   Document data providing basic information about documents (e.g., where the documents is stored, or archived, who is responsible for the document, existing language codes, and version status);

4.   Information structure providing all information that is related to the specific product.

Because many different tools are used during the development phase, products may not be registered in PRIM until they are ready for release. Within Ericsson, there is no other global product data management system with the necessary interfaces to other systems used in different development projects. According to Ericsson Corporate Basic Standards, all released products must be managed in PRIM.

8.4.5.2   GASK

The GASK is the central document and software archive within Ericsson. Ericsson Corporate Basic Standards demands the use of GASK for documentation of released products. Other tools or archives are available for use during project execution, but the GASK's security and global accessibility make it the most suitable for use in a distributed development. GASK is used in the same way as PRIM; the information is stored at the release point or other project milestones.

8.4.5.3   Documentation environment library and transfer aid

Documentation environment library and transfer aid (DELTA) is a project archive tool used in many development projects, especially for the development of the public telephone exchange (AXE) system. Originally, it was a stand-alone tool, not integrated with PRIM or GASK. DELTA has an interface to PRIM, the DELTA Access tool. DELTA Access is a Web document management tool with access to DELTA to search, edit, print, and store documents. DELTA Access can be used to fetch, browse, save to disk, and print documents in GASK.

8.4.5.4   Modification Handling System

The Modification Handling System (MHS) is an old Ericsson-built in-house tool for modification handling. This is an error reporting system that contains functions to register and track errors and many other functions. Global availability and an existing infrastructure are the main reasons for using MHS. Although the system is old and often referred to as due for replacement, it is still used, especially during and after system test. During the development phase, other tools for error reporting are used (e.g., ClearDDTS and ClearQuest). However, not all projects use these tools. For example, in the Phase 10 project CRs are manually managed.

8.4.5.5 DOORS

Requirement management and the satisfaction of demands for traceability are increasingly supported by means of tools. Within Ericsson, DOORS has demonstrated its ability to manage a large volume of requirements of a high degree of complexity. DOORS was used within the Phase 10 project. However, the requirements were still verified manually.

Other tools used alternatively for requirement management within Ericsson are eMATRIX, Requisite Pro, and Requirement Traceability Management (RTM) [2]. However, these tools are not used globally on the corporate level.

8.4.5.6 ClearCase

ClearCase is the SCM tool used on the corporate level. The multisite functionality is especially used when geographically dispersed teams develop a product. Once every night, all information is synchronized. To minimize risks and problems regarding naming, branching, and merging, a common methodology has been developed and used.

8.4.5.7 Tool integration

Prim and GASK are tightly integrated. If a document is stored in GASK, gthe information structure and document attributes are automatically updated in PRIM. MHS has an interface to PRIM. MHS does not accept error reports from products not registered in PRIM. Today, there are integrations between FrameMaker and GASK, Word and GASK, and Excel and GASK to provide storage of documents. The DELTA has an interface to DELTA Access but no other tool. The requirement tool DOORS has no integration to other tools. There is an interface between ClearCase and PRIM, with updates to the information structure in PRIM directly when changed. In some organizations, ClearCase is used as an archive with connection from PRIM (i.e., PRIM has a link to actual ClearCase installation where all documents and source codes are stored). No information is directly fetched from PRIM into ClearCase.

8.4.6 CM methods

The CM methods applied in the Phase 10 project were well defined and understood. The CM methods used within Phase 10 are shown in Figures 8.11 and 8.12. Figure 8.11 depicts schematically many baselines created during the project. Each baseline contains a report including the following documents: minutes of the CCB meetings, TRs, CRs, audit reports, and test reports. All of these documents are registered in PRIM and stored in DELTA. When the products are ready for release, all documents are stored in GASK. Each baseline always documents the four CM corner stones: configuration, quality, deviations, and decision.

The flow of a CR process is shown in Figure 8.12. The product management or a member of the project team can introduce a CR. This CR will be posted to the mailbox of the CCB and also stored in DELTA. New CRs will be

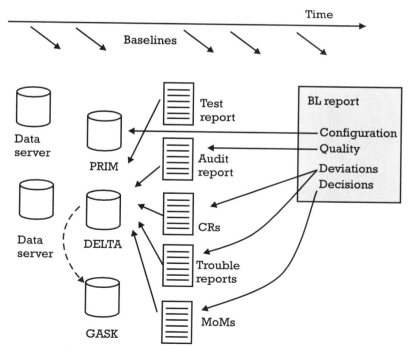

Figure 8.11 The baseline content.

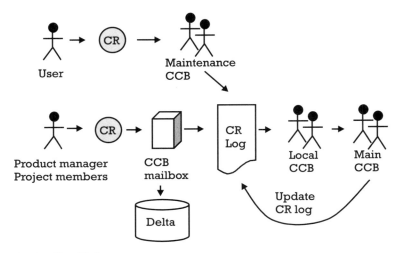

Figure 8.12   The CR flow.

added into the CR log, which contains all information related to the CR. The
CR log is presented and prepared by the local CCB. The main CCB will then
make a decision whether to include the CR in the implementation process.

These illustrations may indicate that all of the necessary methods were
available to keep the product information for the Phase 10 project accurate
and complete. However, the local tools supporting the methods were not
state of the art and not integrated with each other. This required many
manual activities, which may be a source for introducing faults.

8.4.7   Information flow

Figure 8.13 is an overall illustration of the project information flow, involving the tools needed. This is a generic picture at a very high level, intended
to depict the basic flow. In a complete flow, many other tools are involved.

Customer requirements are registered in the tool PEACE. New requirements generated either by product management or project team members
are stored and managed in the requirement tool DOORS. A main requirement specification (MRS) is written and updated from DOORS and stored in
the project archive DELTA. The MRS will be used for design for new or
changed functionality. During the design, the different archives depend on
the product developed. The design documentation is stored in the common
archive GASK. Deliveries are stored both in a local archive, and the software
for AXE archive (SWAXE). PRIM contains the product structure and is
updated with the latest information. When the design is ready for a function

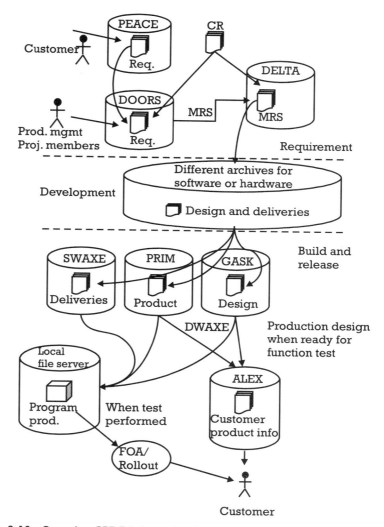

Figure 8.13 Overview PPDC information flow.

test, it will be fetched from the different archives GASK, SWAXE, and PRIM. Builds will be temporarily stored on local file servers. When a system test is performed successfully, the product is ready for FOA or deployment. Customer product information will also be produced. This information [e.g., document products for AXE (DWAXE)] is fetched from GASK, refined, and stored in the archive Active Library Explorer (ALEX) before delivery to the customer. ALEX is designed to handle electronic documentation and provides a user with the means of browsing in document libraries with a standard Web browser.

Figure 8.13 indicates the problem of establishing flow control and traceability. With many tools and many interfaces, the possibilities of accessing correct information from involved systems are reduced. Today's project management is hampered by the lack of an overall PDM system.

In the text that follows, a more detailed generic description of three major phases are presented: RM, software and hardware development, and build management. The purpose of these is to explain the backgrounds of the tools and to give the reasons for their use.

8.4.7.1 RM

The customer requirements are processed by local Ericsson companies. The local product management is responsible for discussions and agreements on contract issues. The Ericsson office then communicates with the Phase 10 project requirement coordinator in Sweden. The coordinator is a representative at the main project level of the product management in Sweden. Study of the requirements will be assigned to one or more of the three major research and development organizations. Figure 8.14 is a part of Figure 8.13, focusing on the flow of requirements from the customer to the start of the development phase.

The requirements from the customer are stored in the PEACE database at the local Ericsson Company and also in the global DOORS database at Ericsson Sweden. All requirements for all PDC systems are stored in DOORS.

All relevant requirements for the Phase 10 project were assembled in a report from DOORS designated MRS. The MRS is stored in the project archive DELTA. The requirements are controlled in a baseline (so-called requirement baseline) and changes are managed with CRs. However, as the different

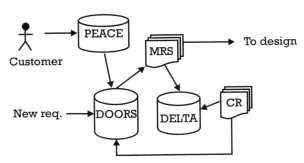

Figure 8.14   The requirement flow in the product specification phase.

requirements are described in an ordinary document and stored in the project archive (DELTA), it is possible to update the document without issuing a CR. Such changes will not be visible in the requirement baseline. The requirement baseline and the CRs are managed manually without tool support.

A number of improvements in the process can be made. For example it should not be possible for project team members to update requests without writing a CR first and following the CR procedure. CRs should be visible together with their corresponding requirement. Furthermore, requirements should be linked or tagged down to test specifications for full traceability of each requirement in the whole system. The requirement baseline should be the only source of requirement information.

8.4.7.2 Software and hardware development

Information flow of software and hardware development is shown in Figure 8.15. The requirements phase of the project is common for software and hardware development. The software development phase is, however, separated from the hardware development process. The software product is developed on the basis of the input from the requirements specification and product specification process stored in DELTA. The software produced during software design is stored in different archives depending on the design organization and product (e.g., ClearCase or local archives). Various software-programming languages are used. AXEs use the internal Ericsson language PLEX. The PLEX language has been used since the 1970s, and the supporting tools have been modernized during the following years. Traditionally, all source code has been stored in GASK. Modern languages, such as C++ and Java, are also used within software development in Ericsson. In some organizations, code is generated directly from UML. In recent years,

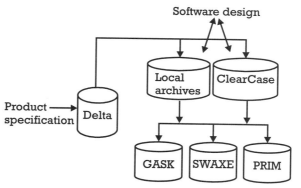

Figure 8.15 Information flow for software and hardware development.

the use of ClearCase for software configuration control has expanded. When the design is ready, the code is archived in an approved archive (i.e., GASK for non-PLEX language and SWAXE for PLEX language). All documents written during software development are archived in local archives. All product documents are stored in GASK. Metadata and files are stored in different archives in different locations. This emphasizes the need for an integrated environment.

Hardware development is much more mature with respect to common methodology and tools in comparison with software. Usually, system studies on functional block level identify the need for a new or updated hardware product. The study specifies the requirements and the specification of the hardware units. The prototype is designed in a CAD environment. When function tests have been performed, the realization phase begins. A hardware design environment helps to adapt layouts to approved standardized boards. The planning of production begins at an early stage in a development project. If needed, the printed board assembly (PBA) is manufactured in a preseries production for testing properties and function. A trial production run is then performed to obtain measurements of the costs and time of common manufacturing. These measurements are compared with the stipulated requirements, and, if acceptable, the production unit approves the product as ready for production. Information prepared for the TTC process is exported from PRIM and GASK to a global order inventory invoicing system (GOLF) database. GOLF is an order system used for the management and administration of customer sales orders. It helps untangle the order management problems from order processing through invoicing, purchase administration, and stock reporting. GOLF keeps track of stock movements, incoming orders, order adjustment, order stock, and invoicing.

Figure 8.16 shows the overall flow for hardware design. Mechanical parts and cables have been traditionally considered within Ericsson as non-system-dependent products. Most often, the PBA and software are structured into function blocks defining the needed software or hardware modules for a certain function. Mechanical parts, cables, batteries, power supply, and cross connectors are structured in a separate structure or separate branches of the functional structure.

While the hardware development process is rather smooth, several things can be improved. For example, there is a lack of traceability of requirements from the top level. Further decomposition of functions is not supported from CM. A function cannot be unverified as a CI (i.e., it is not possible to check out and check in a function). Finally SCM-PDM integration is missing. To further support the development environment,

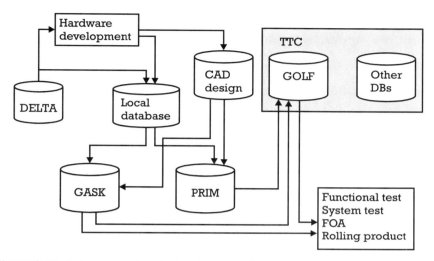

Figure 8.16 Information flow for hardware design.

Ericsson focused on use of the PDM system Metaphase. Also, Ericsson has initiated a project to obtain integration between Metaphase and ClearCase.

8.4.7.3 Build and test management

The build process is centralized. During the later stages of development, all relevant information is collected at one site where the system is built (and some basic tests are performed). This build is then distributed to all subprojects, where it is tested and further developed. In detail, this process is much more complex. When development is completed, the software is sent to a test CM subproject. The test CM prepares a test bed (dump) for other subproject testing. The project deliverables are stored in SWAXE (the PLEX software) and in GASK (software written in C++). Function tests can be started when the test bed is available. The software is also delivered to the subproject SIT, in which the AXE system is integrated with the packet data part. From this phase, all errors are reported as trouble reports in the MHS, a common tool within the Ericsson group worldwide. Customer product information documents are fetched by DWAXE from the archives Delta and GASK. The documents are updated and stored in the archive ALEX. When products are released and documents are approved, all customer product information documents (for operation and maintenance) are translated into the languages of foreign customers. The customer orders hardware directly via the GOLF system. Information flow of the entire build and test process is shown in Figure 8.17.

When function test is finalized, the system test begins. When the system test is finalized, the system is ready to be sent to the FOA and deployment project. The most important system here is, once again, the error report system MHS.

As seen from the figure, the build procedure has a rather complex information flow. Also, there are many manual procedures. For example, it is not possible to perform a fully automatic daily build of changed products or their parts. Neither it is possible to automatically create reports of the delivery (e.g., the content, the included solved TRs that are corrected, known errors, the included requirements, and the list of new features). The test environment still lacks automated tests.

8.4.8 Conclusion

In the Phase 10 project, there was a good understanding of the clearly described PLC and the configuration methods were up to date and competitive. The basic CM methods and the necessary "know how" and "know why" were available. This provided promising prerequisites for a successful process implementation by using PDM and SCM tools in an

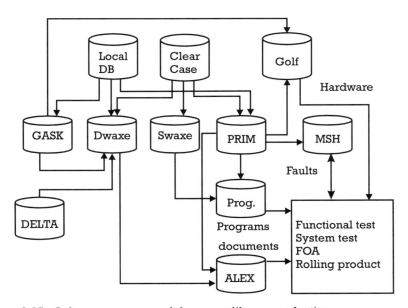

Figure 8.17 Software program and document library production.

integrated environment. However, the total number of tools in combination with their poor interoperability interfaces made the work dependent on manual procedures. The major comments of the project CM manager are related to the lack of adequate tool support. Ericsson is making efforts to change this environment and has projects ongoing to introduce the PDM system Metaphase integrated with ClearCase.

We can summarize the conclusion with several comments:

- Ericsson Corporate Basic Standards provided a good basis for PDM.
- The global systems (PRIM, GASK, and MHS) were of great assistance in this distributed development project, especially during and after system test.
- SCM was well implemented.
- The life cycle model was clearly identified.

In addition to these positive comments, there is obvious place for improvements:

- Far too many of the systems involved were without interfaces and interoperability.
- Too much manual work was required, because of the absence of PDM for the described flow and because PRIM and GASK are old tools soon to be phased out.
- In general, CM tool support for all phases up to system test was weak.
- Generic CM support suffered from the lack of tools linking CRs to baselines.

The importance of supporting the entire PLC is discussed in Chapter 5. Issues about interfaces and interoperability between tools are can be found in Chapter 6.

8.5 Ericsson Mobile Communications AB

Ericsson Mobile Communications AB develops and manufactures mobile phones (so-called terminals). The development is geographically distributed at several sites in the world. Engineering functions such as software, mechanical, and hardware engineering are mirrored at all sites (e.g., in Lund, Sweden, in which the case is studied). The case studies development of PDM support in this organization.

8.5.1 PDM tools

Different development groups use their own specialized PDM tools, often integrated with the development environment, to manage their local development. They are responsible for making available the necessary support in terms of processes and tools. Sometimes this is achieved by means of global solutions used in common with many groups; sometimes it requires home-made solutions. For example, the electronics group uses systems managing their components in terms of CAD data and data about purchase and contractors; the mechanical group has a system for managing revisions of CAD files; the software group uses ClearCase to manage revisions and releases of source code.

Within Ericsson Mobile Communication, several global solutions exist for many domains and phases in the PLC (e.g., RM support). The support systems for overall BOM control towards factory are PRIM, GASK, ESTER, and others. PRIM is the product and document register for the Ericsson group. The BOM for the product and certain other important information such as the relations between the product revision and document version, frozen product revisions, and PLC status are registered in PRIM. PRIM is internally reachable worldwide. GASK is the common Ericsson group archive, internally reachable worldwide. ESTER is the tool for handling of exemption requests. The tool can only be used for nonconforming products registered in PRIM. The use of the tool is compulsory for products to be delivered outside Ericsson with nonconformity, but the tool can also be used for all products, projects, and operations if the product number is registered in PRIM.

8.5.1.1 Current support

PRIM and GASK are used after production release. PRIM is used mainly for the view as designed and SAP R/3 is used for as manufactured (see Figure 8.18). None of these systems are used as much as intended during the early development phase. According to the PDM group at Ericsson Mobile Communication, this is unfortunate. More effective use of these tools, particularly during development, would be of benefit to all parts. Instead, local tools are used and registration in global tools is performed late in the development process. Late registration can cause problems with unique identities of products and documents (e.g., an identity used for one product but not registered can be allocated to and used by others for another product, and much administrative work is necessary to correct this situation).

Ad hoc use of PRIM and GASK results in limited control of versions and their contents. When the product is released, all production documents

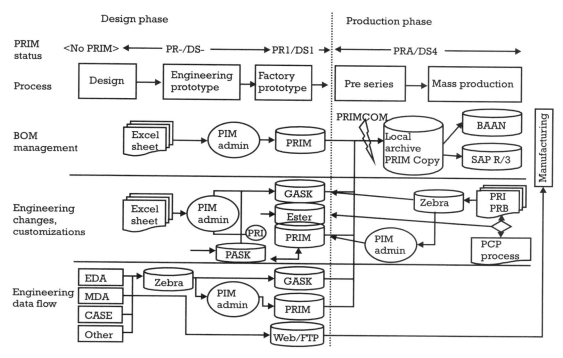

Figure 8.18 Information flow and tools used in the design and manufacturing processes. The following abbreviations are used: Design status (DS), production ready status (PR), design just started (DS-/PR-), ready for preproduction (PR1/DS1), product test doc (PRA/DS4), ready to be sold (PRA), and product revision information (PRI).

and related information are stored in PRIM and GASK, but during earlier phases, before production and to some extent also for work done between releases, this information is often only available locally. Other design data is not stored in PRIM and GASK. The project manager thus has a considerable responsibility to retrieve and send the correct information to the producers and contractors, especially for early prototypes, before correct revisions are registered in PRIM.

PRIM was primarily designed for use in the management of the production of large and complex products such as AXE switches, rather than mobile phones. Complex and rigid rules define the process (e.g., how to release the product, which requires much manual administration and control). These rules also require much of the project manager and make the process too slow to cope with the short development cycles used. It can also be hard for the developers to see what is in it for them, and therefore they do not use them, even though the truth may be that they have gained a great deal using the tools. Another reason for not using the tools is the unfriendliness of the user interface.

An important functionality of a PDM tool is to provide awareness of the progress of a project to all developers and managers. This is best achieved if documents are checked in frequently and made accessible to others concerned. It is thus important to be able to check in work in progress, making it clear at the same time that it is in an unfinished state. This functionality has not been utilized in the process.

8.5.1.2 Improvements in progress

TTM Engineering Platforms at Ericsson Mobile Communication were, at the time of writing, developing a new graphical Web-based user interface on top of Metaphase, designated metaDoc. metaDoc is actually built on top of Collaborative Data Management (CDM), which is an Ericsson-specific layer on top of Metaphase supporting corporate basic standards (e.g., the rules mentioned earlier and all unique identification rules). The PDM architecture is shown in Figure 8.19. CDM is also under development, and only parts of the final functionality are currently provided. In addition to metaDoc, other interfaces are built or are planned to be built upon CDM (for example, an interface to Unigraphics).

The introduction of metaDoc is developed in two phases. In the first phase, metaDoc manages nonproduct documents only (e.g., meeting protocols and general specifications). In the second phase, the metaDoc will include building support for BOM and product documents management.

8.5.1.3 Future plans

The next phase of the PDM program has been initiated and is supposed to support BOM control. It also includes a reimplementation of CDM in order to make the rules less complex and easier to understand and use (i.e., adapt

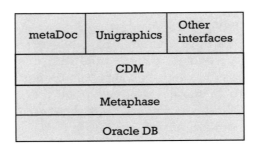

Figure 8.19   PDM tool architecture.

the BOM management to the short development cycles used). Ericsson Mobile Communication actually does not want to develop tools by themselves. Initiatives such as metaDoc are taken only because they could not find something similar at the market. If a vendor provides an adequate interface, they will probably use that instead. It would still be beneficial to integrate the overall PDM tool with the local tools used within each group. There are ongoing tests of an interface between Metaphase and Unigraphics, and, as described in Section 6.4, there is also work on interfaces between ClearCase and both Metaphase and eMatrix. These integrations assume continued use of PRIM in collaboration with other PDM tools.

8.5.2 Product modeling

Ericsson Mobile Communication uses two different ways to model their products: complete product structure, and product (rule) engine. Often, a lot of different products and product variants must be managed, even though only some of them finally reach the market. To create one product tree for each product would be ineffective, so instead a product engine produces the products, as depicted in Figure 8.20. A "super BOM" contains all components that might be constituents in a product configuration. The product engine then defines a lot of rules of how to combine these components to build legal products. Some rules define which components technically can work together, while some rules are more market driven (for example, a color may be reserved for a specific product). The rules do not

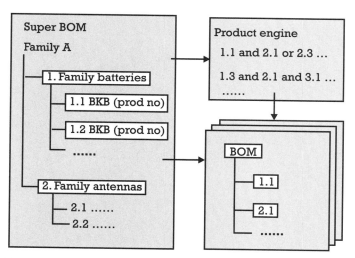

Figure 8.20 Modeling the products by rules describing the products.

define all possible configurations but only those that might be interesting because of different reasons. By adding rules to the engine, it is possible to test new products. However, it is more complex to manage rules than to manage relations.

8.5.3 Traceability

All released products are registered in PRIM (i.e., the entire product structure is registered). Strictly bound configurations are not used, as this had resulted in too many versions, especially on the top level (i.e., the release number of the product does not exactly specify the revision number of all of its components). Full traceability is instead achieved through a generic configuration plus a five-letter code that really specifies its contents. The main reason not to use bound configurations is the large amount of manual administrative work they require in PRIM. Another reason is the need to be able to modify the product without changing its revision number. Customers are sensitive to new revisions, and it is hard to sell a product with an old revision number, irrespective of what the difference to the latest revision really is. The drawback of using generic configurations instead of bound configurations is lack of full traceability. Sometimes the only way to find the correct revision (e.g., to fix a bug) is to follow product revision information (PRI). A PRI describes the changes from one product revision to next product revision. The document is mainly used during the manufacturing phase to upgrade the hardware, as stated in the PRI.

8.5.4 Change management

There is no tool support for global change management. The software group has developed a tool called Fido, which supports the entire CR process and bug tracking. This tool makes it easier to find all products affected by a CR. A bug reported in one product may also exist in other products (e.g., a bug in a revision of a platform common for many products), and the CR created due to the bug therefore lists all affected products. Additionally those responsible for these products are informed through the tool. Fido is also integrated with the SCM tool used and is part of the freezing process of releases.

8.5.5 Conclusion

Ericsson Mobile Communications AB develops and produces many versions and variants of products, and the traceability of any kind is very important.

Particular requirements require particular solutions in the development and integration process. This is the reason that the company has its special rules, procedures, and tools in addition to general and standard support from the corporation. The case study shows that in large organizations, very often the general support of the corporation level is insufficient, but local organizations need adjustments or other types of support that are specific for them. Further, the case emphasizes that there is a need for a permanent improvement of the support. This improvement will usually be incremental, acquiring the existing process into the new one.

The important need for support during the software development phase is elaborated in Chapter 3. A comparison of SCM and PDM functionality is made in Chapter 4. Issues regarding the deployment of new tools or functionality are discussed in Chapter 7.

8.6 ABB Automation Technology Products

ABB is a leader in the field of power and automation technologies that enable utility and industrial customers to improve their performance while lowering environmental impact. The power technologies division serves industrial and commercial customers and electric, gas, and water utilities with a broad range of products, services, and applications for power transmission and distribution. The automation technology products division serves customers in the automotive, chemicals, manufacturing, marine, and many other industries. The technology is based on the industrial information technology concept, which integrates diverse automation and information technologies in real time.

ABB Automation Technology Products consists of a number of units that develop different products for industrial automation (e.g., industrial robots, automation control, operation, and information systems used in a wide range of industrial processes from very small control systems to large plant automation and information systems).

This case study contains a brief description of the PDM and SCM tools used in the ABB Automation Technology Products unit in Malmö, Sweden (referred to as ABB Malmö in the following). ABB Malmö has recently developed the ABB Common Controller used for data acquisition in different processes and for control of these processes. In addition to this new product, the unit has developed and maintains several families of similar products, such as Controller 800M, Controler 800C, I/O 800, and I/O S200.

8.6.1 Data management tools

ABB Malmö previously made use of a system designated construction base, which provides system developers with a degree of support during the production phase. This tool, now obsolete, stored information about the system-building process. It has now been superseded by several tools, both commercial and in-house tools, which together constitute an information, software, and product data management system. The most important of the tools used currently are:

- *Documentum.* Documentum [3] is a commercial document management tool used as a central documentation and product structure archive. (For more about document management tools, see Chapter 11.) Documentum supports distributed management based on a client/server concept. All information about all relevant products, both software and hardware, is stored at a central server accessed via the Internet.

- *Capri.* Capri is a program package developed by ABB, used as a plug-in for Documentum for simpler management of the product structure within the product information model implemented in Documentum. It includes a graphical user interface and procedures for automatic creation of certain documents. Capri is used by technical product and project managers.

- *ABB Library.* This is a structure of a particular data in Documentum, an internally developed tool package that provides views of this structure. The data includes additional information about the products and components (e.g., different manuals and product guides).

- *SAP R/3.* SAP R/3 [4] is a commercial ERP tool. ERP tools include much of the functionality present in PDM or other document management tools. SAP R/3, however, focuses on the commercial aspects of the entire PLC rather than on the development and production phases. ABB uses SAP R/3 for storage of product and manufacturing data, such as information about subcontractors, inventories, and prices. Information about a particular product is transferred from Documentum when the product is released.

- *Visual SourceSafe (VSS).* VSS is a commercial SCM tool (see Chapter 10) used in the development and maintenance of software products. Documents related to the software development process, function specifications, test specifications, and implementation proposals are also saved in a VSS repository. Later, when the product is released, some of these documents can be exported to Documentum.

▸ *PVCS Tracker.* PVCS Tracker is a commercial tool for error handling, change proposals, and issue management.

The relationships between the tools are shown in Figure 8.21.

Today, most of the relevant information is transferred between tools more or less manually. The company is aware that a more automatic transfer would provide more effective support during development cycles, and the overall process would be shortened. Some new tools are being evaluated, and there are certain ongoing activities in which the possibility of a more efficient use of existing tools is under investigation.

8.6.2   Product structure

To manage products, ABB Malmö identifies a product structure that describes realized products. All aspects and parts of the entire product are

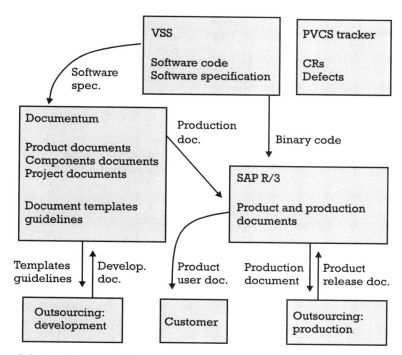

Figure 8.21   Tools supporting product and document management.

included, including product documentation, wrapping, and the product itself, whether realized in hardware or software, outsourced or developed in-house. A product structure includes not only a particular product version, but may contain many optional nodes [see Figure 8.22(a)]. This may be because the volume of production determines when firmware is to be loaded—and by whom—or whether a specific functionality should be realized in hardware or software. Firmware is low-level software loaded on a circuit board (e.g., the software implementing the protocol on an input/output board). The same hardware can be loaded with different firmware, implementing different protocols. The volume of production of a product,

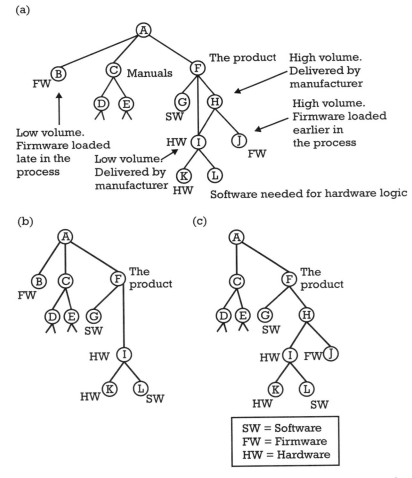

Figure 8.22 Example of a product structure: (a) product structure, (b) product low volume, and (c) product high volume.

which can vary between more than 10,000 per year and 100 per year, affects the optimal product structure. A central processing unit part for several system families may have a generic hardware. The production volume determines to a degree when the firmware is to be loaded into the central processing unit hardware. For a low volume, the firmware is loaded late, at the time of packaging or even by the customer [Figure 8.22(b)]. With a high volume, the firmware is loaded early, often by the manufacturer [Figure 8.22(c)]. This indicates the importance of a flexible product structure.

When a product is to be manufactured, a tree of concrete nodes, referred to as a part list, is specified. It is important to define unambiguously the constituent parts of a product. Each node designated an article or part can be realized in different ways: developed in-house, outsourced, or bought as COTS. Irrespective of its origins, it always has an article number. Figure 8.23 depicts an example of an article and of what it consists (in this case four parts—articles). Each part can, in turn, be complex and can consist of articles itself.

Each part has an article number of its own—down to a certain level. ABB has full traceability down to the manufacturer of a circuit board. (Only approved manufacturers are used by ABB and specified in the SAP/R3.) Some companies have traceability down to the batch number of the circuits used. The "same" hardware has the same part number, irrespective of manufacturer. Thus, it is impossible, in the product structure and in the BOM, to see who manufactured. For example, a resistor (several alternatives may be specified in the SAP/ R3) on a CPU card.

8.6.3 Conclusion

Product data management at ABB Malmö is typical of that of many industrial enterprises. It is often a result of an organic and continuous improvement of process support. A complete support is built from several tools, often of different generations and based on different technologies. Interoperability and process efficiency is achieved by additional, often ad-hoc, building tools and import/export utilities and by specification of rules

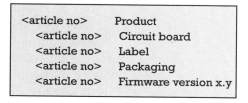

Figure 8.23 An example of an article and its constituent parts.

that permit a semiautomatic information flow. In an ideal case, a few well-integrated tools would be used. However in reality, it is often impossible to achieve as such a migration to new tools, as it can be prohibitively expensive.

Product structures and how they are supported in PDM is explained in Chapter 2. The importance of tool integration and how this could be performed successfully is discussed in Chapter 6.

8.7   SaabTech Electronics AB

The Saab Group develops, manufactures, and supplies advanced products and services for the defense market and commercial markets. Saab's operations are organized in six business units, covering modern defense information technologies, command and control systems, military and commercial aircraft, advanced technical support and services, missiles, space equipment, and aviation services [5].

SaabTech Electronics AB (formerly CelsiusTech Electronics) is a business unit within Saab that develops and manufactures advanced products within the areas of electronic warfare, optronics, and sensors. SaabTech Electronics AB consists of three divisions: optronics, electronic warfare, and sensors. The optronics division is the supplier of advanced optical and optronics sights, chiefly various types of missile and weapon sights. The electronic warfare division is a supplier of electronic warfare equipment, such as advanced radar warning systems and self-protection countermeasures. The sensors division is engaged in radar, microwave applications antennas, signal and image processing, and stealth technology.

This case study describes briefly its currently-used PDM system, developed in-house, and the requirements of the system by which it is to be superseded. The new system is an example of a global PDM system integrated with all the local systems used throughout the company.

8.7.1   The central article and structure register PDM system

The central article and structure (CAS) register system is an in-house PDM system, used for the administration of products. The development of CAS began in the mid 1980s. CAS is the company's main register for articles and structures. Every item, from small components to entire products, is identified by articles. The system contains information about articles, such as article numbers, article structures, type list (a list with approved articles that may be used under current requirements), and a manufacturer and customer register.

All articles and their structures are registered in CAS. The information is then distributed from CAS to adjacent tools [e.g., to the company's Manufacturing and Planning System (MPS)]. Most articles have references (relationships) to the documents describing the articles. A number of different reports and schedules are generated from CAS (e.g., part lists).

8.7.1.1 Environment, system, and authority

CAS is implemented on a VAX/VMS operating system and uses the VAX Database Management System (DBMS) database. The system was developed to permit concurrent usage. CAS has its own access management system, making it possible to control access to different functions for each user. To register data in the system, the user needs a user account on the VAX computer with access rights to enter or update the information in CAS. Access to CAS can be obtained via a terminal or via the company's intranet.

8.7.1.2 CAS architecture and functions

The CAS system is divided into five different subsystems (see Figure 8.24), CAS Register (CASR), CAS Interface (CASF), CAS Lists (CASL), CAS Production (CASP), and a set of functions for transfer of data to other systems:

- *CASR.* Updating and registration of data in CAS is primarily performed in CASR. CASR contains functionality to maintain articles, part lists, type lists, customers, and manufacturers.

- *CASP.* Certain information, exclusively used by the production department, is registered by CASP.

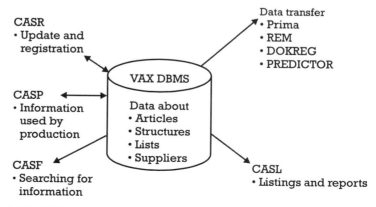

Figure 8.24 CAS system functions.

▸ *CASF.* CASF is used to search for information (e.g., metadata and free text). A separate database has been created to provide good performance for free text search and to reduce the load on the global company database. This copy of the database is updated once a week from the main CAS database. CASF has two user interfaces: HTML and VT100. The HTML interface on the company's intranet is used by those only reading information.

▸ *CASL.* CASL incorporates functions for printing different lists and reports (e.g., document lists, component lists, and structure lists).

▸ *Data transfer subsystem.* CAS is the company's master system for article metadata (i.e., data created, updated, and managed in CAS). Data is transferred to the following systems:

1. Prima—the company MPS-system;
2. VeriBest—electronic CAD (ECAD) development;
3. REM—traceability system for delivered systems and spare parts;
4. PREDICTOR—program for reliability calculations;
5. DOKREG—register for documents.

8.7.2   The new PDM system

There is now a significant need to replace CAS with a new generation of capabilities for product data management, designated CAS II. One reason is that, within the near future, it will become difficult to provide the resources to maintain the existing CAS, in particular, the platform on which CAS is running. There are also requirements for additional functionality and a more user-friendly interface. To provide the expanded functionality and improved availability, the company has concluded that it would be more effective to develop a completely new system than to upgrade the existing one.

CAS II will be developed in a research and development project in collaboration with two other companies and will be based on the commercial PDM tool, Metaphase Foundation from EDS [6]. The use of CAS II will begin within smaller groups and then be gradually extended throughout the entire organization and all products.

8.7.2.1   System architecture

Initially, CAS II will provide the functionality of the existing CAS, but subsequently, as a central PDM system, it will constitute an integrated system (including routines, rules, and tools) that will establish and maintain the product configuration during its entire life cycle (i.e., the configuration of all product data needed to describe the product, detailed enough for its manufacture, use, administration, and further development). This product configuration and the product data may need to be managed in many different development environments and their corresponding information technology support tools. Such development environments are, for example, electronics, mechanics, software, and user and customer documentation.

The system architecture was designed on the basis of experience from the PDM/CM area at the company during 1980–2000, together with trends on the market, as depicted in Figure 8.25.

As seen in Figure 8.25, the CAS II is an umbrella tool integrated with all archives, development environments, integrated logistic support (ILS), and production tools. It should provide support for managing the total product configuration, including the management of relationships between different parts of the product during its entire life cycle. It will be necessary to control identity and versions of articles centrally.

8.7.2.2   Cooperation of the main system and local tools

The main system will cooperate with local tools on an appropriate level for each type of activity. An important requirement is the storage and transfer of data in standardized formats. A further major requirement is the ability to store data safely for a long period (20 to 30 years) relying on well-established and stable standards. All articles and related data needed during the product development process are created and processed by other tools. When a new version of an article is released, the development result will be

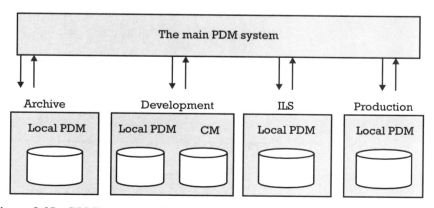

Figure 8.25   CAS II system architecture.

managed in the main PDM system, either directly or by references. However, this is often only a subset of all of the information managed in the local IT system.

8.7.2.3   Supporting the generic PLC

The company's generic life cycle model is shown in Figure 8.26. According to this model, the project manager decides which functional and physical articles should be under CM, how the structure shall be designed, and which documents should be included in the baselines. The PDM system will support the process of obtaining product configurations by establishing relationships between versions of articles, documentation, and changes during the entire life cycle.

In order to support this concept, the main PDM system should provide support for:

- Document management—support for the creation, identification, registration, archiving, presentation, searching for, and reuse of documents. The system should also support different workflows (e.g., reviewing and approval and release).

- Article management—support for the creation, identification, registration, presentation, searching for, reuse, connection of information, and structure management.

- Configuration management—support for the identification, control, review, and status accounting of managed objects in the PDM system.

- Change control, including:

  1. Support for the creation and management of documents from change proposal to approved change orders;
  2. Workflows for review, approval, and release;
  3. Status accounting (e.g., a change proposal can be in one of the states, created, approved, or implemented).

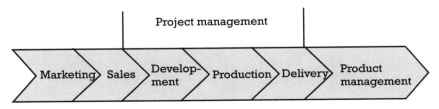

Figure 8.26   Life cycle model.

▸ Workflow—support for the creation and change of processes, or work-flows (e.g., the document release process).

▸ Program management, or WBS support for the relationship of a WBS activity to an object managed by the PDM system. This enables status accounting of documents.

Furthermore, it should also be possible to integrate the PDM system with other information technology systems by efficient and standardized interfaces.

When integrating with the local information technology systems, three different types of local information technology systems can be identified:

▸ Embedded PDM/CM systems [e.g., UG/manager for managing mechanical CAD (MCAD) data developed in Unigraphics];

▸ Local CM support (e.g., the archive Dokreg and CVS for software management);

▸ Manual CM support (e.g., manual naming of directory structures and files in the NT environment, say for documents created in Microsoft Office).

Export and import of information, both between two internal information technology systems and between information technology systems and external PDM systems, should be distributed through the main PDM system whenever possible. The information format used can be either application dependent or application independent. In most cases, it should be application independent.

Support for CM and change management is fundamental and should be implemented for all phases in the company's life cycle model. For the initial phases, marketing and sales, the primary need for support is in document management. In succeeding phases, such as project management, development, production, delivery, and maintenance, the main needs for support will be, for example, article and structure management.

8.7.2.4   Gradual completion of the product structure

The product structure is gradually built up in the main PDM system (see Figure 8.27). During the initial phase of the product development process, the main activity is to create requirement documents defining a functional structure managed in the main PDM system. The system design and associated documents are reviewed, approved, and established following the

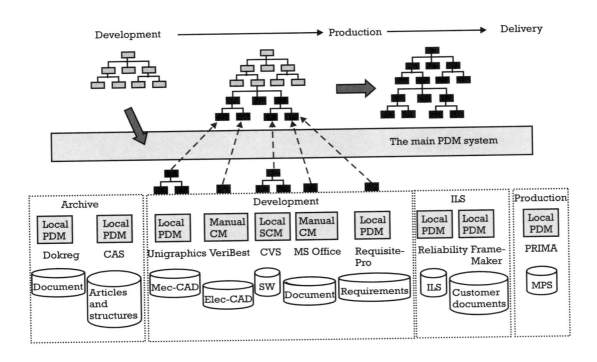

Figure 8.27 Overall system architecture and its relationship to the development phase during the product development process.

workflow supported in the main PDM system. In the succeeding phases, the system design is realized in the relevant local development environments. The project manager creates WBS activities, which refer to the articles in the functional structure managed by the main PDM system. When the realization is finished and realization structures have been developed in the local environments, these are released (exported) to the main PDM system, gradually building up the total product structure. This is done latest, at the establishment of a formal version in the local information technology system. Examination/approval/establishment is performed with the help of the workflow in the main PDM system.

In preparation for manufacture, all the required information is collected in the main PDM system and transferred to the current MPS system. Subsequently, in all succeeding phases, the individual articles will be registered and updated in the main PDM system. During the product maintenance phase, all necessary information for each product or article, including the serial number, will be found in the main PDM system. When larger modifications or upgrades of existing products are performed, a new project is begun and proceeds through the development process. Obsolete systems are phased out after a formal decision.

8.7.3 Conclusion

SaabTech Electronics AB is in a period of transition between two generations of PDM systems. In the same way as many other large companies, the company has an established PDM process but is in a situation in which its technology is aging and there are increasing demands for new PDM tools based on emergent technology. In this transition period, the company strategy is to retain the present system but to improve its efficiency by introducing new tools and improving the interoperability between the tools. Although the use of a commercial PDM system has been decided on, much effort will be required to adjust it to the existing process and to integrate the system with other tools.

The evaluation and deployment of new tools was discussed in Chapter 7. Tool interoperability and integration was further analyzed in Chapter 6.

8.8 Summary

The case studies have shown a large diversity in requirements, in current states and future goals related to support of PLCs. There are some common characteristics, though, which might indicate that there are some current states and general trends in this area.

First of all, we can see that all companies are in a dynamic state. Most of them have a solution, but it is not completely satisfactory, and there are plans or ongoing activities for improvements. Many companies still have their own solutions with internally built tools. These tools are becoming obsolete due to various reasons, but mostly due to:

- Old technologies that have difficulties coping with the new tools used in the development process;
- Moving to a distributed development, which requires new methods and tool support for intercommunication and increased awareness of parallel processes;
- Time-to-market requirements, which in turn demand more efficient and more automated processes;

‣ Increased competition and demands for better contacts with customers, which requires better information access regularly implemented through the Web.

A second common remark is the complexity of the development process and information flow. Usually, several tens of tools are part in the process, and very often it is the humans who are the integrators of the information. This, in many cases, unnecessary complexity is often a result of organic increase of the company or the result of merges between companies. In many companies, there are clear needs for simplifying and improving the processes.

The improvement process (e.g., the process to improve the product development process) is of a different nature than the process for product development itself. While development of the products is very much related to the market, and the new products are clearly distinguished from the previous versions or variants, the improvement processes are of more continuous nature with less strict plans and less precise goals. The main activities in the improvement processes are related to integration—of data and of applications. The improvement processes are even more complicated due to the problems of integrating internal tools, usually built upon an old technology, and commercial tools that use new technologies. For this reason, integration requires significant effort and often expertise from the tool providers. Many modern PDM tools provide means for integration based on client-server and multitier architecture, Web, middleware, and component-based technology. However, these technologies cannot be easily integrated with monolithic applications built on old platforms.

While there is a clear trend toward integration of PDM tools with other tools used in the development process, PDM-SCM integration is still not the main issue of the improvement processes. Software companies use SCM tools as their main support for managing source code and documentation. In addition to SCM, many companies use a document management system or ERP systems. For the hardware-oriented companies, the software question is rapidly becoming more important, but many companies are in the process of or learning how to manage software. PDM-SCM integration is an increasing issue, which probably will dominate in the near future.

The companies focus on the processes rather than on the tools supporting these processes. While the processes are fairly constant, tools are changed more often. This approach has clear advantages, even if it includes risks of introducing a mismatch between tools and processes. There is also a risk that the processes do not follow the trends being supported by modern tools.

References

[1] Mentor Graphics Corporation, www.mentor.com/corp_info, 2003.

[2] Integrated Chipware, Inc., www.chipware.com, 2003.

[3] Documentum, www.documentum.com, 2003.

[4] SAP R/3, www.sap.com, 2003.

[5] The SABB Group, www.saab.se, 2003.

[6] EDS PLM Solution, www.eds.com, 2003.

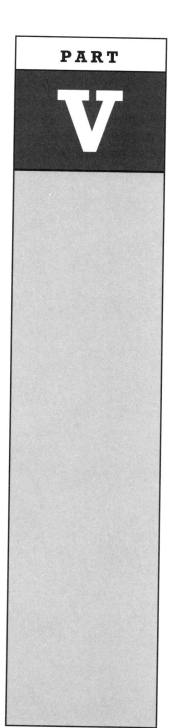

PART

V

Tools and Standards Survey

CHAPTER

9

Contents

A survey of PDM tools

Competition creates better products, alliances create better companies.
—Brian Graham

Commercial PDM systems have been on the market since the middle of the 1980s. Many different systems with a wide range of functionalities and sizes are available today. A common characteristic of these tools is the complexity and constant changes in technologies and business. In their marketing, most of the producers of PDM systems do not refer directly to the PDM systems; rather, they focus on the support of PLC of all of the activities of an enterprise. This support is classified as PLM, customer relationship management (CRM), supply chain management, and ERP [1, 2]. PLM is an approach to the management of the creation and dissemination of engineering data throughout the extended enterprise. According to this definition, PLM is very similar to PDM. The difference is the emphasis on processes within PLM, with PDM originally focused on product data. ERP systems manage such enterprise operations as contract management, production, procurement, cost accounting, and finance. This flow of information concentrates on logistics data associated with parts (e.g., schedules, quantities, quality, and costs) [3]. CRM focuses on the customer interface and all related activities, such as marketing management, human resource management, and production management. Supply chain management is a process for managing all materials,

249

components, and finished products, and in general the flow of information between customers and suppliers. It supports sales, purchasing, production, and delivery activities. PDM is often identified as a support for the underlying structure and processes and as an instrument for integration of different tools and processes, as shown in Figure 9.1.

Large vendors usually cover all of these areas with their own line of products, of which PDM is only one. Some vendors concentrate their support on PDM and on a particular tool (e.g., a CAD/CAM tool). Integration capabilities are an important factor in this type of system and very often modern integration technologies are used. Many vendors also focus on particular tools. These can be large ERP tools, particular tools such as change management tools, supply chain tools, or tools used in particular domains. It is worth mentioning that many vendors traditionally related to a particular domain show a strong tendency to also cover other areas of the PLC. For example, some ERP tools (such as SAP R/3) may include functions for supply change management, project management, change management, and similar.

This chapter gives a short overview of certain PDM tools, with emphasis on their integration capabilities. PDM resources on the Internet, which provide information relating to PDM tools and tools from associated areas, are listed in Section 9.1. A list of PDM tools is presented in Section 9.3 at the end of this chapter.

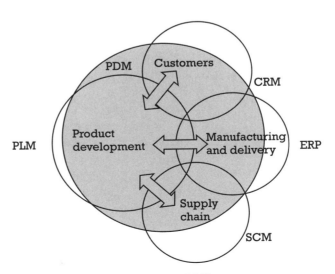

Figure 9.1 Different management tools and PDM systems.

9.1 PDM resources on the Internet

9.1.1 Product Data Management Information Center

The Product Data Management Information Center (PDMIC) [2, 3] is an organization assembling relevant information and assisting in the development and evolution of the PDM industry. The ambition of PDMIC is to concentrate all information relating to PDM in one place. This includes information about the latest PDM products and technologies and about trends in PDM and related domains. It contains many articles, both introductory and advanced, within the PDM domain.

9.1.2 John Stark Associates

The John Stark Associates Company [4] makes available a number of references to introductions to PDM, PDM frequently asked questions (FAQs), PDM implementations, PDM performance reviews, PDM systems, and PDM publications. The Web page also includes references to PLM, CAD management, collaborative product development, collaborative engineering, product development knowledge management, and similar. The company publishes an electronic publication, *2PLM e-zine*, every 2 weeks with the latest news related to all of these areas.

9.1.3 CIMdata

CIMdata [5] is a company providing PLM consultation and program support, research, and education for both industrial organizations and suppliers of technologies. The CIMdata Web page includes references to many articles, PDM and PLM vendors, standards, and similar. It also contains a list of interesting magazines and periodicals. CIMdata also organizes conferences in the United States and Europe on topics related to PDM.

9.1.4 CADCAMnet

Although the main focus of this resource is on the CAD/CAM domain, CADDAMnet [6] includes a PDM page with many articles of current interest.

9.2   PDM systems

Four of the larger PDM systems are presented here in more detail, in order to give an overview of the functionality such systems offer. Besides those presented (MatrixOne, TeamCenter, Windchill, and ENOVIA), SAP R/3 (which is classified as a typical ERP system) is also among the larger players on the PDM system market.

9.2.1   MatrixOne

MatrixOne [7] is a set of tools supporting collaborative product development. It is also known under the name eMatrix. eMatrix began as a simple and easy-to-customize PDM toolbox, but has grown considerably. The eMatrix system consists of a common platform and a set of application modules: a system administration tool, a data modeling tool, Web collaboration servers, and interfaces. The data model can easily be redefined with a menu-based tool supplied with the product. This feature makes it possible to adapt the product to a company's needs, and the customers can do part of this job themselves. However, the system configuration and adaptation process can consume time and effort, as it often takes more time to determine what the needs are than it takes to configure and customize the system. Therefore, eMatrix offers the *value chain portfolio*, which includes several business-oriented applications ready for use together with the system.

The following products are included in the value chain portfolio:

▸ *Configurator Central* is a product configurator that manages product engineering data and processes throughout the PLC. During the concept phase of development, integrations with CAD tools permit the automation of the capture of the mechanical and electronic product structure. During the production phase of product development, integrations with ERP systems facilitate the seamless transfer of product engineering information.

▸ *Engineering Central* includes support for managing a collaborative digital workplace of global team members, designated a WorkSpace. Geographically distributed team members can use a WorkSpace. Within the WorkSpace, members can create folders, organize views, reviews, mark ups, and approve different type of information.

▸ *Request Central* is a customer-oriented application. It enables customers to send in requests for quotations, checks if requests are valid, and then tracks them all the way through design and manufacturing.

▸ *Software Central* coordinates hardware and software development. It contains software-oriented features for requirements management, project management, and change management. Integration with ClearCase provides a connection to the software development environment (see Section 6.3.1).

▸ *Supplier Central* is used for collaboration with suppliers within a virtual team. The suppliers are given access to their customers' product data, they can exchange information with the customer, and they can view change requests. The customer is provided with a single point of supplier information.

▸ *Team Central* enables the members of a project to work in a virtual team. In this virtual team, the members can share data, take part in discussion groups, and receive notification of project events.

By using a standard component-based technology, Java 2 Platform, Enterprise Edition (J2EE), MatrixOne enables easy integration with applications that use the same technology. J2EE is a general-purpose component-based technology, which can be used in any type of Web-based and Internet-based application. For example, it provides support for the development of server-based applications (servlets) with thin clients or the programs running on the client side (applets) with thick clients. The difference between J2EE technology and a standard client-server technology lies in the additional services provided, such as a component-specification standard, components deployment into the system, communication between components, security issues, and similar. Thus, by using J2EE, eMetrix ensures a broad base for integration with applications from different domains. For developing user-specific applications and for customizing standard eMatrix applications, eMatrix provides additional services included in the Application Development Kit (ADK).

In addition to the general development tool ADK, eMatrix is delivered with the eMatrix Adaplet Development Toolkit, which is used for communication with the databases of systems integrated with eMatrix. Finally, for direct management of data in databases, eMatrix uses a superset of standard query language (SQL), designated Matrix Query Language (MQL), and, as a part of ADK, the EmbeddedMQL package. Figure 9.2 shows two different solutions for application integration using MQL. The basic architecture is client-server based. The first type of integration is implemented by using an MQL application interface package designated MQLIO, and the second type, by using eMatrixMQL. The solutions are similar, but in the latter case the communication can be achieved over the Internet using standard HTTP,

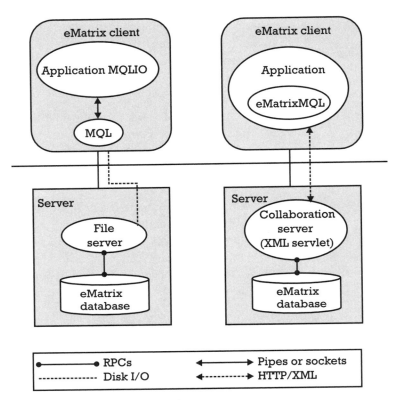

Figure 9.2 eMatrix integration solutions.

which gives increased flexibility and more security. In addition, the use of XML enables easier and more efficient specification of different data formats. The entire data model can be specified and processed by means of XML (for more information about XML, see Chapter 12). The eMatrixMQL technology is used for the integration of many other applications. Integration of eMatrix and ClearCase, described in Section 6.3.1, is one example of use of this technology.

9.2.2 TeamCenter

EDS [8] offers a product designated TeamCenter, a PDM tool developed from the Structural Dynamics Research Corporation (SDRC) product portfolio. SDRC has its roots in computer tools for mechanical engineering, such as the CAD tool IDEAS. SDRC entered the PDM market with Metaphase, which is incorporated in TeamCenter.

The standard edition of TeamCenter consists of several modules.

- *TeamCenter Collaboration Foundation* provides the traditional core functionality that manages product information throughout a virtual enterprise. This foundation allows globally dispersed teams to author, share, and access product information. It also includes capabilities for product definition, life cycle states, release management, and event notification.

- *TeamCenter Product Collaboration* includes part and document management, change management, and advanced product configuration. It has a Web-based user interface.

- *TeamCenter Design Collaboration* is a CAD-neutral collaboration environment. It allows users to create, share, and manage virtual prototypes, independent of where they are located (in-house or supplier) and the CAD tool used.

- *TeamCenter Project Collaboration* is used for project management and collaboration. Projects can be scheduled; documents can be shared among team members; and tasks can be specified, sent, and followed up.

- *TeamCenter Requirements Collaboration* is a systems engineering tool for requirements management.

- *TeamCenter Enterprise Collaboration* draws information from dissimilar information systems and integrates it in different user views. It supports integration with ERP systems and enables supplier integration with the local tools.

TeamCenter applications are integrated in a common framework, and they are adjusted to a commonly used PLC model. Figure 9.3 shows the model and TeamCenter tools supporting it.

TeamCenter offers ready-to-use integrations with several mechanical and electrical CAD tools and ERP systems, as well as integration with Clear-Case. Communication with other tools and systems is obtained by using the STEP standard (for STEP, see Chapter 12). A module in TeamCenter maps information from an internal data model to a STEP protocol. The STEP data can then be used in another application.

TeamCenter Integrator solutions are built on top of commercially available enterprise application servers that are J2EE compliant. This includes a set of foundation services, such as XML information mapping between different structures, security services, event-driven messaging over the Internet, and similar. These foundation services also include

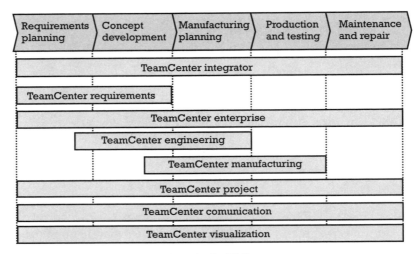

Figure 9.3   TeamCenter applications in the PLC.

ready-to-use components for thin-client information access and support functions for building a Web portal that can be used as an information server accessible via standard Web browsers.

9.2.3   Windchill

Among the larger PDM systems, Windchill [9] has been most recently introduced on the market. Windchill was developed by PTC, which, as a former SDRC company, is a well-established provider of CAD systems. Windchill has had a Web-centric approach since it was introduced and is based on standard technology. It is Java based and uses a Web browser as client.

Windchill has an architecture, similar to the other two tools described, consisting of a product platform, the *Windchill foundation*, and components to support collaboration in various parts of the PLC. The Windchill foundation contains the basic PDM functionalities.

> *Document management* includes standard functionalities, such as data vaulting, check in and check out, and version control, and, additionally, full text search of documents.

> *Structure management* creates hierarchical relationships between parts and associates documents with parts. The structure can be viewed from various perspectives, depending on the role of the user.

‣ *Life cycle management* controls the maturity of product information. A life cycle consists of a sequence of phases and gates that identify the state of an object and the conditions to be satisfied before the object enters the next phase.

‣ *Workflow management* can be used to support processes within and between life cycle phases. Workflows can be defined, executed, and monitored.

Additional Windchill components include:

‣ *Windchill PDM*, which provides extended functionality for product structure management and change management.

‣ *Windchill ProductView*, which enables users to view graphical information (three-dimensional models and two-dimensional drawings), product structures, and other information through a Web-based interface.

Windchill foundation is used together with the other components to support the PLC. A number of different applications are offered. Some of them are:

‣ *Windchill ProjectLink* for manufacturers/public business-to-business exchange is used to share information in project teams. It enables project members to store and view product information and to attend collaborative meetings.

‣ *Windchill customer collaboration* makes it possible for a company's customers to configure their own products and to submit product information queries. From a manufacturer's perspective, its products are presented in a searchable on-line catalog.

‣ *Windchill manufacturing collaboration* is intended to be an interface between design and manufacture. It can be used to increase knowledge capture and reuse, optimizing manufacturing processes and sharing knowledge across the enterprise.

‣ *Windchill product development collaboration* supports the development process, both within a company and between partners.

‣ *Windchill supplier collaboration* enables a company to make its procurement process more effective. Suppliers publish their product information in a standardized way, which makes it easier to select between parts available and to reuse parts.

In the same way as the PDM tools, Windchill uses a component-based and Internet-based technology. In addition to full Web-services support provided through the Windchill Info*Engine technology, PTC also provides support for traditional enterprise application integration. The Windchill runtime architecture is divided into multiple tiers: client, application and data, and integration. On the client tier, users access Windchill solutions with a Web browser. The application and data tier consists of the Windchill java application server, which handles business logic and processing along with the necessary security services, database communication, and system administration tools. The data portion includes the data model, which provides a product structure and its associated digital product content. The integration tier consists of messaging services that integrate enterprise systems and other systems via XML, SOAP, WSDL, JMI, JNDI, 3270/5250 mainframes, and other native APIs. Figure 9.4 illustrates the Windchill architecture.

9.2.4 ENOVIA

ENOVIA Solutions [10] provides e-business support across the development life cycle for enterprise intellectual property as it relates to product, process, and resource data. ENOVIA PLC applications ensure collaboration between multiple engineering groups. Pervasive use of graphical product, process, and resource representations throughout the development process ensures

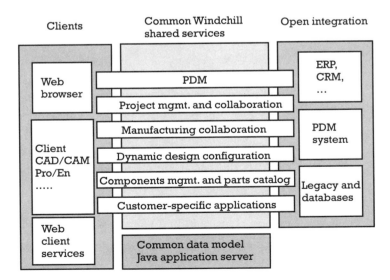

Figure 9.4 Windchill runtime architecture.

that product development participation can extend beyond the engineering teams to sales, service, procurement, and other enterprise functions.

The life cycle application foundation covers application requirements for PLC management in both the virtual product data management (VPDM) and PDM domains. An end-to-end solution builds on total use of and deployment of the three-dimensional digital mock up throughout product development, including product design, process definition, change management, and three-dimensional document control.

ENOVIA PLC application consists of three different suits:

1. *ENOVIAVPM* is a set of powerful role-based applications very closely integrated to the CATIA and DELMIA authoring tools. The highlights in the product are event notification and propagation, private or local vaulting for documents and product information, definition of engineering actions, configuration definition, configuration definition at the part feature level, maturity promotion and demotion, storage and management of technological links, authoring and visualization tools plug-ins, generative document management, and ENOVIAPM interoperability.

2. *ENOVIAPM* is a PDM solution for managing and enforcing structured business processes. The suit consists of functions for definition, storage, and management of all product- and process-related data for a PLC in a complex environment. This is achieved by improving processes used to introduce new parts, build structures, attach context to them in terms of effectivity, and change levels, versions, and feature variants. It provides also built-in functions for change management, release control (e.g., request for engineering action and engineering change specification), document management, and integration with external applications. Highlights in the product are common PDM functions (see Chapter 2 for description), such as PLC configuration, life cycle management, document management, location of control, ERP integration, supply chain, workflow, and project management.

3. *ENOVIALCA* is comprised of several families of interoperable product lines. In the VPDM domain, they include ENOVIAVPM, and in the PDM domain, ENOVIAPM. Covering both domains simultaneously, ENOVIALCA ensures deployment of digital mock up and three-dimensional product knowledge throughout the enterprise, based on a unique product-process-resource (PPR) foundation.

ENOVIALCA provides functions for customers with extensive integration requirements.

9.3   List of PDM tools

Table 9.1 provides a list of PDM systems resources.

Table 9.1   PDM Systems Resources

PDM Systems	Web Site
Active Sensing, Inc.	www.acseni.com
Agile Software	www.agilesoft.com
Aras Corporation	www.aras-corp.com
Bom.com	www.bom.com
Cimage Enterprise Systems	www.cimage.co.uk
CMStat Corporation	www.cmstat.com
CoCreate Software, Inc.	www.cocreate.com
CONCENTRIC Asia Pacific	www.concentric.com.au
CONTACT Software GmbH	www.contact.de
Dassault Systems	www.dsweb.com
EDS—Metaphase/TeamCenter	www.eds.com
Eigner	www.eigner.com
Enovia	www.enovia.com
EPM Technology	www.epmtech.jotne.com
Eurostep Commercial Solutions	www.share-a-space.com
Exertus	www.exertus.se
Freeborders, Inc.	www.freeborders.com
Gerber Technology	www.gtisd.com
IDFM, Inc.	www.idfm.com
INCAT	www.incat.com
Integrated Support Systems	www.isscorp.com
Intersect Software	www.intersectsoft.com
Lascom—Advitium	www.lascom.com
Lotsia Soft Company	www.lotsia.com
Matrix One—eMatrix	www.matrixone.com
Media concept ORCON GmbH	www.orcon.de
Modultek—Aton	www.mudultek.com
NetIDEAS, Inc.	www.netideasinc.com
Parametric Technology Corporation Windchill	www.ptc.com, www.ptc.com/windchill
Pragmax Ltd.	www.pragmax.com

Table 9.1   (Continued)

PDM Systems	Web Site
PROCAD	www.procad.de
ProSTEP GmbH	www.prostep.de
RAND Worldwide	www.rand.com
SmarTeam Corporation Ltd.	www.smarteam.com
Step Tools	www.steptools.com
The BEST Group	www.martir.com
Thetis Technologies, Inc.	www.thetistech.com
UniGraphics Solutions, Inc.—IMAN	www.ugs.com
Waware Systems	www.freepdm.com
Workgroup Technology Corporation	www.workgroup.com

9.4 Summary

The PDM system scene has changed significantly within a period of a few years First, many companies have merged or large companies have acquired smaller ones and merged their tools. Second, the focus has moved from pure PDM functionality to a spectrum of different services for managing information and different processes. Third, the technology used has dramatically changed from proprietary solutions to standard Web and Internet technologies. All of these changes have had an important influence on the improvement of tools and customer support. Unfortunately, it cannot be said that all of the changes have had a positive impact. As a consequence of many mergers of companies and tools, the purposes and the business advantages of using these tools have became more diffuse. In many cases, it is not clear which tools and options should be used for a particular type of business. Also, as the tools become more general, the focus on particular support has been decreased. On the other hand, their usability and flexibility has enormously improved. PDM and similar tools have been known as tools difficult to acquire, use, update, or replace. They have also had problems with scalability and compatibility. The newest trend of using middleware and component-based technologies such as J2EE, .NET, or CORBA, and associated distributed architectures, solves many of these problems. The applications are built in a standard way, and they are easier to integrate, more flexible and scalable, and most importantly significantly more user friendly.

Integration with SCM tools is still not a primary focus for PDM systems vendors. Even if we do find certain integrations, the awareness of software development in the PDM world is still low. We can, however, expect that the use of standard technologies will make it simpler to integrate these tools and in this way favor their use in combination.

References

[1] EDS PLM Solution, Vendor of the PDM system Metaphase, www.sdrc.com, 2003.

[2] The PDM Information Center, www.pdmic.com, 2003.

[3] Bourke, R. W., "New Directions in the Aerospace and Defense Industry: The Integration of Product Data Management and Enterprise Resource Planning Systems," *PDMIC 2002*, www.pdmic.com/articles/misscrit.html, 2003.

[4] John Stark Associates, www.johnstark.com, 2003.

[5] CIMdata, www.cimdata.com, 2003.

[6] CADCAMnet, www.cadcamnet.com, 2003.

[7] MatrixOne, www.matrixone.com, 2003.

[8] Electronic Data Systems, www.eds.com, 2003.

[9] Parametric Technology Corporation, www.ptc.com, 2003.

[10] ENOVIA,www-3.ibm.com/solutions/engineering/esenovia.nsf/Public/enovia_ overview, 2003.

Survey of SCM tools

An apprentice carpenter may want only a hammer and saw, but a master craftsman employs many precision tools. Computer programming likewise requires sophisticated tools to cope with the complexity of real applications, and only practice with these tools will build skill in their use.
—Robert L. Kruse, Data Structures and Program Design

SCM is today a well-established software engineering discipline, and probably more than 100 SCM tools are currently available. These cover a wide range of functions, differing in functionality, complexity, and price. Although SCM was first developed in the 1970s, it was not until the late 1990s that there was an explosion of SCM tool availability.

The question of which tool is the best is irrelevant. There is no best tool, but there is the most appropriate tool, depending on the business objectives of the users. Many simple tools contain basic functions such as version management and CM, sufficient enough for small development teams. Advanced tools supporting distributed development, change management, and sophisticated building are used in large enterprises. In any case, a single SCM tool without continuous process support is not sufficient for its successful utilization. Even the most sophisticated tools must be integrated into the process with other tools. Also, administration resources must be available. It is naive to believe that more sophisticated tools will require fewer resources for SCM activities. However, the overall results in productivity and product quality can be significantly improved.

This chapter gives a short survey of the SCM tools available on the market. Because of the large number, descriptions of all of them cannot be given here. Some of the most frequently used are described very briefly, to give the reader an idea of the main characteristics of such tools. A list of most used SCM tools based on [1–3] is also presented. The tools are separated into two categories, commercial and free tools. More information about SCM tools can be found on the Internet; the most interesting resources are listed in the next section.

10.1 SCM resources on the Internet

10.1.1 CM Yellow Page

A good starting point when exploring SCM is the CM Yellow Page site [1]. The page includes a number of white papers and technical papers relating to SCM, references to other SCM pages, an extensive list of commercial and noncommercial tools, future conferences and seminars, consultation and education, and job opportunities.

10.1.2 CM II Users Groups

The CM II Users Groups [4] has an excellent CM resource guide on-line page. This page includes a number of references to articles, reports and proceedings, journals and newsletters, books, conferences, providers of education/training, evaluation of PDM and software CM tools, copies of standards, lists of organizations, user groups and research groups, CM software vendors, standards, guidelines and position papers, and SCM Web sites.

10.1.3 FAQs relating to CM

CM FAQs [5] presents many questions in a wide range, from the very general (such as "What is CM?" or "How does problem management relate to CM?") to concrete ("Where else can I look for CM information?" or "Is there a tutorial someplace on RCS?"), and gives concise and precise answers. The page also lists a number of SCM references, such as SCM books, and a list of SCM tools and vendors.

CM FAQs is very much related to the news group comp.software.config-mgmt. This news group is very active and up to date, and it is possible there to find information or state a question related to SCM of any type. Like most FAQ lists, these parts are archived at rtfm.mit.edu and at various other sites that archive FAQs, such as www.faqs.org or www.google.com.

10.2 Commercial SCM tools

There is a wide range of commercial tools, from simple ones (intended for small systems and development groups), to those that cover the needs of large enterprises. We shall focus here on some of these, giving a short overview and in some cases showing characteristic or interesting parts.

10.2.1 AllFusion Harvest Change Manager

AllFusion Harvest Change Manager [6], formerly known as CCC/Harvest, is an enterprise change and CM tool. The tool is intended to provide a comprehensive, integrated, repository-based change management and CM solution for managing complex, enterprisewide development activities. The tool is intended to provide a means of tracking software changes and managing the application development process in distributed environments. This is a tool best suited for middle-size projects with a well-defined development process. The tool can be adjusted to the existing process.

The main features of AllFusion Harvest Change Manager are the following:

- *Process-driven, integrated change management and CM.* The tool helps to create and modify models of a development process by automating workflows, such as notifications, approvals, and change migrations from one phase to another.

- *Problem management.* Problem management can be automated and tracked with associated change packages, which give historical information regarding specific changes and events that take place within a development process.

- *Application development tools integration.* This feature is enabled through its open architecture, customization options, and support for the Microsoft source code control interface (SCCI) standard.

- *Management reporting and metrics capabilities.* Different reports providing data from the repository can be created using Visual Basic or Java scripts.

- *Inventory management.* This feature provides authorized users with status information regarding any software asset in the entire organization—who, what, why, when, and where.

▶ *Automated build management.* The tool includes automated build management through the Openmake facility, which is integrated in the tool and different IDEs.

Change management and CM provide support for managing the life cycle of software products by combining cooperative objects (for example, states and processes). The change process is based on promoting the change package (a set of changes), not on individual files. Figure 10.1 shows an example of the possibilities of defining a process, including several projects sharing common parts and in which the states are mutually dependent.

10.2.2 Rational ClearCase

Rational ClearCase [7] is one of the leading SCM tools for the support of software development and maintenance life cycle. It is a tool for larger organizations that can take full advantage of SCM by providing control of all of the assets in the development and maintenance processes.

The tool consists of several products covering different phases and aspects of the software life cycle and scaling up support for small and middle size development teams up to large distributed enterprise projects (see Figure 10.2):

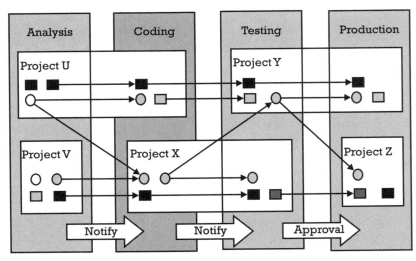

Figure 10.1 Development process managed by AllFusion Harvest Change Manager.

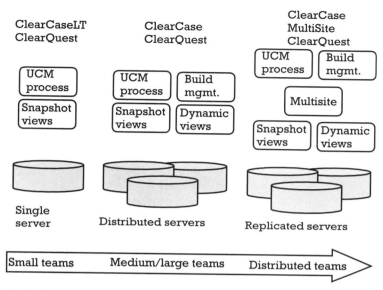

Figure 10.2 Rational ClearCase Family products for development projects of different sizes.

• *Rational ClearCase* covers the basic SCM functions: version management, CM, change management, and build support. A light version, Rational ClearCase LT, is intended for smaller development projects.

• *Rational ClearCase MultiSite* is a product option included in Rational ClearCase. A component of the Rational integrated change management solution, it enables parallel development across geographically dispersed teams.

• *Rational ClearQuest* is a defect and change tracking system that captures and manages all types of CRs throughout the development life cycle.

The ClearCase product family is to a large extent integrated with other Rational tools and supports Rational's Unified Change Management (UCM). UCM defines an activity-based process for managing changes that teams can apply in their development projects, from the specification of requirements and design through implementation and delivery. It permits the management of changes at a higher level, in terms of activities or components. With UCM, an activity is automatically associated with its change set, which encapsulates the particular versions of the project artifacts used to implement the activity.

ClearCase is a very powerful means of obtaining an invariant view of the version management and CM. When accessing versioned files, developers work in a predefined view that is obtained by a selection filter for accessing a particular version of files or folders or any other type of object under version control. In everyday work, developers see the working structure as any ordinary file system, but they actually work directly on the repository. The repository, which is different from most SCM tools, is a version-management file system, which is mounted to the developers' standard file system. The rules for providing views are powerful, consisting of a combination of a set of simple rules, such as working version, latest version, particular BL, and particular branch.

Extensive support of distributed development is provided by a multisite option with a primary role in the synchronization of repositories. The synchronization is achieved at object version level, or more precisely on the branch level of objects. Different sites can be assigned as owners of different branches. A site can generate new versions of a file in a particular branch and can read other branches. The branches are synchronized at a specified frequency. The merge process from the branches must be performed manually. The example on Figure 10.3 shows two sites, where site A can check in new file versions in the main branch, while site B is allowed to update the bugfix branch. The branches are periodically replicated. In the example, only site A can do a merge from different branches and create a new version in the main branch.

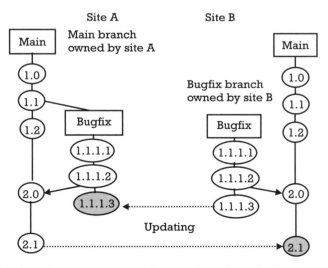

Figure 10.3 Multisite management of different branches of a file.

ClearCase is integrated in many IDEs. It also includes Microsoft SCCI and can therefore be integrated with other tools that support that interface. ClearCase also includes a simple script that manipulates with assets under version control. Triggers related to particular events and actions from users or from ClearCase itself can start these scripts. However, an API covering all ClearCase functions is not available in the present version. ClearCase is one of the few SCM tools that provide solutions for integration with PDM tools (see Section 6.3).

10.2.3 CM Synergy

CM Synergy [8] (previously known as Continuus) manages objects that can be source code, binary files, folders, or documents. All objects are under version control, saved, in the same way as in PDM systems—in a relational database and in the file system. In order to modify files, they must be checked out in the local file system.

Telelogic Synergy includes the following tools:

▸ *CM Synergy* is change management software used for the development and maintenance of software and systems. It provides a distributed repository and support for a team-oriented workflow approach to development teams of different sizes.

▸ *Change Synergy* is a change request tracking and reporting system that manages the process of change request management.

▸ *CM Synergy Distributed Change Management* is used for remote and distributed change management. DCM enables geographically distributed development teams to work together.

▸ *CM Synergy ObjectMake* provides a build management capability.

▸ *Project Synergy* for Microsoft Project enables project management, with greater visibility into project activity and more accurate project schedules.

For integration with other tools, CM Synergy uses Microsoft SCCI. It permits integration with different IDE tools such as PowerBuilder, Microsoft(R) Visual C++, Visual Cafe, VisualAge for Java, and Visual Basic. The ActiveCM plug in enables automatic execution of SCM commands by monitoring the development environment and triggering the SCM activities that would normally be provided by a developer.

CM Synergy can specify a life cycle model for the development process by defining workflows using states of objects and activities as transitions between the states. Different life cycles can be defined for different types of objects (e.g., for source code, a life cycle model defines the states *work, integration, test, SQA,* and *release,* and for a task, *registered, assigned,* and *completed*). A script language is used for modeling life cycles.

The process models can be classified in two categories:

1.   *Object-based models.* This category of model identifies different object types and a life cycle model for each type. It is easy to add new types of objects and new life cycles for them.

2.   *Task-based process models.* This model is focused on tasks. Objects can be associated with tasks. An action applied on a task is propagated to all associated objects. For example, if a task is checked out, all files associated with this task will be checked out.

The tool supports parallel development and it distinguishes three different types of concurrent development: concurrent development of objects, development of variant releases, and development of parallel releases. Distributed development is supported by Distributed Change Management, which manages the synchronization of repositories. Entire repositories, objects, or particular structures can be synchronized. The objects are updated over multiple sites using the following methods (see Figure 10.4):

▸ *Object replication.* One site (a master site) is responsible for all changes in an object, while other sites can use the object.

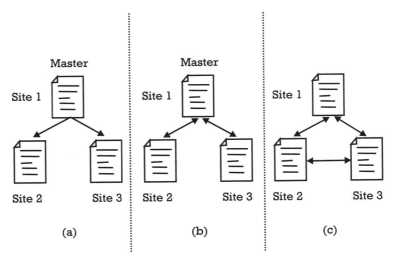

Figure 10.4   Different principles in sharing of data: (a) Object replication, (b) hub-and-spoke parallel development, (c) peer-to-peer parallel development.

▸ *Concurrent development.* All sites work with the same object, and two approaches are used for sharing the object: hub and spoke (in which a particular side includes a master version to which all other versions are synchronized), and peer to peer (in which versions of all sites are synchronized in particular order) [2].

10.2.4 MERANT PVCS

Merant PVCS [9] products cover SCM functions and also focus on similar activities in other domains, in particular Web content management (WCM) and application change management (ACM) in corporate-packaged application suites from Oracle.

PVCS is a family of the following products:

▸ *PVCS Professional* is a single suite for SCM that includes PVCS Version Manager, PVCS Tracker, and PVCS Configuration Builder.

▸ *PVCS Version Manager* organizes, manages, protects software assets during revision, and promotes team collaboration. PVCS Version Manager is integrated with numerous development environments and tools.

▸ *PVCS Tracker* captures and manages changes, issues, and tasks, providing basic process control to ensure coordination and communication within and across development teams.

▸ *PVCS Configuration Builder* ensures that applications can be reliably built in a reproducible manner, ensuring the use of components from the same version.

▸ *PVCS Dimensions* integrates SCM functions under process definition to automatically manage workflow and change implementation. It is used for larger projects.

▸ *Merant Collage* is a Web life cycle toolset that manages a Web site infrastructure and combines it with task management and workflow.

▸ *PVCS Change Manager* for Oracle speeds adoption of custom development and updates and new releases from Oracle for ERP suites.

Both PVCS Professional and PVCS Dimensions address version management, build management, and issue management. Process and workflow management, BL management, and release management are addressed in a basic way with PVCS Professional. PVCS Dimensions has more advanced capabilities for build, release, and process management. It relies on a single metadatabase repository, and it integrates all management functions into a single system. PVCS Dimensions manages all areas of SCM and the items, components, roles, and processes involved, including enforcement of workflow steps, checkpoints, and approvals. PVCS Tracker is a link between a development process and users' requirements. It is used for registering feature requests, defect reports, customer feedback, general project issues, tasks, action items, and responsibilities. These issues are integrated with the development process by linking them with particular changes performed in the development projects. Figure 10.5 shows the high-level differences between PVCS Professional, PVCS Dimensions, and PVCS Tracker.

PVCS tools are intended for medium-size projects. They support parallel and distributed development processes. In particular, PVCS includes WebDAV functions, which make it possible to access file structures over the Internet.

All of the tools are integrated with most existing IDEs. A special facility, TrackerLink, IDE integration, is used for integration with other products. The integration is based on Microsoft SCCI specification, which is supported by many IDEs.

10.2.5 Microsoft Visual Source Safe

Microsoft Visual SourceSafe (VSS) [10] is a version management tool with rudimentary configuration functionality. The main feature of VSS is its good integration in Visual Studio (it is actually a part of Visual Studio, although the integration is not perfect). Unlike most SCM tools, VSS is neither file oriented nor change oriented; it is project oriented. Version management is performed within a frame of a project. Parallel development and file versioning is obtained on a project level, not a file level. Although VSS belongs to a low-level class of SCM tools, it is very popular because it is supplied with MS Visual Studio.

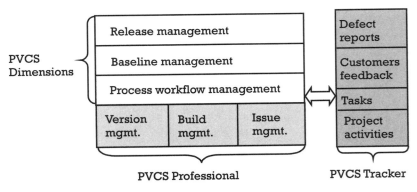

Figure 10.5 PVCS tools collaboration.

The main features of VSS are:

▸ It is practical for individual developers or small groups;

▸ It is integrated into Visual Studio, so there are no extra costs if using Visual Studio;

▸ Easy start for inexperienced programmers and SCM users;

▸ Many tools on the market have adopted VSS and built additional functions (such as change management and distributed development).

10.3 List of SCM commercial tools

Table 10.1 presents process-based CM tools, and Table 10.2 lists CM and version control tools.

10.4 Freeware SCM tools

In addition to commercial SCM tools, there is a large number of free SCM tools. It is interesting to note that two SCM tools dominate in free software market: RCS and CVS. We give a short description of them and a list of other free SCM tools.

Table 10.1 Process-Based CM Tools

SCM Tool	Web Site
AccuRev—AccuRev/CM	www.accurev.com
AccuRev/Dispatch	www.accurev.com
Intasoft—Allchange	www.intasoft.net,
Computer Associates—CCC/Harvest	www.cai.com
Serena	www.serena.com
Rational—ClearCase	www.rational.com
ExpertWare—CMVision	www.cmvision.com
Merant—Dimensions	www.merant.com
Softlab—Enabler	www.softlab.com
Visible Systems—Razor	www.razor.visible.com
McCabe & Associates, Inc.	www.mccabe.com
TRUEchange	www.mccabe.com
Telelogic Synergy	www.telelogic.com
Prosoft—Xstream	www.prosoftcm.com

Table 10.2   CM and Version Control Tools

SCM Tool	Web Site
+1 Software Engineering, +1CM—Solaris	www.plus-one.com
AccuRev—AccuRev/CM	www.accurev.com
Sequel UK—Alchemist	www.sequeluk.com
BitMover, Inc.	www.bitmover.com/bitkeeper
Aldon	www.aldon.com
Industrial Strength Software ChangeMaster	www.industrial-strength.com
Reliable Software	www.relisoft.com
Agile Software Corp	www.agilesoft.com
Collabnet, SourceCast	www.collab.net
NCI	www.nci-sw.com
ComponentSoftware, CS-RCS—Windows	www.ComponentSoftware.com
Data Services—ECMS	www.configdata.com/w002product.htm
Lockheed Martin	www.lockheedmartin.com
Quality Software components	www.qsc.co.uk
JavaSoft, JavaSafe	www.javasoft.com
JSSL—Librarian	www.winlib.com
Tesseract—Life cycle Manager	www.tesseract.co.za
British Aerospace—LifeSpan	www.lifespan.co.uk
Realcase—Multi-Platform	www.realcase.com
Perforce Software—Perforce Fast SCM System	www.perforce.com
Data Design Systems—PrimeCode	www.datadesign.com
Merant—PVCS	www.merant.com
Synergex—PVCS	www.synergex.com
Qumasoft—QVCS—Windows	www.qumasoft.com
Inroads Technology—Rapid	www.inroadstech.com
Ultracomp—Red Box	www.ultracomp.co.uk
Software Ever After	www.s-e-a.com.au
Lucent Technologies—Sablime HP, NCR, SUN	www.bell-labs.com
MKS, Source Integrity	www.mks.com
SourceGear—SourceOffSite	www.sourceoffsite.com
SiberLogic – SourceTrack	www.siberlogic.com
Giant Technologies, Visual SourceMail	www.giant-technologies.com
Microsoft Visual SourceSafe	msdn.microsoft.ssafe
Mainsoft Corporation—Visual SourceSafe on Unix	www.mainsoft.com
Starbase Corporation—StarTeam	www.starbase.com
Interwoven—TeamSite	www.interwoven.com

Table 10.2   (Continued)

SCM Tool	Web Site
SoftLanding SystemsTurnOver	www.softlanding.com
Burton Systems—TLIB	www.burtonsys.com
George James Software—VC/m	www.georgejames.com
UNI Software Plus, VOODOO	www.unisoft.co.at/Home.html
Sun—Forte TeamWare	www.sun.com/forte/teamware

10.4.1 RCS

RCS is one of the oldest SCM tools. It is very simple and includes rudimentary SCM functions applied on files. The simplicity of RCS is outstanding and the reason for its widespread use. RCS is also used as a basic tool for many other SCM tools. Even more interesting is that the principles introduced in RCS (and partially previously SCCS) are still applied in other, more advanced SCM tools.

RCS is file oriented, and the SCM repository is simply a directory that contains versioned files. One versioned file contains one or several versions of that file. Baselines are achieved by setting a label on specific versions of the files. RCS includes difference and merge functions, which can be used by users and by check-in and check-out commands.

The main features of RCS are:

- Contains basic SCM functions (versioning, check in, check out, baselines, difference, and merge);
- SCM repository is the RCS underlying directory;
- Simple and easy to use;
- Practical for using on individual bases or in small groups;
- Can be used as a base for building more sophisticated tools.

10.4.2 CVS

CVS uses RCS as a basic SCM tool. However, in contrast with RCS, it manages directory structures. All files in a directory tree structure can be checked out or synchronized with working versions of files. CVS supports multiuser projects directly, as it uses a server-client architecture. A TCP/IP connection is used for the client-server communication. There are many CVS clients, for example, WinCVS (www.wincvs.org), jCVS (www.jcvs.org), command-line interfaces, and emacs commands. In the same way as RCS, CVS is a widespread tool because of its simplicity and flexibility.

The main features of CVS are:

▸ Contains basic SCM functions (versioning, check in, check out, base-lines, difference, and merge);

▸ It is a client-server application in which the server manages the file repository;

▸ Enables parallel development with concurrent changes of files;

▸ Includes monitoring of files—operations (e.g., check in and check out) on the specified files are reported to the users;

▸ Simple and efficient;

▸ Practical for use in small distributed groups.

10.4.3   List of free SCM tools

The first SCM tools were developed by researchers, which has an implication: Many SCM tools are freely available on the market. There are, however, different categories of free software [11] (e.g., public domain free software [11], open source [12], and free software [13, 14]), which treat the software ownership, maintenance, and support in different ways.

Table 10.3 lists some of the free SCM tools available on the market.

Table 10.3 SCM Tool Free Software

SCM Tool	Web Site
Aegis	http://aegis.sourceforge.net
CERN—CMZ	www.info.cern.ch/cmz
CVS	www.cvshome.org
DVS	www.cs.colorado.edu/serl/cm/dvs.html
Inversion	inversion.tigris.org
JCVS	www.jcvs.org
Keep-It	www.keep-it.com
ODE	www.accurev.com/ode/index.html
PRCS	http://prcs.sourceforge.net
RCS	www.gnu.org/software/rcs/rcs.html
SCCS (free implementations)	www.cvshome.org/cyclic/cyclic-pages/sccs.html
TCCS	www.oreilly.com/homepages/tccs
TkCVS	www.twobarleycorns.net/tkcvs.html

10.5 Summary

This chapter gives a concise survey of SCM tools. From the tables, we can see that many SCM tools are available on the market. A few of them, perhaps ten or fewer, cover most of the market. From this large number and from the fact that many tools (including the leading ones) have changed their names or the vendor, we can conclude that the SCM market is still not stable. This is not easy for users, as even well-established tools or vendors can disappear from the market. For this reason, it is important that the organizations using these tools are prepared for changes, and this is possible only if they have control of their development process and understand the activities related to SCM.

Another interesting conclusion that we can derive from this survey is that several large SCM systems use system architectures very similar to that of PDM. The total information consists of data and metadata. While data is usually stored in the file system, metadata is saved in databases, usually relational databases. The similarity in architecture of these two systems should lead to easier integration.

References

[1] CM Today Yellow Pages, www.cmtoday.com/yp/configuration_management. html, 2003.

[2] Burrows, C., and I. Wesley, *Ovum Evaluates: Configuration Management*, London, UK: Ovum Ltd, 1998.

[3] Leon, A., *A Guide to Software Configuration Management*, Norwood, MA: Artech House, 2000.

[4] Configuration Management II Users Groups, www.cmiiug.com/Sites.htm, 2003.

[5] Frequently Asked Questions Relating to Configuration Management, www.daveeaton.com/scm/CMFAQ.html, 2003

[6] Computer Associates, www3.ca.com/Solutions/Product.asp?ID=255, 2003.

[7] Rational, www.rational.com/products/clearcase, 2003.

[8] Telelogic, www.telelogic.com/products/synergy, 2003.

[9] Merant, www.merant.com/pvcs, 2003.

[10] Microsoft, msdn.microsoft.com/ssafe, 2003.

[11] Categories of Free and Non-Free Software, www.gnu.org/philosophy/ categories.html, 2003.

[12] Open Source Initiative, www.opensource.org, 2003.

[13] Free Software Definition, www.gnu.org/philosophy/free-sw.html, 2003.

[14] Free software, www.free-soft.org, 2003.

Document management systems

Information is a source of learning. But unless it is organized, processed, and available to the right people in a format for decision making, it is a burden, not a benefit.

—William Pollard

The demands for improved document management have increased with the increasing volume and diversity of documentation produced. The development of technologies that make wide use of digital documents (i.e., documents produced by different software in an electronic format) has enormously increased the efficiency and flexibility of the creation, change, and distribution of documentation. However, not all of the consequences of this are positive. For example, a digital document is often less reliable than a paper document. A digital document has on average a lower life length, as its existence depends not only on the media in which it is stored but also on the tools by means of which it can be reproduced. In addition, the massive increase in volume of documentation makes it significantly more difficult to locate the information required. Although document management is relatively new in the world of computers, it has a long tradition elsewhere. Document management originated in ancient Mesopotamia and Egypt. For centuries, the main activities were document creation, its classification, and its archiving. These functions are parts of document management even today, but it is not now possible to perform them in a traditional way by using manual procedures. Also, certain new functions, nonexistent before the electronic age, have become very important. In modern technology, the content of a document is separate from its media. Similarly a document format is separated from its content. A particular document can be a part of a larger document or can be composed of different documents. These new functions provide many new opportunities for the effective exploration of documentation, but they also require the use of new tools. Document management has in recent years emerged as a new information and engineering discipline. The purpose of document management is similar to that of PDM ("to provide the right users with the right information at the right time" [1]). A document management system (DMS) is a collection of different tools, intended for use in the management of the life cycles of documents.

This chapter contains a survey of basic document management functions to give the reader an introduction to the use of document management. A list of certain document management Internet resources and an extensive list of document management products and service providers at the end of the chapter give the reader more possibilities for further exploration of this area.

11.1   Document management and PDM

Many functions of a DMS are the same, or are very similar to, those of PDM; data storage, CM, and workflow support are parts of both domains. On the other hand, a DMS includes some functions that are only marginally included in PDM or are entirely absent. Document conversion and, in general, different techniques for importing documents of different format or from other media are specific functions of a DMS. Similarly, archiving (long-term storage) of documents is a function characteristic of document management, which is hardly present in PDM. In recent years, we have witnessed that the term document management is often replaced by the term content management. However, these terms are not equivalent. The meaning of document management is slightly different from that of content management. Content management considers in the first place, information (i.e., content itself) and its organization. Many tools include only content management, and many DMSs do not include all of the functionality of content management. However, in general, content management is an integral part of document management. Figure 11.1 shows the overlap of PDM and DMS. There is less overlap between SCM and document management. The document management functions present in both PDM

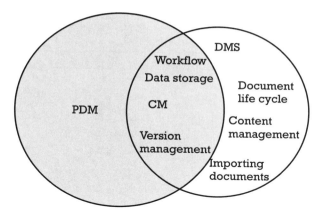

Figure 11.1   The overlap of DMS and PDM functions.

and SCM (e.g., CM and version management) are much more similar to PDM functions than SCM functions. In many PDM tools, document management is its integral part, as described in Section 2.5.2. Several suppliers of PDM have integrated a DMS with their PDM tools. All this makes the boundary between PDM and document management indistinct.

Enterprises, the core business of which is information delivery, are by definition in need of a document management tool that keeps effective their internal processes and facilitates the flow of information to customers. If using a DMS, such enterprises have no need for PDM or SCM tools. It may be asked if companies already using a PDM or SCM tool need additional support for document management or if the functions already available are sufficient? The answer to this is that it depends on the intensity of the documentation and information management and the type of documentation handled. A DMS focuses on the life cycle of a document, which is not necessarily the same as a PLC.

11.2   Document life cycle and document management

Document management functions are focused on providing services for documents during their life cycle, from their creation to their disposal. As Figure 11.2 shows, a document management system includes the following functions that support document life cycle:

▸ Document creation and import of document;

▸ Data storage;

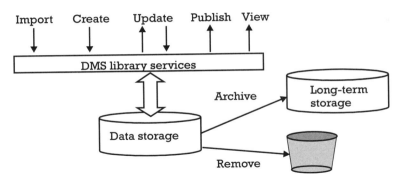

Figure 11.2   Document life cycle and basic DMS functions.

> • Document editing;
> • Publishing;
> • Viewing;
> • Archiving (long-term storage);
> • Document disposal.

11.2.1   Document creation and the import of documents

Documents can be created in many different ways outside the control of a DMS. They can be created by different tools, such as CAD/CAM tools, word processors, modeling tools, or other computer-based tools. They can also be created in a completely different way (e.g., manually as a text or as a drawing on a piece of paper). To be able to manage documents, a DMS provides a mechanism for importing documents into the system. The quality of a document management service depends very much on the level of the DMS integration with the editing tools. The minimum level of such integration is the ability to import and export a document. Here, the DMS is able to identify a document as an entity without being able to look at its content. Examples of such low-level integration are scanning and imaging procedures. The problem of importing documents is the same for PDM, and many services provided by a DMS are integrated functions of PDM (e.g., image processing as described in Section 2.2.8).

11.2.2   Data storage

Data storage or data vault in document management is very similar to PDM data vault support (see Section 2.2.1) but is much simpler. For example,

STEP is usually not a part of document management. Metadata support may be a part of document management, but in a much simpler form. While PDM can describe any type of object, document management is focused only on documents (i.e., on a very particular type of object). A DMS uses databases, mostly relational databases, and file systems as document repositories. Mechanisms for data distribution, replication, and access are very similar to the solutions from PDM.

11.2.3 Documentation editing

Documentation editing includes documentation creation and updating. In most cases, the same tools are used for document updating as for document creation. The requirements and problems are the same as for PDM. Integration with different tools and data transformation are the key issues. In the same way as PDM systems, a DMS provides support in starting different applications and for import/export functions.

11.2.4 Publishing

Publishing is the most specific important function of document management. It includes activities related to document presentation. The possibilities of different presentation of the same content are the results of the increasing ability to separate document content from its format. These also facilitate the presentation of information in different ways in different kinds of media. The same content may be presented on a desktop computer, on paper, on a personal digital assistant, or on some other device. Separation of content from format requires a standard way to describe formats. XML [2], an overview of which is presented in Section 12.6, is widely used for this purpose today. Publishing functions use XML technology for combining formats and content to generate presentations suitable for particular users and for the different media in which the information is presented. Another important function of publishing is the composition of different documents and ways to make them accessible to users (e.g., by publishing them on a Web portal). Another task of publishing is to keep the information consistent (e.g., by keeping consistent hyperlinks on Web pages).

11.2.5 Viewing

In a classical approach, the tools for documentation viewing are the same as the tools for documentation editing. This approach has severe limitations, as it requires a reader to have the same tool as the document editor. It also requires that a reader is familiar with the use of the tool. In the new approach, the objective is to enable consumers to reach information in as simple, flexible, and fast a manner as possible. This is achieved by making it possible to use one or only a few tools for information presentation. Instead of focusing on particular presentation tools, document management uses standard formats—again XML, HTML, or PDF—for information presentation. In this way, presentation tools (different Web browsers or PDF readers) are not part of document management. Despite this apparent paradox, the accessibility of information is greatly improved.

11.2.6   Archiving (long-term storage)

One of the serious problems associated with digital documents is their short life cycles, resulting not only from the short lifetime of the tools by means of which they are produced but also from the short lifetime of the media on which they are presented. Tapes and even CDs have a limited lifetime, between 10 and 20 years. Comparing this with classical media, such as paper, or such older media, such as stone or clay (Sumerians created a cuneiform script more than 5,000 years ago, which still exists on clay tablets), this time is negligible. Of course, flexibility, usability, and many other factors are in favor of electronic media, but the maintenance of documents stored in such media requires periodical refreshing of the data. Archiving is frequently a separate service not integrated with other parts of document management.

11.2.7   Document disposal

One consequence of the massive production of digital documents and information in general is the continued existence on record of enormous quantities of information that is obsolete, incorrect, or simply irrelevant. This produces many problems, not only the danger resulting from the accessibility of false information, but also the increasing cost of information administration and the increasing difficulty of locating correct information. Unfortunately, there is no systematic support for the deletion of superfluous documents in either DMSs or other tools.

In addition to functions related to document life cycle, document management also includes:

- Document and content search functions;
- Location transparency support;

- Management of compound documents;
- Version management and CM;
- CM and product management;
- Workflow management;
- Access control.

11.2.8 Document and content search functions

DMSs combine search functions characteristic of PDM and standard text searching. The basic level of searching is to locate a particular document for which the search criteria is a document name and document metadata (i.e., document attributes, its location in the database, its relation to other documents, or similar). Another type of searching includes finding documents with a particular content. This type of searching is widely used on intranet or on the Internet and is implemented via different search engines and information indexing and caching mechanisms. Many document management tools include such general purpose searching machines.

11.2.9 Location transparency support

Users should treat a document independently of whether it is stored locally in the file system, in a database saved locally or remotely, or placed on the intranet or Internet. Location transparency support is to a large extent implemented in DMSs as in PDM systems.

11.2.10 Management of compound documents

Document management has no information model as developed for PDM systems; there is no term such as object or entity. A basic entity in document management is a document. However, documents may be composed (e.g., a book can consists of several chapters, each of which is implemented as a separate entity, or a set of documents may be used for a particular purpose). The term document also becomes vaguer when extensive use is made of hyperlinks, which are typical for HTML or XML documents. Document management usually provides support for the identification and processing of documents that are compositions of other documents. Such documents are designated compound or virtual documents. Composition issues are always related to version management and CM, which simplifies the determination of which versions of parts belong together.

11.2.11   Version management and CM

Version management in document management is similar to version management in PDM. Many DMSs provide rudimentary version management support. Versions are identified as elements in a linear sequence of document history in which the latest version is normally assumed to be the only modifiable version. Configuration management is usually very simple. Two basic variants of configuration are used: the latest version configuration, in which a composition is obtained from the latest versions of all elements, and explicitly defined versions, in which a particular composition consists of particular versions of elements. There is no support for versioning compositions or identifying configurations by using different attributes.

11.2.12   Access control

Document management access control is also similar to PDM access control. It may be somewhat simpler as the objects in document management are simpler. On the other hand, access control is a very important issue, as it is directly related to security problems. Documents published on the Internet are exposed to widespread intrusion, and there is a need for systematic protection.

11.2.13   Workflow management

Workflow management is the same as for PDM.

11.3   Document management and related technologies

There are several types of technologies related to document management. They can be classified as document production (creation and editing), document storage, and document publication technologies. Document production tools, which are usually very interactive, are those mostly frequently and extensively used. An efficient, intuitive, and user-friendly interface is extremely important for document editing tools. Another important characteristic of an editing tool is its ability to manage different types of information. A document need not only be text; it may include a drawing, an image, or a graph or similar type of information. A user working with a document does not want to work with different parts of documents separately using different tools and in different work environments. A user prefers an integrated approach in which he or she can use different tools directly in a document for creating its content. Modern component-based technologies make this possible. Different applications may be integrated dynamically as components in a one-document processor. For example, a Microsoft Word file can include a Microsoft Excel document, and a user can edit the Excel part directly within an Microsoft Works environment. Another example is OpenOffice [3], in which different components for creating graphs, spreadsheets, and similar documents can be a part of one document and manipulated directly in that document. Similar technology is used in other editing tools. Figure 11.3 shows an example of a document that is a unique document from a user's perspective, but is a document container including different types of documents from the application and system point of view.

Another way of composing different documents and, to some extent, different types of documents, is to use hyperlinks in HTML or in a more advanced XML format. Hyperlinks are references from one document to another. Important features of a hyperlink are its location and application transparency. A hyperlink can refer to text in a local document, to a document from a local file system, or to a document placed on intranet or Internet. The hyperlink behavior is the same, irrespective of the location of the object referred to. The same applies to application association. In principle, any type of application may be related to a particular hyperlink. The associated application is invoked by clicking on a hyperlink.

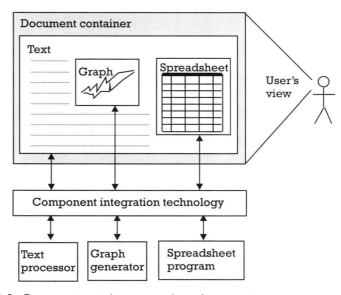

Figure 11.3   Document container as a unique document.

Document storage technologies are very much the same as those used in modern PDM tools. Usually, a three-tier architecture, as described in Chapters 9 and 10, is used. Documents and data in general are saved on database servers, which are accessed via the Internet. Different application components may be used to manage the data either on the server or on the client site. The user-interface part of applications is separated from the data-managing parts. The same architecture and technology is used for publication. The user-interface part is directly integrated into Web browsers. The data management part and data storage are two additional separated tiers. This separation makes it easy to publish information at different places and in different media. Document management support has been improved significantly by using modern Web-based and component-based technologies.

11.4 Document management resources on the Internet

As PDM systems in general consider document management and in particular information management as an integral part of PDM, many PDM resources include references to DMSs (see Chapter 9). Many resources related to Web-based applications and services also include references to document management. In addition, many document management services directly address document, content, and knowledge management. Some of these are listed next. They in turn contain a vast number of additional references.

11.4.1 Cms-list

Cms-list [4] is a forum Web page intended to help content management professionals teach each other about content management trends, tools, and ideas. The forum is focused on Web-based implementations.

11.4.2 CMSWatch

CMSWatch [5] is an independent source of information, news, opinion, and analysis about Web content management. It publishes a CMS report, which gives analysis of content management systems tools, the current problems and solutions, and similar items. The site also includes information about related technologies, such as XML, digital asset management, and content syndication.

11.4.3   Document Management Avenue Ltd.

Document Management Avenue [6] is a Web portal that provides information about document management and content management resources. It includes a discussion forum, FAQ, a glossary, and news. An extensive list of document management suppliers is provided.

11.4.4   Information Management Internet Directory

The Information Management Internet Directory [7] provides a large number of Web resources classified in different areas of document management and related disciplines: documentation format processing, data mining and warehousing, publishing, workflow, network management, and distributed systems.

11.4.5   Intranet Journal

The *Intranet Journal* [8] provides comprehensive information related to the Web and the Internet: technologies, standards, case studies, white papers, and product and service providers. Although most of the information is focused on Web technologies that are only indirectly related to PDM and SCM, the resource includes references and white papers from knowledge and content management, data and information workflow, and standards such as XML and HTML (for standards see Section 12.6).

11.4.6   Knowledgestorm

Knowledgestorm [9] provides a directory of more than 20,000 business-to-business products, services, and providers. Document management, content management, document publishing, information management, and middleware systems are included in the directory.

11.5   List of document and content management systems

Many companies are providing services or delivering products related to document and content management. The market is still not stabilized, and we shall experience many changes in the near future; many companies will disappear and new companies will emerge. In addition, document management services will increasingly become standard parts of other types of services and systems. Table 11.1 lists some of the companies that explicitly

Table 11.1 Document and Content Management Tools

Company	Web Page	Products and Services
170 Systems, Inc.	www.170systems.com	Document management and imaging system, workflow management system
Access Systems LLC	www.asllc.com	Information management, data and content management, workflow
ACS Software Inc.	www.acssoftware.com	Document management and workflow solution, multisite enterprise support
AiP Safe	www.aipsafe.com	AiP Safe, WorkFlow, SafeChange, document delivery
Arimtec International, Inc.	www.arimtec.com	Document management, system integration
Capsoft UK	www.capsoftuk.co.uk	HotDocs—Document assembly software
Cimage Enterprise Systems	www.cimage.com	Document Manager, DM-Net, ImageMaster
Cimtech Ltd.	www.cimtech.co.uk	EDM and workflow consultancy, courses, publications, and conferences
Datamatics	www.datamatics.com	Document, workflow management content and knowledge management
DataServ, LLC	www.dataserv-stl.com	Document-centric solutions
Dataspace UK Ltd.	www.data-space.co.uk	Off-site records management of files
DDMS Technologies	www.ddms-technologies.com	Document management software
Decos Software Engineering	www.decos.com	Decos Document—Web edition
Documentum, Inc.	www.documentum.com	Document and Spece management, Smartspace, Viewspace, RightSite, iTeam
DocuXplorer Software	www.docuxplorer.com	DocuXplorer Pro
Dynamic System Solutions, Inc.	www.dssihq.com	Solutions provider for document management, workflow, e-forms, reports, and system integration
Electronic Document Management Solutions Ltd.	www.edmsco.co.uk	Document management solutions
Excosoft AB	www.excosoft.com	Excosoft Content Manager

Table 11.1   (Continued)

Company	Web Page	Products and Services
FAICO Information Solutions	www.faico.net	Viewers, search engines for the distribution and management of hypertext documents
Feith Systems and Software, Inc.	www.feith.com	Feith Document Database
Fatwire Software	www.fatwire.com	Dynamic document management software
FileControl.com	www.FileControl.com	FileControl.com's document management system
FileNet	www.filenet.com	Panagon 2000, Visual WorkFlow
Formtek	www.formtek.com	Enterprise content management
Grafnetix	www.grafnetix.com	Document technologies
Gemini Resourcing Ltd.	www.gemini-resourcing.com	Document management, content management, activity management
GTOS Ltd.	www.gtos.co.uk	Document management solutions, workflow consultancy
Hitec Laboratories	www.hiteclabs.co.uk	DataStore
Hummingbird	www.hummingbird.com	DOCS Open, DOCSFussion
Hyland Software, Inc.	www.onbase.com	OnBase Integrated Document Management, OnBase Online
IBM Lotus Notes	www.lotus.com	Integrated messaging and Web application software platform, knowledge management
Imanage	workdocs.imanage.com	Collaborative content management
Ingeniux	www.ingeniux.co.uk	XML content management system
Interowen	www.interwoven.com	Content and document management
InSystems Technologies	www.insystems.com	Document assembly, DMS, workflow and multichannel delivery
Manedge Software	manedge.com	Carmen Documents 4.0
Mechworks	www.mechworks.com	Workflow integrated module support for multiple geographical sites

Table 11.1   (Continued)

Company	Web Page	Products and Services
Mystic Management Systems, Inc.	www.mysticpdm.com	Managing document life cycle
Open Archive Systems, Inc.	www.openarchive.com	Document/drawing management, indexing, viewing
OpenText	www.opentext.com	Collaboration and knowledge management
Optix	www.mindwrap.com	Document management and workflow system
Pallas Athena	www.pallas-athena.com	FLOWer Case Management and Enhanced Workflow
Prescient Information Systems	www.prescientinfo.com	Document imaging, faxing, management, and workflow
Progressive Information Technology	www.pit-magnus.com	Target 2000 (content management, XML)
Quickstream Software	www.quickstream.com	Quickstream—content management platform
Scancapture	www.scancapture.co.uk	Data capture, document management, and market research services
SoftCo	www.softco.com	Electronic document and content management
Spicer Corporation	www.spicer.com	Document life cycle support
Synergis Adept	www.synergis-adept.com	Document management—specializing in CAD and engineering documents
Tower Software UK Ltd.	www.towersoft.co.uk	TRIM (electronic document and records management system)
UltraSoft Technologies Ltd.	www.ultrasoft-tech.co.uk	Document, project, and client management system
Vignette	www.vignette.com	Content management suite

define their activities as document and content management. According to CMSWatch, there exist more than 250 providers of content management tools, without taking document management tools into account.

Most of the DMS and content management systems are commercial products. There are, however, some providers with open source and freeware solutions. Some of them are listed in the Table 11.2.

Table 11.2   Open Source Document and Content Management Tools

Company	Web Page	Products and Services
Apache Cocoon	xml.apache.org/cocoon	XML publishing framework
Cofax	www.cofax.org	Multimedia publication system
Midgard Project	www.midgard-project.org	Open source application server
OpenCms	www.opencms.org	Open source content management system
OpenACs	openacs.org	Toolkit for building Web applications
Zope	www.zope.org	Content management framework

11.6   Summary

Document and content management systems have many functions in common with PDM systems. In many cases, PDM will be sufficient for satisfactory management of documents. If publishing and the provision of information in general is a core business, PDM alone will probably not be sufficient to provided adequate support. The focus of DMSs is on document and information management (i.e., finding, creating, formatting, and composing information). As information becomes an increasingly important part of any business activity, document management tools are becoming more important and more widely available on the market. To a greater extent than PDM systems, DMSs vary in costs, complexity, and functionality.

SCM tools do not provide specific support for document management, although SCM can be used for document management to a relatively large extent. By using advanced version management and CM within SCM, it is possible to save and search for documents with particular state, automate publishing, and implement similar functions related to document management. In most cases, additional tools not provided with SCM must be used.

It is very likely that in the future, most of the document management functions will be directly included in other tools or basic platforms such as operating systems.

References

[1]   Documentum, www.documentum.com, 2003.

[2]   XML, www.xml.com/webservices, 2003.

[3]   Open Office, www.openoffice.org, 2003.

[4]   Cms-list, www.cms-list.org, 2003.

[5]   CMSwatch, www.cmswatch.com, 2003.

[6]   Document Management Avenue Ltd., cgi.parapadakis.plus.com/index.php, 2003.

[7]   Information Management Internet Directory, www.dm-kmdirectory.com, 2003.

[8]   *Intranet Journal*, www.intranetjournal.com/km, 2003.

[9]   Knowledgestorm, www.knowledgestorm.com, 2003.

12

Contents

Standards and de facto standards in PDM and SCM

The best thing with standards is that there are so many to choose from.
—C. Northcote Parkinson

We have seen that PDM and SCM systems usually consist of several tools that exchange or use common data. We have also seen the importance of the ability to integrate these tools with other engineering tools. As these tools have neither common data nor a common information model, exchange of information is one of the major problems in their use. To avoid this interoperation problem, tool providers and, in many cases, tool users define the standards with which these tools comply. Many of these standards originate in defense industry applications. As early as the 1960s, U.S. defense industries addressed the problem of poor quality and high costs caused by ordering and integrating inappropriate parts by introducing rules and later standards in CM. The introduction and application of these standards has significantly improved development procedures and production quality. CM became an established concept in the defense industry and spread to other industries; NASA adopted the first standard for CM, AFSCM 375-1 [1], for development of the Saturn V spacecraft. Later, many CM standards appeared internationally on civilian commercial level. Organizations such as ANSI, ISO, and IEEE introduced many standards related to SCM and CM.

In addition to formally established standards, de facto standards are used in many tools. Most of the de facto standards originate in large companies with a major influence on the market. The de facto standards have origins in other communities (e.g., the open source community). De facto standards have become so important for a large range of users that all tool providers have been forced to use them.

Standards and de facto standards vary considerably in their scope, in their purpose, in the formality of their acceptance, and in their use.

With respect to PDM and SCM systems, we can classify standards as those used for information exchange in its broadest meaning or those that specify processes in particular domains. Further, some standards are applicable to SCM only or to PDM only, or standards that are valid for both PDM and SCM and, in many cases, for other domains. Several CM standards were acquired by SCM. Finally, some standards can be directly implemented by software (typically, the implementation of particular protocols or the management of particular data formats); others involve human activities and can possibly be supported, but not automated, by tools (usually process-related standards).

Models are closely related to standards. Models may specify a particular activity, process, or technology in a manner similar to standards, but may be of a more general nature and not as precisely specified as standards.

In this chapter, we present certain standards, de facto standards, and models that are extensively used in PDM and SCM.

12.1   PDM standards

Although PDM uses many standards, there are no standards that are exclusively intended for PDM systems. Many standards are however closely related to PDM and originate from PDM-related requirements. Standards are enablers of interoperability, and, as interoperability is one of the most important goals of PDM, it is natural that PDM acquires many standards that are used in other domains. Examples of these domains are configuration management, documentation and content management, product life cycle management, etc.

12.1.1   ISO 10303 STEP

STEP is an ISO standard, the aim of which is to provide a standard means of modeling, specifying, and exchanging product information. STEP consists of a number of parts, each identified by a unique part number under

ISO 10303. These parts are classified in the main groups [2–4] shown in Figure 12.1:

▸ *Description methods.* This group provides specifications and methods for products models, product structures, and application protocols. Important parts of this group are the members of the EXPRESS language family.

▸ *Implementation methods.* This group contains bindings, from models built with description methods to implementations. Parts from this group are interchange file format (ISO-10303-21), repositories (ISO-10303-43), and programming language support, such as for C++ (ISO-10303-36).

▸ *Conformance testing.* This group provides a framework for testing that is based on other parts of the STEP standard. Examples of units in this group are "abstract test methods for application protocol implementations" or "abstract test methods for standard data access interface implementations."

▸ *Integrated resources.* This group contains concepts that are commonly used by different application protocols, such as "fundamentals of

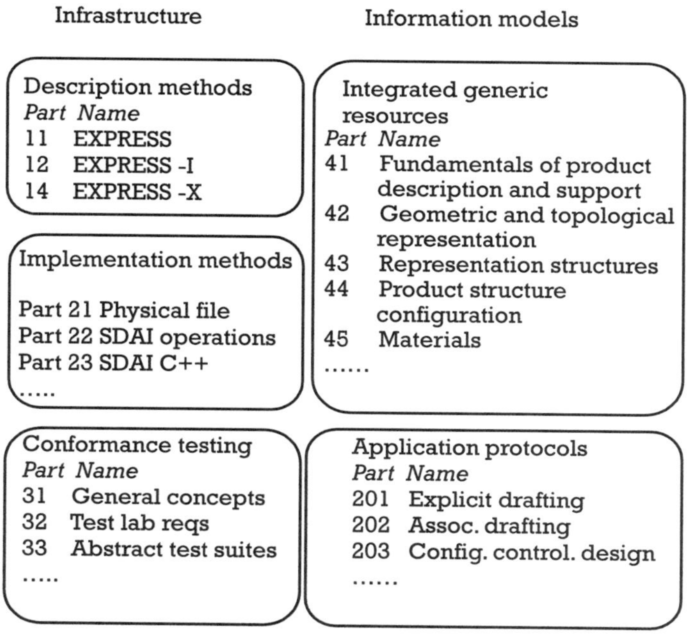

Infrastructure   Information models

Description methods
Part Name
11   EXPRESS
12   EXPRESS -I
14   EXPRESS -X

Integrated generic
resources
Part Name
41   Fundamentals of product
     description and support
42   Geometric and topological
     representation
43   Representation structures
44   Product structure
     configuration
45   Materials
......

Implementation methods

Part 21 Physical file
Part 22 SDAI operations
Part 23 SDAI C++
.....

Conformance testing
Part Name
31   General concepts
32   Test lab reqs
33   Abstract test suites
.....

Application protocols
Part Name
201   Explicit drafting
202   Assoc. drafting
203   Config. control. design
......

Figure 12.1   High-level structure of STEP.

product description and support," "geometric and topological representation," or "product structure configuration."

▸ *Application protocols.* This group contains domain-specific data models for the exchange of data between applications. Some examples of these parts are "core data for automotive mechanical design processes," "plant spatial configuration," "technical data packaging core information and exchange," or "systems engineering data representation."

The core part of STEP is EXPRESS, a modeling and product specification family of languages. EXPRESS has is roots in entity-relationship modeling and database modeling. The basic elements are entities, attributes, and the relationship between the entities. The language semantic in reminiscent to some extent of object-oriented languages with data encapsulation and relationship principles. The language also includes the object-oriented concept of inheritance. Figure 12.2 shows graphical elements of the language EXPRESS-G.

The fundamental elements of EXPRESS-G language are entities. An entity describes an object that may represent a product, a component, or an abstract object. The language includes basic types (such as STRING or INTEGER), to which further types can be added. A relationship is defined as an attribute of the entity from which it originates. A data type can be a basic type, a user-defined type, or another entity. Entities can be grouped in sets designated selections and enumerations. The only difference between lists and enumerates is that an element is always selected in a selection, but not in an enumeration.

EXPRESS-G uses graphical notation and is suitable for product or information modeling. Figure 12.3 shows an example of a schema expressed in the EXPRESS-G language.

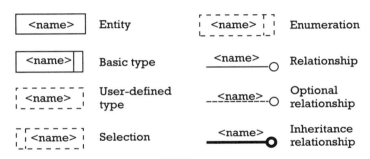

Figure 12.2 Basic elements of EXPRESS-G.

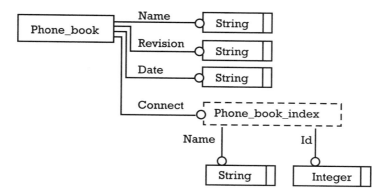

Figure 12.3   Example of EXPRESS-G language.

Another language designated EXPRESS-X is a textual representation of the EXPRESS language, suitable for automatic interpretation. The corresponding expression in EXPRESS-X appears as follows:

```
SCHEMA PHONE_BOOK_V1;
  ENTITY Phone_book;
    Name       : STRING;
    Revision   : STRING;
    Date       : STRING;
    Content    : LIST [1;?] OF Phone_book_index;
  END_ENTITY;

  ENTITY Phone_book_index;
    Name       : STRING;
    Id         : INTEGER;
  END_ENTITY;
END_SCHEMA;
```

By using EXPRESS, STEP is able to provide information models in which product definitions and product definition structures are specified in a standard format. The standardized format makes it possible to exchange information between different systems, either by on-line conversion and communication or by saving information in a so-called STEP file and then loading the file using the application protocol. When the information is exchanged between two databases or tools, the information models need not necessarily be the same. If they differ, particular data or the entire model can be transferred to the destination database through the mappings defined by the mapping schema and by a data converter. The information models and the mappings are specified in EXPRESS (see Figure 12.4).

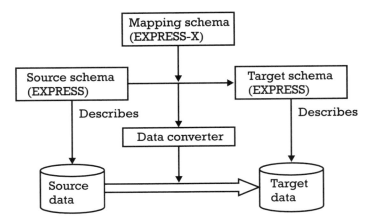

Figure 12.4 System interoperability using EXPRESS specifications.

STEP is a set of standard specifications, and not an implementation. To implement STEP means to implement an application that uses these standards to exchange product information or that makes it possible for other applications to do so. STEP is acquired by many PDM tools, but also by other tools, (e.g., CAD/CAM tools or change management and CM tools). Many of these tools comply with a particular STEP standard (e.g., Standard Data Access Interface [SDAI]). SDAI defines the functionality of an API of a product model. API is standardized and implemented in different programming languages, such as C, C++, and Java, and also for CORBA/IDL. The development of applications that manage information within a system or between systems is greatly facilitated by using SDAI.

For many PDM systems, STEP is the main means of achieving interoperability between different tools. A disadvantage of using STEP is its relative isolation; it is used in PDM and related domains, but is unknown in other domains. Further, with the emergence of SGML and XML, the use of STEP has decreased—even in PDM-related domains—even though neither SGML nor XML can replace STEP (see Section 12.5).

12.2 CM standards

CM standards have had an understandably strong impact on both PDM and SCM, as CM is an integral part of both PDM and SCM.

CM practices were first formalized in the defense and space industry communities, bringing related industry best practices together under a common framework. These practices have become entrenched as standard approaches in various industry segments for a variety of reasons. Software developers practice makes use of CM to identify and control versions of their product. The automotive industry utilizes CM to support the spare parts market, to track warranties, and to be able to perform recalls when necessary. The nuclear power and armaments production industries use CM to maintain both products and facilities. Each industry segment emphasizes particular aspects of this multifaceted process and has evolved its own terminology and methodology for the selected CM practices they employ.

12.2.1   MIL-STD-973 CM

The MIL-STD-973 is from the mid 1990s. The standard is mostly used within industries working with products for U.S. Department of Defense purposes. It defines CM requirements, which are to be selectively applied throughout the life cycle of any CI, either fully or partially developed, with government funds or designated for CM for reasons of integration, logistical support, or interface control.

The following requirements are specified in the standard:[1]

- *Basic requirements.* An internal CM system should be implemented for control of all configuration documentation, physical media, and physical parts representing or consisting of the product. The implemented CM system should consist of the following activities: configuration identification, configuration control, configuration status accounting, and configuration audits.

- *Planning.* A CM program shall be planned in accordance with the requirements of this standard. If needed, the standard may be adjusted for particular CIs.

- *Computer-aided acquisition and logistic support.* Configuration documentations shall be provided via hard copy data (printed manuals on paper), transfer of data files, interactive access to data through integrated technical information services, or a combination of these.

---

1. The following text is an abbreviated extract from the standard.

> • *Data distribution/access*. Distribution statements shall be included in the distribution of technical data.

> • *Automated processing and submittal of data*. Automated processing and electronic submittal techniques shall be used for delivery of data. When data is submitted by electronic transfer to the customer, acknowledgment of receipt will be generated at the end of the transmission. The supplier shall maintain the current status (working, released, submitted, approved) of all digital technical data in a database at all times. The supplier shall provide procedures to identify and control data during the review and update cycle (performed by supplier and customer).

> • *Interactive access to digital data*. In addition to these requirements, the supplier's integrated information service shall provide predefined queries and extraction of data.

MIL-STD-973 refers to the standards shown in Table 12.1.

12.2.2 MIL-STD-483 CM Practices for Systems, Equipment, Munitions, and Computer Programs

The MIL-STD-483 is from the late 1970s. This standard defines CM practices, which are to be adjusted to specific programs and implemented by the contract work statement. The standard is approved for use by the Department of the Air Force and is available for use by all departments and agencies of the Department of Defense. The standard is arranged in two parts: general requirements for CM and appendixes, which supplement or add CM requirements not contained in some other military standards. The scope of the first part is to establish requirements for CM in the following areas: CM plan, configuration identification, configuration control, configuration audits, interface control, engineering release control, and CM reports/records. The purpose is to establish uniform CM practices that can be adjusted to all U.S. Air Force systems. This standard supplements

Table 12.1   References and Connections to Other Standards

MIL-STD-1806	Marking technical data prepared by or for the Department of Defense
MIL-STD-881	Work breakdown structures for defense material items
MIL-STD-490	Specification practices
MIL-STD-961	Military specifications and associated documents

or adds CM requirements not contained in MIL-STD-480, MIL-STD-481, MIL-STD-482, and MIL-STD-490.

12.2.3 ISO 10007:1995 Quality Management—Guidelines for CM

This standard is from the mid 1990s and is a guidance document only. It provides a set of guidelines that may be used to improve performance in the field. The standard provides a management overview and describes the process, organization, and detailed procedures. It is applicable to the support of projects from concept through design, development, procurement, production, installation, operation, and maintenance and to the disposal of products.

The CM process comprises the following integrated activities:

‣ *Configuration identification*—product structure creation, selection of CIs, documentation of CIs, numbering, and establishment of configuration baselines.

‣ *Configuration control*—to control all changes of CIs. Control includes evaluation, coordination, approval, and implementation of changes.

‣ *Configuration status accounting*—to record and report information of all CIs and all exemptions from the specified configuration baseline. All waivers and deviations must also be processed.

‣ *Configuration auditing*—to ensure that the product complies with its contracted or specified requirements and that the configuration documents accurately reflects the product.

The standard amplifies the CM elements found in ISO 9004-1. Other referenced standards are shown in Table 12.2.

Table 12.2 Referenced Standards

ISO 8402:1994	*Quality Management and Quality Assurance—Vocabulary*
ISO 9004-1:1994	*Quality Management and Quality System Elements—Part 1: Guidelines*
ISO 10011-1:1990	*Guidelines for Auditing Quality Systems—Part 1: Auditing*
ISO 10011-2:1991	*Guidelines for Auditing Quality Systems—Part 2: Qualification Criteria for Quality Systems Auditors*
ISO 10011-3:1991	*Guidelines for Auditing Quality Systems—Part 3: Management of Audit Programmed*

12.2.4 EIA-649 Nonconsensus Standard for CM

A joint committee of the Electronic Industries Association (EIA) and the Institute of Electrical and Electronic Engineers (IEEE) developed this standard. The standard discusses CM principles and practices from an enterprise view; it does not prescribe which CM activities individual organizations or teams within the enterprise should perform. Each enterprise assigns responsibilities in accordance with its own management policy.

In this standard, CM is described in terms of the following interrelated processes:

> ▸ *CM planning and management.* This process contains activities such as define application environment; select tools, techniques, and methods suitable for the environment; plan implementation; integrate CM with enterprise-defined processes, prepare procedures, perform training, and measure performance.

> ▸ *Configuration identification.* This process contains the following activities: define product structure to be managed, assign unique identifiers, select configuration documents, define product attributes and interfaces, review and coordinate configuration documentation, establish release process and baseline configuration documentation for design control, and ensure marking or labeling of products and documentation with applicable identifiers.

> ▸ *Configuration change management.* This process contains the following activities: identify a need for change, document each request for change, evaluate each change, classify each request, obtain required approvals, plan change implementation, implement change, and verify reestablished consistency of services, training, and product, documentation, operation, and maintenance information.

> ▸ *Configuration status accounting.* This process contains activities such as identify and customize information requirements; capture and report information about product configuration status, configuration documentation, current and old baselines, change requests, change proposals, and change notices; and provide availability and retrievability of data consistent with the needs of the various users.

> ▸ *Configuration verification and audit.* This process contains activities such as verify product; assure consistency of release information and product/modification information; conduct formal audit when required; review performance requirements, test plans, results, and other evidence to determine that the product performs as specified; record

discrepancies; review to close out or determine action; record action items; and track action items to closure via status accounting.

‣ *CM of digital data.* This process contains the following activities: apply identification rules to document representations and files, use business rules based on status for change management and archiving of data, maintain data-product relationships, apply disciplined version control, assure accurate data transmittal, and provide controlled access.

EIA 649 was prepared in partnership with the Department of Defense CM Advisory Group, with the intent that MIL-STD-973 be canceled when a nongovernment standard (EIA 649) and MIL-STD-2549, CM Data Interface Standard, are available.

Table 12.3 shows standards that EIA 649 refers to:

EIA 649 is compatible with certain other standards shown in Table 12.4.

12.3 SCM standards

12.3.1 IEEE STD 828—1998 SCM Plans

This standard provides minimum requirements for the preparation and content of SCM plans. SCM plans document the methods to be used for identifying software product items, controlling and implementing changes, and

Table 12.3 Related Standards

ANSI/IEEE 610-12:1990	*Standard Glossary of Software Engineering Terminology*
IEEE 828:1990	*Software CM Plans*
ANSI/IEEE 830:1994	*Guide to Software Requirements Specification*
ANSI/IEEE 1042:1987	*Guide to Software CM*

Table 12.4 Compatible Standards

EIA 632	*Processes for Engineering a System*
ANSI/EIA JSTD-016	*Software Development Process*
ISO/IEC 12 207	*Information Technology—Software Life Cycle Processes*

recording and reporting change implementation status. The standard applies to the entire life cycle of critical software.

According to this standard the content of an SCM plan should be as follows:

▸ *Introduction.* Describes the plan's purpose, scope of application, key terms, and references.

▸ *SCM management.* This identifies the responsibilities and authorities for accomplishing the planned activities. (Who?)

▸ *SCM activities.* This identifies all activities to be performed in applying to the project. (What?)

▸ *SCM schedules.* This identifies the required coordination of SCM activities with the other activities in the project. (When?)

▸ *SCM resources.* This identifies tools and physical and human resources required for execution of the plan. (How?)

▸ *SCM plan maintenance.* This identifies how the plan will be kept current while in effect.

12.3.2   IEEE STD 1042—1987 IEEE Guide to SCM

This guide describes the application of CM of software engineering projects. The guide serves three groups of people: software developers, software managers, and those responsible for the preparation of SCM plans. Software CM consists of two major aspects: planning and implementation. This guide focuses on SCM planning and provides broad perspectives for the understanding of SCM.

Software developers can use this standard to determine how CM can be used to support the software engineering process. Management can determine how the SCM plan can be adjusted to the needs and resources of a project.

12.4   Life cycle processes

For different engineering domains, there are different standards and models for different PLCs. Some of the standards address the life cycles of systems, and others address a particular domain (e.g., software). Life cycle standards are closely related to PDM and SCM, as PDM and SCM provide infrastructure and support for these processes.

12.4.1 ISO/IEC FDIS 15288 Systems Engineering—System Life Cycle Processes

This standard provides a common framework for covering the life cycle of a system. This life cycle span is from the conception of the system to its retirement.

The standard defines a set of processes and terminology. These processes can apply at any level in the hierarchy of a system structure. The standard also provides processes that support the definition, control, and improvement of the life cycle processes used in an organization or project.

The system life cycle processes are:

▸ *Agreement processes.* The process specifies the requirements for the establishment of agreements with organizational entities, internal and external to the organization.

▸ *Enterprise processes.* This process manages the capability of the organization to acquire and supply products or services through the initiation, support, and control of the projects. They provide resources and infrastructure necessary to support projects.

▸ *Project processes.* This process provides the establishment and evolution of project plans, to assess actual achievement and progress in relation to the plans and to control the execution of the project through fulfillment.

▸ *Technical processes.* The process defines the requirements for a system to transform the requirements into an effective product, to permit consistent reproduction of the product where necessary, to use the product to provide the required services, to sustain the provision of those services, and to dispose of the product when it is retired from service.

This standard is related to ISO/IEC 12207 *Information Technology— Software Life Cycle Processes—Amendment 1.*

12.4.2 ISO 12207:1995 Software Life Cycle Processes

This standard covers the life cycle of software from conceptualization of ideas through retirement and consists of processes for acquiring and supplying software products and services. The standard may be adjusted for an individual organization, project, or application. It may also be used when software is a stand-alone entity or an embedded or integral part of the total system.

The standard categorizes all life cycle processes into three main groups: primary life cycle, supporting life cycle, and organizational life cycle.

The primary life cycle processes are defined in the standard as follows:

- *Acquisition process.* The process begins with the initiation of the need to acquire a system. The process continues with the preparation and issue of a request for proposal, selection of a supplier, and management of the acquisition process through the acceptance of the system.

- *Supply process.* The process may be initiated either by a decision to prepare a proposal to answer a request for a proposal or by signing and entering into a contract with a vendor to provide the system. The process continues with the determination of procedures and resources needed to manage and assure the project software product.

- *Development process.* This process contains activities and tasks for the developer, such as requirement analysis, design, coding, integration, testing, and installation and acceptance.

- *Operation process.* The process contains operator activities and tasks such as operation of the software product and operational support to users.

- *Maintenance process.* This process contains activities and tasks for the maintainer. The process is started when the software product undergoes modifications due to a problem or the need for improvement or adaptation. The process includes migration and ends with the retirement of the software product.

To support the primary life cycle processes, there are eight different processes supporting life cycles. They are:

1. *Documentation process.* This process records information produced by a life cycle process or activity.

2. *CM process.* The process applies administrative and technical procedures to identify and define software items in a system; control modifications and releases of the items; record and report the status and modification requests; ensure the consistency, and correctness of the items; and control storage, handling, and delivery of the items.

3. *Quality assurance process.* This process provides assurance that the software products and processes in the PLC correspond to the specified requirements and the established plans.

4. *Verification process.* The process provides activities to determine whether the software products of an activity fulfill the requirements or conditions.

5. *Validation process.* This process provides activities to determine whether the requirements and the final as-built system or software product fulfill its specific intended use.

6. *Joint review process.* The process evaluates the status and products of an activity of a project. Joint reviews are held at both project management and technical levels.

7. *Audit process.* The process determines compliance with the requirements, plans, and contract.

8. *Problem resolution process.* The process analyzes and resolves any problems encountered during the execution of development, operation, maintenance, or other processes.

The standard also identifies organizational life cycle process. The activities and tasks in an organizational process are the responsibility of the organization using that process. The organizational processes are:

▸ *Management process.* The manager is responsible for product management, project management, and task management for applicable processes such as supply, development, operation, maintenance, and supporting processes.

▸ *Infrastructure process.* The purpose is to establish and maintain the infrastructure needed for any other process, including hardware, software, tools, techniques, standards, and facilities for development, operation, or maintenance.

▸ *Improvement process.* The purpose is to establish, assess, measure, control, and improve a software life cycle process.

▸ *Training process.* This process provides the required trained personnel.

Normative references are found in Table 12.5.

12.4.3 ISO 9000-3:1997 Quality Management and Quality Assurance Standards—Part 3

ISO 9000 Part 3 has a long title, *Guidelines for the Application of ISO 9001:1994 to the Development, Supply, Installation and Maintenance of Computer Software.* It

Table 12.5 References to Other Standards

ISO/AFNOR:1989	*Dictionary of Computer Science*
ISO/IEC 2382-1:1993	*Information Technology—Vocabulary—Part 1: Fundamental Terms*
ISO/IEC 2382-20:1990	*Information Technology—Vocabulary—Part 20: System Development*
ISO 8402:1994	*Quality Management and Quality Assurance—Vocabulary*
ISO 9001:1994	*Quality Systems—Model for Quality Assurance in Design, Development, Production, Installation, and Servicing*
ISO/IEC 9126:1991	*Information Technology—Software Product Evaluation—Quality Characteristics and Guidelines for Their Use*

provides guidance in applying the requirements of ISO 9001:1994, in which computer software design, development, installation, and maintenance are treated together as an element of a commercial contract entered into by a supplier, as a product available for a market sector or as software embedded in a hardware product.

The quality system requirements are:

- *Management responsibility.* This is to define the quality policy of the organization and to identify and ensure the availability of the resources required to satisfy the quality requirements.

- *Quality system.* This is to develop and describe a quality system and to implement procedures in accordance with the quality policy it describes.

- *Contract review.* This is to develop and document procedures to coordinate the review of software development contracts.

- *Design control.* This is to establish and maintain documented procedures to control and verify the design of the product to ensure the satisfaction of the specified requirements.

- *Document and data control.* This is to develop procedures to control all documents and data relating to the requirements. CM procedures should be used to implement document and data control.

- *Purchasing.* This is to develop and maintain procedures to ensure that purchased products conform to specified requirements. These procedures should control the selection of subcontractors, the use of purchasing data, and the verification of purchased products.

- *Control of customer-supplied product.* This is to establish and maintain documented procedures for the control of verification, storage, and maintenance of customer-supplied products.

- *Product identification and traceability.* This is to develop a procedure for identifying the product during its life cycle. A CM system may provide this capability.

- *Process control.* This is to identify and plan the production, installation, and servicing processes that directly affect quality and ensure that these processes are executed under controlled conditions.

- *Inspection and testing.* This is to develop procedures for inspection and testing activities to verify the satisfaction of the product requirements specified. If third-party products are to be included, procedures shall be developed for the verification of such products in accordance with the requirements of the contract.

- *Control of inspection, measuring, and test equipment.* This is to develop procedures for the control, calibration, and maintenance of inspection, measuring, and testing equipment.

- *Control of nonconforming products.* This is to develop procedures to prevent the inappropriate use of nonconforming products.

- *Corrective and preventive action.* This is to develop procedures for implementing corrective and preventive action.

- *Handling, storage, packaging, preservation, and delivery.* This is to develop and document procedures for the handling, storage, packaging, preservation, and delivery of the products of the organization. In addition, this is to develop product handling methods and procedures that prevent product damage or deterioration and to designate secure areas in which to store and protect the products.

- *Control of quality records.* This is to identify and define the quality information to be collected. It is also to develop a quality record-keeping system and develop procedures for its maintenance and control.

- *Internal quality audits.* This is to develop internal quality audit procedures that determine whether quality activities and results comply with documented quality plans, procedures, and programs, to evaluate the performance of the quality system, and to verify the effectiveness of corrective actions.

- *Training.* This is to develop quality-training procedures.

‣ *Servicing.* This is to establish and maintain procedures for performing servicing procedures and verifying and reporting that the servicing meets the specified requirements.

‣ *Statistical techniques.* This is to select the statistical techniques to be used to establish, control, and verify process capabilities and product characteristics.

From this comprehensive list, we can see that many quality requirements need systematic support for documentation, version management, CM, and requirements management (i.e., just the support provided by PDM and SCM tools).

12.5 CMM® and CMM Integration®

12.5.1 CMM®

The CMM® for Software is a model for identifying the maturity of an organization in software process development. CMM® was developed by the Software Engineering Institute [5] and released as a full version in 1993. It has become a de facto standard for assessing and improving software processes. Its aim is to help software organizations improve the maturity of their software processes from ad hoc, chaotic processes to mature, disciplined software processes. The use of the CMM® spread rapidly to many organizations and soon became the preferred means of determining the maturity of the software development processes of an organization.

In addition to software processes themselves, the CMM® focuses on software process capability, performance, and maturity as defined in [6]:

‣ Software process capability describes the range of results that can be expected to be achieved by following a software process. The software process capability of an organization provides one means of predicting the most likely outcome expected from the next software project the organization undertakes.

‣ Software process performance represents the actual results achieved by following a software process. Thus, software process performance focuses on the results achieved, while software process capability focuses on the results expected.

‣ Software process maturity is the extent to which a specific process is explicitly defined, managed, measured, controlled, and effective.

The main principle of the CMM® is simple. It distinguishes five levels of maturity. Each level is identified by a certain number of key process areas. To achieve a particular level of maturity means to comply with all key process areas of that and previous levels. Each key process area is described in terms of key practices that describe the activities and infrastructure that contributes most to the effective implementation and institutionalization of the key process area. The key practices provide a description of the essential elements of an effective software process (i.e., they describe what is to be done, and not how the process should be implemented).

The key practices are intended to communicate principles that apply to a wide variety of projects and organizations, which are valid across a range of typical software applications, and which will remain valid over time. Therefore, the approach is to describe the principles and leave their implementation as the responsibility of each organization, according to its culture and the experiences of its managers and technical staff.

The CMM® specifies five levels of maturity as shown in Figure 12.5. The five CMM® levels are [7]:

1. *Initial.* The software process is characterized as ad hoc, and even chaotic. Success depends much on individual effort and heroics. There are no or few processes that are defined.

2. *Repeatable.* The main goal of this level is to achieve a stable development environment and establish a project management. Basic project management processes are established to track cost, schedule, and functionality. The processes needed to repeat earlier successes with projects with similar applications are identified at this level.

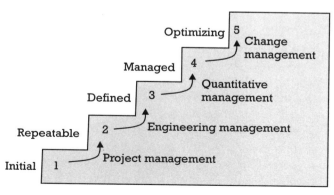

Figure 12.5 The software CMM levels.

3. *Defined.* To achieve this level, it is necessary to establish the organization's common processes and engineering methods. The software processes for both management and engineering activities are documented, standardized, and integrated into a standard software process for the organization. All projects use an approved, adjusted version of the organization's standard software process for developing and maintaining software.

4. *Managed.* This level specifies how to manage the continuous changes to which an organization is exposed. Detailed measurements of the software process and product quality are collected. Both the software process and products are quantitatively evaluated and controlled.

5. *Optimizing.* Continuous process improvement is enabled by quantitative feedback from the process and from piloting innovative ideas and technologies.

The key process areas at level two focus on the ability to repeat software projects, so it concerns processes related to establishing basic project management controls. The key process areas are requirements management, software project planning, software project tracking and oversight, software subcontract management, software quality assurance, and SCM.

The key process areas at level three address both project and organizational issues. The key process areas are organization process focus, organization process definition, training program, integrated software management, software product engineering, intergroup coordination, and peer reviews.

The key process areas at level four focus on establishing a quantitative understanding of both the software process and the software work products being built. They are quantitative process management and software quality management.

The key process areas at level five cover the issues that both the organization and the projects must address to implement continual, measurable software process improvement. They are defect prevention, technology change management, and process change management.

On these levels, SCM is a key process area on the second (repeatable) maturity level. On level five are technology change management and process change management, but these types of change are not directly related to the change management that is a part of SCM. The SCM key process area includes the same types of key practice as other key process areas. The basic principles of the key practices are ensuring the availability of resources for the activities concerned, planning them, performing them, measuring them, and analyzing them. A verification process also achieves quality assurance goals.

The following key practices for SCM are specified:

1. Commitment to perform:
    ▸ The project follows a written organizational policy for implementing SCM.

2. Ability to perform:
    ▸ A group that is responsible for coordinating and implementing for the project (i.e., the SCM group) must exist.
    ▸ Adequate resources and funding must be provided for the performance of their activities.
    ▸ A manager is assigned specific responsibilities for SCM.
    ▸ Members of the SCM group are trained in the objectives, procedures, and methods for performing their SCM activities.

3. Activities performed:
    ▸ An SCM plan is prepared for each software project according to a documented procedure.
    ▸ A documented and approved SCM plan is used as the basis for performing the SCM activities.

4. Measurement and analysis:
    ▸ Measurements are made and used to determine the status of the SCM activities.

5. Verifying implementation:
    ▸ The SCM activities are reviewed with the project manager on both a periodic and event-driven basis.
    ▸ The software quality assurance group reviews and audits the activities and work products for SCM and reports the results.

The CMM® has rapidly become widely accepted, and many organizations in both military and civil industries have used it to measure their ability to produce software of high quality and to improve their software development processes. For example, the deployment of SCM tools has increased tremendously during the 1990s, thanks to the popularity of CMM®. Experience indicates, however, that acquiring CMM® is difficult. The vast majority of organizations are not able to reach even level two. In

2002, less than 150 organizations in the world reached levels four or five. Indian companies with approximately 80 organizations, which comply with these levels, occupy leading positions. One of the problems with using CMM® is its extensive and very detailed documentation, which makes it difficult to understand and to process. One of the common complaints about the CMM® is that its use is only feasible in very large organizations, despite documented evidence that it is also applicable in small organizations [8]. Although the intention of CMM® is not to require or espouse a specific model of the software life cycle or a specific organizational structure, but rather to give basic elements of each process, there are complaints that the CMM® is most applicable with the waterfall model, and that it is not applicable with other types of development processes (such as incremental development). There have been, however, positive experiences with the use of different development models in combination with the CMM® (e.g., extreme programming [9]). The CMM® has been a very positive influence in encouraging the use of SCM, which has led to a wider understanding of the need to use SCM tools and for planned and measurable SCM processes in software development.

12.5.2 CMM Integration®

Although the objectives of the CMM® are the improvement of software development, most of the principles identified in the CMM® are valid for other types of life cycles. Many organizations now apply the CMM® in their processes, which are not necessarily pure software development processes. Learning from these experiences, SEI has developed a new model, CMM® Integration® (CMMI®), which is an extension of the CMM®. The targets of CMMI® are system and integration processes [10]. In particular, CMMI® is a result of combining CMM® for Software version 2.0 with the EIA Interim Systems Engineering Capability Model Standard and the CMMI® Product Development, Draft Version 0.98. A CMM® for Software version 2 draft was the major contributor to CM in the CMMI® [11]. This version was never released but included about 200 user requests from lessons learned in CMM® for Software implementation, defining a better understanding of software maturity, and achieving better consistency with the other software industry standards and terminology [12]. The staged structure of the model is adopted from the CMM®. Like the CMM®, CMMI® is composed of five ascending levels. The designation of level two was changed from repeatable to managed, and that of level four was changed from managed to quantitatively managed. The term key process area has been changed to process area.

CM is a process area at level two that belongs to a class of support area processes together with process and product quality assurance, measurement and analysis, decision analysis and resolution, and causal analysis and resolution. In the same way as SCM in the CMM®, the purpose of CM is to establish and maintain the integrity of work products using configuration identification, configuration control, configuration status accounting, and configuration audits [13]. The main configuration management activities are grouped in establishing baselines, establishing integrity, and tracking and controlling changes (see Figure 12.6).

CMMI® has not yet been accepted as widely as the CMM®, but it is certain that the model will have significant impact on process improvements in many engineering domains.

12.6 SGML and XML

The same motivation that led to the introduction of EXPRESS language as a part of the STEP standard is valid for SGML, ISO 8879:1986 standard [14]. The main purposes of languages such as SGML are to separate data from tools, formats from contents, and to provide a means of specifying formats

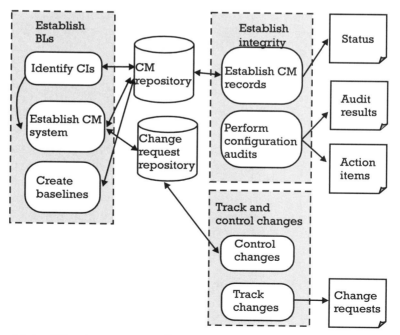

Figure 12.6 CM activities in CMMI®.

in a standard way. The first purpose makes it possible to use different tools for obtaining the same information (e.g., to edit the same document using different word processors)—to be independent of a particular tool or a particular tool version. The second purpose provides the ability to present the same information in different formats. The third purpose enables the exchange of information between different tools that use different formats and different protocols for data exchange.

SGML is a markup language. We can define markup as a text encoding (i.e., as any means of making explicit an interpretation of a text). A markup language specifies which markups are allowed, which markups are required, how markups are distinguished from text, and what the markups mean. HTML is a markup language. For example, an HTML sequence <B>home</B> includes <B> and </B> markups, which means that the text *home* will be presented in boldface style. SGML is slightly different from HTML. SGML provides the means of doing the first three factors; the last part—the meaning of the markup—is not a part of SGML. Additional definitions are required to describe the meaning of the markup.

In general, we can distinguish three characteristics specific to SGML: it uses descriptive markup, it includes a document-type concept, and it is independent of any one system for representing the script in which a text is written. A descriptive markup means a use of codes that simply provide names to categorize parts of a document (e.g., a paragraph or a list). Another type of markup system, a procedural markup system defines the processing that is to be carried out at particular points in a document (e.g., define margin or begin in the next line). With descriptive instead of procedural markup, the same document can be directly processed by different software and for different purposes. SGML uses the notion of a document type and, according to this, a document type definition. Its constituent parts and their structure formally define the type of a document. For example, the definition of a book might be the following: a book consists of a title and an author, followed by a sequence of chapters that contain text. Any document lacking a title, according to this formal definition, would not formally be a book. If documents are of known types, special programs (designated as parser) can be used to process a document of a particular type and check that all of the required parts are present and correctly ordered. More importantly, different documents of the same type can be processed in a uniform way.

With such characteristics, SGML was a promising approach, and not surprisingly much work related to STEP and SGML was begun. Several word processors were supplemented with support for the SMGL documentation format. However, the complicated structure of SGML and the lack of support for tools resulted in less acceptance of SGML than expected. In the meantime, the boom in Web and HTML made it clear that a simpler format than SGML and compatible with HTML would be more successful. This indeed appeared. With the introduction of XML [15, 16], its use exploded in virtually all known engineering and computer domains.

XML is a subset of SGML and contains almost all of its characteristics. Any XML document is a type of SGML document. XML separates contents from a format and format from a presentation in the same way as SGML. The following document shows an example of an XML file.

```
<xml version="1.0" ?>
  <Book Author="Thea Smith">
   <Title>Sample Book</Title>
   <Chapter id="1">
    This is an ordinary text that belongs to Chapter 1.
   </Chapter>
   <Chapter id="2">
      This text belongs to Chapter 2.
   </Chapter>
</Book>
```

The grammatical rules for this XML file are expressed in a document type definition file.

```
<!DOCTYPE Book [
  <!ELEMENT Book (Title, Chapter+)>
  <!ATTLIST Book Author CDATA #REQUIRED>
  <! ELEMENT Title (#PCDATA)>
  <!ELEMENT Chapter (#PCDATA)>
  <!ATTLIST Chapter id ID #REQUIRED>
]>
```

XML is used for the specification of formats of data, for exchanging data, for protocols between different components, for storing data, for specification of new languages, and in general for any kind of information management process. In many domains, XML is used to formalize the domain's information model, and many tools manage XML documents. XML has had a large impact on STEP. XML representation for EXPRESS-driven data is included as a part of the STEP standard. XML binding with STEP is a revolutionary change that makes STEP data much easier to use. Traditional STEP implementation methods require programming by expensive, expert programmers, but by using this binding, the facilities of XML can be used to directly enable simple description and processing of STEP data.

12.7 Summary

In all engineering domains, standards have a long tradition. It is a common belief that standards can help improve life cycle processes, in product quality, development, and production efficiency. Further, standards are used as a means of communication between different stakeholders and between different tools.

This chapter has shown that many standards can be classified per engineering domain, per type of the process they cover, or per the technology they use or address. It is impossible to make a clear orthogonal classification, as they are often overlapping, and it is certain that the same standard can fall into several different categories. Many standards are closely related, and it is not seldom that some standards are the products of mergers, further evolvement, or the adaptation of old standards.

PDM uses and complies with many standards. STEP is a standard that is directly related to PDM. It provides the means to specify an information model in a standard way using EXPRESS language. STEP also includes a number of parts that apply in particular engineering domains or that provide support for different tools. Other standards extensively used by PDM are CM standards. These standards are also used by SCM, for process management only and not as directly integrated in the SCM tools. Most of the several SCM standards originate from CM standards. Probably, the most influential de facto standard for use of SCM is the CMM®. The CMM® identifies SCM as one of the key process areas in the maturity of an organization for software development management. A special category of standards is related to technology. The standards from this category can be incorporated in the tools. Besides, certain parts of STEP, SGML, and even more so XML are used extensively by PDM and PDM-related tools.

We can expect many new standards related to system and software engineering in the future. The development of technologies and increasing competition will lead to the appearance of many new tools that need to interoperate. The requirements for interoperability and reduced development costs will increasingly demand the use of standards.

References

[1] Leon, A., *A Guide to Software Configuration Management*, Norwood, MA: Artech House, 2000.

[2] Pandikow, A., *A Generic Principle for Enabling Interoperability of Structured and Object Oriented Analysis and Design Tools*, Ph.D. thesis, Linköping University, Linköping, Sweden, 2003.

[3] LKSoft Company, www.lksoft.com, 2003.

[4] National Institute of Standards and Technologies, "The STEP Project," www.nist.gov/sc4/www/stepdocs.htm, 2003.

[5] SEI, "List of High Maturity Organizations," www.sei.cmu.edu/cmm/ high-maturity/HighMatOrgs.pdf, 2003.

[6] Paulk, M. C., et al., "Capability Maturity Model, Version 1.1," *IEEE Software*, Vol. 10, No. 4, July 1993, pp. 18–27.

[7] Paulk, M. C., et al. (eds.), *The Capability Maturity Model: Guidelines for Improving the Software Process*, Reading, MA: Addison-Wesley, 1995.

[8] Paulk, M. C., "Using the Software CMM in Small Organizations," *The Joint 1998 Proceedings of the Pacific Northwest Software Quality Conference and the Eighth International Conference on Software Quality*, Portland, OR, October 13–14, 1998, pp. 350–361.

[9] Paulk M. C., "Extreme Programmig from a CMM Perspective," *IEEE Software*, Vol. 18, No. 6, November/December 2001, pp. 19–26.

[10] Capability Maturity Model Integration, 2002, www.sei.cmu.edu/cmm.

[11] U.S.A.F. Software Technology Support Center, "Mapping of CMMI-SE/SW Version 1.1 to and from SW-CMM Version 1.1," www.stsc.hill.af.mil/ consulting/cmmi/cmmiseswippdv11.pdf, 2003.

[12] Starbuck, R., "A Configuration Manager's Perspective," *Cross Talk, The Defensive Journal of Software Engineering*, July 2000, www.stsc.hill.af.mil/crosstalk/2000 /07/starbuck.html.

[13] Ahern D., A. Clouse, and R. Turner, *CMMI Distilled, A Practical Introduction to Integrated Process Improvement*, Reading, MA: Addison-Wesley Professional, 2001.

[14] On-line resources for markup-type languages, xml.coverpages.org, 2003.

[15] The World Wide Web Consortium, www.w3.org, 2003.

[16] www.xml.com/webservices, 2003.

List of Acronyms

ACM	Application change management
ADK	Application Development Kit
ALEX	Active Library Explorer
API	Application program interface
ASIC	Application-specific integrated circuit
AXE	Public telephone exchange
BL	Baseline
BOM	Bill of material
BS	Base station
BU	Business unit
CAD	Computer-aided design
CAE	Computer-aided engineering
CAM	Computer-aided manufacturing
CAS	Central article and structure
CASF	CAS Interface
CASL	CAS Lists
CASP	CAS Production
CASR	CAS Register

CCB	Configuration control board
CDM	Collaborative Data Management
CI	Configuration item
CM	Configuration management
CMM	Capability Maturity Model
COTS	Commercial off the shelf
CPC	Collaborative product commerce
cPDm	Collaborative product definition management
CPM	Collaborative product management
CR	Change request
CRM	Customer relationship management
CRM/PRM	Customer/partner relationship management
CVS	Concurrent versions system
DELTA	Documentation environment library and transfer aid
DMS	Document management system
DR	Defect report
DSM	Deep submicron
DWAXE	Document products for AXE
ECM	Engineering change management
EDA	Electronics design automation
EIA	Electronic Industries Association
ePDm	Electronic product data management
ER	Enhancement request
ERP	Enterprise resource planning
FAQ	Frequently asked question
FOA	First office application
FPGA	Field programmable gate array

GASK	General archive system for communication
GMSC	Gateway exchange
GOLF	Global order inventory invoicing system
HDL	Hardware description languages
HTML	Hypertext markup language
HTTP	Hypertext transfer protocol
IDE	Integrated development environment
IEEE	Institute of Electrical and Electronic Engineers
ILS	Integrated logistic support
INCOSE	International Council on Systems Engineering
ISDN	Integrated Services Digital Network
J2EE	Java 2 Platform, Enterprise Edition
KBE	Knowledge-based engineering
MHS	Modification Handling System
MPS	Manufacturing and Planning System
MQL	Matrix Query Language
MRD	Marketing requirement document
MRP	Manufacturing resource planning
MRS	Main requirement specification
NC	Numerical control
PAC	Product approval committee
PCB	Printed circuit board
PDC	Personal digital cellular
PDF	Portable definition file
PDM	Product data management
PDMIC	Product Data Management Information Center
PIM	Product information management

PLC	Product lifecycle
PLM	Product life cycle management
PMSC	Packet mobile switching center
PPDC	Packet data PDC
PRI	Product revision information
PRIM	Product information management
PSM	Product structure management
PSTN	Public switched telephone network
RCS	Revision control system
RFQ	Request for quotation
RM	Requirement management
RTL	Register transfer level
RTM	Requirement Traceability Management
SCCI	Source code control interface
SCCS	Source code control system
SCM	Software configuration management
SDAI	Standard Data Access Interface
SDRC	Structural Dynamics Research Corporation
SE	Systems engineering
SGML	Standard generalized markup language
SIT	System integration and test
SMS-C	Short message center
SoC	System on chip
SQL	Standard query language
SRM	Software Release Manager
STD	State transition diagram
STEP	Standard for the Exchange of Product Model Data

SWAXE	Software for AXE
TDM	Team data manager
TR	Trouble report
TTC	Time to customer
TTM	Time to market
TTS	Theory of Technical Systems
UCM	Unified change management
VMSC	Voice mobile switching center
VPDM	Virtual product data management
VSS	Visual SourceSafe
WBS	Work breakdown structures
WCM	Web content management
WebDAV	Web-distributed authoring and versioning
WIP	Work in process
WWW	Worldwide Web
XML	Extensible markup language

About the authors

Ivica Crnkovic, Mälardalen University, Department of Computer Science and Engineering, Västerås, Sweden

Ivica Crnkovic is a professor of industrial software engineering at Mälardalen University, where he is the administrative leader of the software engineering laboratory and the scientific leader of industrial software engineering research. His research interests include component-based software engineering, SCM, software development environments and tools, and software engineering in general. Professor Crnkovic is the author of more than 40 refereed articles and papers on software engineering topics. He has coorganized several workshops and conferences related to software engineering (in particular, component-based software engineering) and participated in program committees of SCM symposia and workshops. He also participated in several projects organized by the Association of Swedish Engineering Industries.

From 1985 to 1998, Professor Crnkovic worked at ABB, Sweden, where he was responsible for software development environments and tools. He was a project leader and manager of a group developing SCM systems and other software development environment tools and methods for distributed development and maintenance of real-time systems. From 1980 to 1984, he worked for the Rade Koncar company in Zagreb, Croatia. Professor Crnkovic received an M.Sc. in electrical engineering in 1979, an M.Sc. in theoretical physics in 1984, and a Ph.D. in computer science in 1991, all from the University of Zagreb, Croatia.

He can be reached at ivica.crnkovic@mdh.se or http://www.idt.mdh.se/~icc.

Ulf Asklund, Lund University, Department of Computer Science, Lund, Sweden.

Ulf Asklund is an associate professor of configuration management at Lund University, Sweden. His research interests include SCM and software engineering in general. He is especially interested in the developer view in software engineering, focusing on tool support and IDEs. His research also includes computer-supported cooperative work and PDM, and how these can be combined and integrated with SCM. Dr. Asklund also takes an active interest in undergraduate and graduate education.

Dr. Asklund is the author of more than 10 refereed journal articles and conference papers. He has also coorganized several workshops and a conference for the IEEE, participated in the Program Committee of the IEEE Conferences and Workshops on Engineering of Computer-Based Systems 2002 and 2003, and reviewed several submissions for journals within software engineering.

Ulf Asklund is a regular presenter at national and international conferences regarding SCM and PDM. He has participated in two projects organized by the Association of Swedish Engineering Industries, and is the author and coauthor of the resulting reports. He is an active member of the local Software Process Improvement Network (SPIN) organization.

Dr. Asklund received his M.Sc. in electrical engineering in 1990 and earned his Ph.D. in computer science in 2002. He is now an associate professor with the Department of Computer Science and a senior researcher with the Lund University Center for Applied Software Research (LUCAS).

Ulf Asklund can be reached at ulf.asklund@cs.lth.se or http://www. cs.lth. se/~ulf.

Annita Persson Dahlqvist, Ericsson AB, Business Unit Transmission and Transportation, Mölndal, Sweden

Annita Persson Dahlqvist has been a nominated specialist in CM, SCM, and PDM for more than 5 years with Ericsson AB. She is the manager of the CM managers group. She is also responsible for training, starting up new projects, process development, and supporting the organization regarding CM and PDM issues. Ms. Persson Dahlqvist's interest is in CM (especially SCM), PDM, and how to automate processes and interoperability between tools for these activities.

Ms. Persson Dahlqvist has been chairperson for three projects (within the SCM and PDM areas) sponsored by the Association of Swedish Engineering Industries. In the latest project, she also acted as cowriter of the resulting report.

Ms. Persson Dahlqvist has been a member of the Program Committee of SCM symposia during 1997–1999, 2001, and 2003. She has also been a member of the Program Committee to the Euromicro Conference, a component-based software engineering track conference, from 2001–2003.

She is also a frequent presenter for national and international conferences regarding CM, SCM, and PDM, and she is the author of more than 10 refereed articles and papers on SCM and PDM topics.

Ms. Persson Dahlqvist earned her B.Sc. in computer science from the University of Gothenburg, Sweden, 1985.

She has been working for Ericsson AB since 1985, where she started as a software designer. Later, she worked as subsystem designer, project manager for software and quality projects, CM manager, and team manager for CM Managers. She has also worked part-time for the Ericsson Group regarding SCM, CM, and PDM.

Ms. Persson Dahlqvist can be reached at Annita.Persson@emw.ericsson.se.

Index

.NET, 261
3G mobile systems, 206

A

ABB Automation Technology Products, 231
Access control, 286
AllFusion Harvest Change Manager, 265
Application Development Kit, 253
Application program interface (API), 76, 134
AXE, 221, 227

B

Baseline, 39, 68, 101, 111, 114, 139, 149, 217
Bill-of-material (BOM), 25, 31, 48, 104, 111
    "super BOM," 229
Boeing, 52
BOM. *See* Bill-of-material
Branch, 62, 64, 66, 72, 98, 101, 151, 268
    permanent, 65
    temporary, 65
Build management, 69, 103, 113, 184
Business item, 25, 31, 93, 94, 100

C

C3P, 51
CAD. *See* Computer-aided design
CADCAMnet, 251
Capability Maturity Model®
        (CMM), 61, 84, 312
    CMM levels, 313
        defined, 314

initial, 313
managed, 314
optimizing, 314
repeatable, 313
    key practices, 315
Capability Maturity Model Integration®
        (CMMI), 316
Capri, 232
CAS, 236
CCB. *See* Configuration control board
CCC/Harvest. *See* AllFusion Harvest
        Change Manager
CDM. *See* Collaborative data management
Change management, 43, 72, 103, 185,
        200, 230
    CCB, 73
    process, 73
    release document, 75
    traceability, 73
Change request (CR), 73, 118, 120
Change Synergy, 269
Check-in/out, 22, 64
CI. *See* Configuration item
CIMdata, 251
Class, 32
Classification management, 28
ClearCase, 72, 81, 203, 216, 266
        integration with eMatrix, 148
        integration with Metaphase, 155
        MultiSite, 267
ClearQuest, 204, 216, 267
CM. *See* Configuration management
CM plan, 84, 117, 183, 305, 306

For further information on these and other Artech House titles, including previously considered out-of-print books now available through our In-Print-Forever® (IPF®) program, contact:

Artech House
685 Canton Street
Norwood, MA 02062
Phone: 781-769-9750
Fax: 781-769-6334
e-mail: artech@artechhouse.com

Artech House
46 Gillingham Street
London SW1V 1AH UK
Phone: +44 (0)20 7596-8750
Fax: +44 (0)20 7630-0166
e-mail: artech-uk@artechhouse.com

Find us on the World Wide Web at:
www.artechhouse.com